Work Study

by

R. M. CURRIE, C.B.E.
M.I.MECH.E., M.I.C.E., M.I.PROD.E.

Head of I.C.I. Central Work Study Department
President of the Work Study Society

WITH A FOREWORD BY
SIR EWART SMITH, F.R.S.

A

PUBLICATION

London:
SIR ISAAC PITMAN & SONS, LTD.

First published 1960
Reprinted 1960
Reprinted 1961

SIR ISAAC PITMAN & SONS, LTD.
PITMAN HOUSE, PARKER STREET, KINGSWAY, LONDON, W.C.2
THE PITMAN PRESS, BATH
PITMAN HOUSE, BOUVERIE STREET, CARLTON, MELBOURNE
22–25 BECKETT'S BUILDINGS, PRESIDENT STREET, JOHANNESBURG

ASSOCIATED COMPANIES
PITMAN MEDICAL PUBLISHING COMPANY, LTD.
39 PARKER STREET, LONDON, W.C.2

PITMAN PUBLISHING CORPORATION
2 WEST 45TH STREET, NEW YORK

SIR ISAAC PITMAN & SONS ((CANADA), LTD.
(INCORPORATING THE COMMERCIAL TEXT BOOK COMPANY)
PITMAN HOUSE, 381–383 CHURCH STREET, TORONTO

PRINTED IN GREAT BRITAIN BY THE WHITEFRIARS PRESS LTD.
LONDON AND TONBRIDGE

F1—(B.630)

Foreword

KNOWLEDGE of work study, as defined by the author of this book, is now becoming widespread, and its methods are being used with signal success in many branches of industry and the public services. That this should be so is, to a major extent, due to the enthusiasm with which Mr. Currie himself has developed, applied and expounded work study techniques during the post-war years.

In my experience, work study, properly understood and applied, can affect work at every level. I say " at every level " advisedly, for its influence can be felt in the board-room, as on the shop floor. It is a general tool of management but perhaps its most important result is to inculcate an attitude of mind that seeks continuous progress in a systematic manner and that does not rest content till it is achieved. Because of this, the detailed techniques and applications of work study are themselves developing all the time, and the author has been wise to concentrate on the basic principles of approach and practice. Even some of these are not very old and no doubt revision and extension will be necessary in the years to come.

To those student readers who will be taking up some form of managerial activity for the first time, I would emphasize that an understanding of work study cannot but be of help in developing a dynamic and objective approach to their own work. This is also necessary for every " line " manager if he is to take proper advantage of the help which specialists, such as fully trained work study officers, are able to provide. But let no one think that to read a book—however good—is to become such a specialist himself; like a doctor, he must also have practical training under skilled teachers, if he is to become a skilled practitioner, rather than a danger to those with whom he has to deal.

I have been in close touch with Mr. Currie's work for the past twelve years, and I have seen at first hand what work study can do in raising productive efficiency. Thus, I am naturally predisposed in favour of this guide to its principles and practice. I hope it will be widely read and wisely followed, so that these benefits may be still further extended.

EWART SMITH

20*th July*, 1959

Preface

THIS book is an attempt to put together experience and knowledge of Work Study, gained more particularly since 1947, while I have been concerned with its development and growth in one of Britain's largest industrial enterprises, Imperial Chemical Industries Limited. The scope of this growth may be judged from the fact that prior to 1947 there were only thirty men in the whole of I.C.I. operating the techniques which may be said to have preceded work study, and there are now 1,500 staff engaged on work study. It should, however, be realized that this rapid and impressive growth has been made possible by I.C.I.'s progressive management policy, which has resulted in sound and excellent labour relations. It is only against a background of mutual understanding between management and men that work study can achieve its greatest results.

Over the past few years demands for information and instruction on work study, as practised in Great Britain, have grown steadily both at home and abroad and the need for an authoritative book on the subject has become increasingly evident. The British Institute of Management have been " holding the fort " with three booklets in the " Outline of Work Study " series, and at their request I have revised this material and expanded it by the addition of extra chapters in the hope of taking a long step towards filling the requirement.

This need is even more obvious now that the Institution of Mechanical Engineers have included Work Study in Part II of the examination for Corporate Membership and the Institute of

Production Engineers have taken similar steps. The City and Guilds of London Institute now offers a Work Study Certificate; and another significant stage in the progress of Work Study was reached with the fusion of the Work Study Society and the Society of Industrial Engineers.

In compiling this book—which is intended to be basic rather than exhaustive—I have also had in mind the extension and broadening of the examinations entry to the Work Study Society.

This book is, however, addressed not only to examination students and to those wishing to become members of the Work Study Society, but also to all those desiring information on the subject, whether they are in industry or not. It is intended primarily to provide a basis from which more specialized knowledge may be built up as required. With this in view I have felt it important to show the historical background against which the work study techniques have gradually developed. It is indeed fascinating to look back into the past and to see how management methods have slowly changed under the impact of the early pioneers. They made many mistakes and were often misunderstood, but modern industry owes them a great deal.

I have devoted a chapter to explaining what I consider to be the main purposes and functions of work study so that these may be clearly understood from the outset. Included in this understanding must be a real appreciation of the human implications of work study. This is a side of the subject which I think has sometimes been overlooked in the past and yet is undoubtedly the most important aspect of all. Work study has a very big part to play in ensuring that every worker feels his job is worth while, that he is doing it as efficiently as possible and is receiving a fair reward for his labour. A great deal has been written and said about human relations in industry and it all comes to the same thing—treating people as individuals with hopes and fears, needs and desires similar to our own.

The chapters on the techniques of work study must necessarily be somewhat longer and more detailed than others in the book, because they deal, after all, with the " tools of the trade." These are the tools which have been and are being used so successfully not only by industry but by organizations in many other fields. Needless to say, with such a rapidly developing subject as work study, changes and improvements in the techniques are taking place all the time and there is no doubt that regular revisions of these chapters will be required should the book be found to serve usefully the purpose for which it is intended. One factor that I hope will commend itself is that the terminology used is that decided upon by the British Standards Institution.

In the concluding chapter I have tried to give a picture of the service to be gained by management from work study and to show how this service is growing. This is particularly evident in pre-production planning, design of buildings plants and products, construction, estimation of labour requirements and so on. I hope that this chapter may give readers the feeling that work study is more than just a set of routine techniques to be used (important though this is) for improving methods or working out incentive schemes. It is a part of management, which nothing else can replace.

As this book is in the nature of a " pioneer " in the field there must obviously be many omissions and perhaps errors in the handling of the material. I should, therefore, be most grateful for suggestions from readers so that, if there should be a demand for a second edition, matters may be put right. Perhaps in the future it may be found desirable to increase the scope of the book and to include exercises, specimen charts and more examples.

It goes without saying that this book could not have been written without the assistance of everyone concerned with work study in Imperial Chemical Industries Limited. It would be invidious if I were to single out names but I feel that I must mention my especial gratitude to the past and present members of my own Central Department, who have helped so much, including Mr. Thomas Fassam who has patiently nursed this first edition through the press. I wish also to pay tribute to the whole-hearted encouragement I have received at all times from the members of the I.C.I. Board, without whose enthusiastic and continuous support the story of work study in I.C.I. might have been so different.

R. M. CURRIE

Contents

xii   *Contents*

List of Illustrations

Historical : The Pioneers

WORK Study is as old as industry itself. The first man who succeeded in simplifying his job by the use of his reason can be considered its unconscious founder; for behind the many techniques which constitute the ever-growing province of work study lies a basic scientific attitude. It is essentially a ruthlessly analytical and inquisitive approach to the use of manpower, materials and equipment coupled with a desire to apply the facts from such inquiry to improve existing methods by the elimination of waste in every form. Such an attitude of mind has always been a prerequisite of industrial progress, but the techniques of work study now developed can make a notable contribution to success.

The British Pioneers

While there is nothing essentially new in work study the novelty is apparent in the intensity of the analytical approach. It has always been practised as an unconscious art, an attribute of individuals, gained through experience and lost in the same way. For instance, in some respects one might consider Britain's Robert Owen (1771–1858) as a precursor of method study. He foreshadowed the work of America's Gilbreths by his work in his New Lanark Mills. Records show his intense interest in problems of layout, in the need for new methods to embody better working conditions, and in making provision in the " time allowed " for a job to include compensating rest and to cover the effects of fatigue.

Owen's attitude is summed up in an essay addressed to " the superintendents of factories," where he wrote: " Many of you have long experienced in your manufacturing operations the advantages of substantial, well-contrived and well-executed machinery. If, then, due care as to the state of your inanimate machines can produce such beneficial results, what may not be expected if you devote equal attention to your vital machines, which are far more wonderfully constructed ?"

The Beginning of Work Measurement

As far as work measurement is concerned there is some evidence that hundreds of years ago monks recorded " overall times " in the construction of stonework when building their monasteries. As far as is known the earliest attempt at the more detailed timing of manufactory operators was made in 1760 by a Frenchman, Jean R. Perronet. Perronet made overall-timed studies of the complete cycle of operations in the manufacture of pins. It is believed that parallel developments were taking place in Britain, for a document exists suggesting that timed studies were not uncommon in British industry in 1792. It is worthy of note that this is sixty years before the great American pioneers were born.

The document refers to the Old Derby China Manufactory—

I Thomas Mason, this 22nd day of December, 1792 solemnly pledge myself to use my utmost caution at all times to prevent the knowledge transpiring that I am employed to use a stop watch to make observation of work done in Mr. Duesbry's manufactory; and to take such observations with the utmost truth and accuracy in my power and to give the results thereof faithfully to Mr. Duesbry.

This " oath " is interesting, in that it establishes two important points—that the object is to get accurate facts, and to report them objectively to management. Secrecy is nowadays regarded as a violation of the confidence that should exist between management and employees (*see* Chapter 3). Forty years later an Englishman, Charles Babbage (1792–1871) carried out similar time studies, also in the manufacture of pins. Babbage, whose primitive computer " Difference Engine No. 1 " may be seen in the Science Museum at South Kensington, anticipated many modern developments. He was among the first management writers who pointed out the possibility of developing general principles based on scientific analysis to govern the conduct of industrial undertakings. It is interesting to record that Babbage was led to time study by a desire to improve factory organization. No attempt appears to have been made in these early studies to break down the cycle of operations into elements. They were merely the record of the overall " elapsed time " in production.

The American Pioneers

For refinements of the broad method studies of pioneers like Robert Owen and the overall time studies of Perronet, Babbage and many others we have to thank two great citizens of the U.S.A. for the undoubted advantages of more detailed method study and more accurate time study.

To Frederick W. Taylor (1856–1915), among many other claims to fame, must go the credit of having first evolved the principle of breaking a job down into detailed elements to determine by time study a time to be allowed for the job.

Taylor was rather a remarkable man. Having served an apprenticeship in several trades he was rapidly promoted until at only 31 he was made chief engineer of the Midvale Steel Works. He began to concentrate attention on such basic industrial problems as " Which is the best way to do a job?" " What should constitute a day's work?", etc., and deliberately set out to give answers to many of these questions.

He extended his studies further and endeavoured to establish basic principles of management which would apply to all fields of industrial activity. Many years later Taylor explained his objectives as having been the following—

1. The development of a science for each element of a man's work, thereby replacing the old rule-of-thumb method.
2. The selection of the best worker for each particular task and then training, teaching and developing the workman; in place of the former practice of allowing the worker to select his own task and train himself as best he could.
3. The development of a spirit of hearty co-operation between management and the men in the carrying on of the activities in accordance with the principles of the developed science.
4. The division of the work into almost equal shares between management and the workers, each department taking over the work for which it is best fitted; instead of the former condition in which almost all of the work and the greater part of the responsibility were thrown on the men.

It was these principles, extended and applied, which formed the basis of what has been called " scientific management."

In 1898 Taylor went out to the Bethlehem Steel Works, where he undertook his famous studies of shovelling. What worried Taylor was the disparity of load handled between the six hundred individual shovellers on the plant and between the wide variety of materials shovelled. For instance, he found that shovellers were lifting loads of 3½ lb when handling rice coal, and up to 38 lb when moving ore.

Taylor, therefore, set out to discover what shovel load permitted a good shoveller to shovel most in a day. He experimented with different sizes of loads and with shovels of varying weights and designs. Finally he came to the conclusion that a load of 21½ lb enabled the average man to shovel the maximum tonnage of material in one day. Therefore he provided different types of shovels for use in handling different types of material, but each was so constructed that it could hold only 21½ lb.

In addition Taylor established a planning department in order to determine in advance the amount of work to be done in the yard during the ensuing day. Furthermore, instead of working as an anonymous member of a large gang, each man was made responsible for his own work and paid a bonus for reaching his target, based on Taylor's standards.

To him must go the credit for christening his technique " Time Study," for of necessity time studies became the principal feature of his " scientific management." Fundamentally management cannot become scientific without an adequate knowledge of how long it should take to do work.

Taylor started by breaking down the cycle of the operation into small groups of motions called *elements*. Each element was timed separately and the elapsed time of each element determined. Taylor realized that an overall time did not give accurate enough information and gave no indication as to where time was wasted or used inefficiently. By timing the individual elements, one obtained a complete breakdown of the total operation into an easily analysable form, while at the same time one could always ascertain the overall time by simple arithmetic. Furthermore, he realized that each cycle must be studied for a long time and each study must be repeated a number of times, if an adequate degree of accuracy were to be attained. Thus Taylor was able to show by time study that there were in industrial operations very large and preventable losses of efficiency which could be recognized, isolated and eliminated.

Taylor's fundamental contribution to the development of work study was to approach production problems in a more intensive manner. In the words of Eric Farmer, the Cambridge industrial psychologist, Taylor " approached problems, which had been thought either not to exist or to be easily solved by common sense, in the spirit of scientific inquiry."

Another American pioneer was Henry L. Gantt, (1861–1919) chiefly known now as the originator of the " Gantt chart " widely used in work study today. The chart is a visual display based on time rather than dimension, weight, etc., and gives a continuous picture of progress, thus enabling management to exercise closer control over production. Gantt was, however, a great contributor to the development of incentive schemes and planning and control systems generally; and his title for inclusion in this chapter is based on his expressed conviction: " In all problems of management the human element is the most important one."

The Beginnings of Method Study

The industrial world owes an incalculable debt to Frank and Lillian Gilbreth, for the development of what they christened " Motion Study," an intensification of the broad pioneering method studies of Robert Owen and many others.

Frank B. Gilbreth (1869–1924) was a New England contractor and industrial consultant and another pioneer in the field of scientific management. He was always greatly assisted by his wife, Dr. Lillian Gilbreth, a trained psychologist, who, happily, is still able to play an active part in the continuation of her husband's work. The Gilbreth's partnership through life makes a long and fascinating story. Gilbreth started as a bricklayer and became a successful contractor. His wife worked for many years to win her doctorate in psychology; yet she was able at the same time to assist her husband materially in his work and bring up the famous *Cheaper by the Dozen* children! Together they developed the techniques of motion study.

In 1885 Gilbreth, at the age of 17, eschewed that Harvard education which was the convention of old New England families. Instead, he went to work for a building contractor in Boston, where he began by learning the bricklayer's trade. His ambition was to work his way through the various ranks of the building trade until he himself could become a partner. But when he tried to learn to lay bricks, he discovered that no two workers used the same technique, nor did the worker use himself the same method as the one which he endeavoured to teach to the apprentice. Furthermore he noticed that a bricklayer used one set of motions when he worked slowly and another when he worked fast.

This started Gilbreth thinking. While learning the craft as best he could himself, he determined to work out the most efficient method of laying bricks so that he personally could get ahead. He began by studying the motions of the individual bricklayer and endeavouring to analyse and rationalize these motions. This was the beginning of motion study. Many years later Gilbreth said about his intentions at this time—

> The only thing I had in mind was to figure out a good way, con-centrate on it, pass my examination and get a position as foreman; I had no idea of motion study, but I did have an idea of finding the best way for me to get on with my job.

So far Gilbreth had done no more than numerous other men must have done under differing industrial circumstances. But he was not content to leave the matter there: he continued to study the problem of laying bricks. He ascertained that eighteen separate movements were made in laying each brick. By analysing these movements, he was able to reorganize the pattern of work so that the movements were reduced to five per brick. From a study of bricklaying Gilbreth moved on to other constructional jobs, to the redesigning of scaf-folding and the general layout of the work-site, all of which were included in his own field of general contracting.

From their various studies, the Gilbreths together developed the laws of human motion, from which they evolved " principles of motion economy." The Gilbreths held that most manual work could be broken down into a few elementary motions, which are repeated over and over again. Variety lay not in the number of elemental motions, but in the different combination of elemental motions, which constitute various jobs. These elemental motions they named *therbligs* (a simple anagram of their own name) and symbols were devised for recording them.

The term *motion study* was coined by the Gilbreths to cover their field of research in order to distinguish it from the time study of F. W. Taylor. In 1917 the Gilbreths propounded the first definition of motion study: that it consists of dividing the work into funda-mental elements; analysing these elements separately and in relation to one another; and from these studied elements, when timed, build-ing methods of least waste.

Like Robert Owen, but to a much more adequate extent, the Gilbreths also investigated the problem of fatigue and its elimination. From their studies they held that it was possible to eliminate " need-less fatigue." The three principal methods by which this could be done were—

1. lightening the load;
2. introducing rest periods;
3. spacing the work.

Here we can distinguish the early conception of what today we call " Relaxation Allowance " or " Compensating Rest."

Two Basic Attitudes

At this time the ideas of F. W. Taylor and his colleagues in " scientific management " were prevalent in American industrial circles. Gilbreth, as might be expected, became interested in them. but he was reluctant to accept them whole-heartedly. He found that many of the details of Taylor's work conflicted with his own experience. All through his life Gilbreth retained immense admiration for Taylor's courage and analytical abilities, but he never allowed it to obscure the certain weaknesses in Taylor's theses. To begin with, Gilbreth held that it was bad practice to make a time study to set times until one had ensured that the best and most economical method of performing the operation had been properly established. Furthermore Gilbreth objected to the habit of making secret time studies of reluctant employees. He maintained stoutly that both motion study and time study required the active interest and co-operation of the workers concerned.

The difference between the two respective approaches of Taylor and the Gilbreths is signified in the two terms which are associated with their names, time study and motion study. Taylor was interested principally in the time factor. He approached the problem of method and motion in a far less scientific manner, simply as an ancillary task in the practice of his time studies. The Gilbreths, on the other hand, were mainly concerned with devising the most economical methods and the most effective layout of work space, followed by the motion study. They regarded elapsed time as a secondary consideration. They felt that in any case a reduction in elapsed time would follow from the proper use of motion study.

Rated Time Study

From 1911 onwards another American industrial consultant, Charles E. Bedaux, tried to construct an objective system of measuring work. He evolved the concept of a common unit by which work done on any particular job could be evaluated. It was intended to provide an objective standard upon which to base financial incentive schemes and by which to compare different types of work. This unit he called B unit after himself.

The technique used by Bedaux to establish his unit values was a development of Taylor's time study; but he made an important refinement to time study practice. Previously time study had been composed simply of the average elapsed time for each element. Bedaux introduced a new factor, *rat ng assessment*. As each element was timed, the time study man assessed a rating value for the speed and effectiveness with which the element was carried out. Thus a serious attempt was made to bring a qualitative element into time study. Furthermore, Bedaux followed Gilbreth's conception of introducing a rest allowance for the recovery from fatigue into the basic calculations of a *B* unit value.

There is no doubt that Bedaux, by introducing rating assessment and including a rest allowance, made an important contribution towards establishing an empirical basis for the measurement of work. Unfortunately, his efforts in industry met with serious opposition from organized labour, both in America and in Great Britain. The reasons were many, but most important was the failure of management by word and deed to obtain labour's confidence, and the failure of labour to realize that time study if properly used could contribute towards justice.

It is also true that some of the Bedaux techniques were still fairly primitive, e.g. fatigue allowances were not on a truly analytical basis. It must, however, be recognized that the advances made by Bedaux were considerable in spite of the fact that the results were often misused. His contributions, for all their imperfections, have been of great consequence to the subsequent development of " Work Measurement."

The British Contribution

Particularly in the last ten years the British contribution towards the development of modern work study has been considerable. The ever closer integration of the two techniques method study and work measurement has been largely British. Britain is largely responsible for the growing international adoption of the name " Work Study." Many do not favour the American equivalent title of Industrial Engineering because—apart from the possibility of comparison with the professional engineer—the scope of work study extends far beyond the activities known as engineering, and certainly well beyond industry proper into the fields of agriculture, the armed services, public administration and so on.

The zero point as far as acceptance of work study was concerned could probably be set at the end of the 1914–18 War. During those four years, in which the national need for increased production led to the recruitment of more and more unskilled workers, including women and juveniles, the seeds of scientific management as well as of welfare were sown. Of course, the equivalent techniques to work study were not known at that time by the comprehensive name, and they were extremely primitive.

In the 1920s methods of the Bedaux type were introduced into

Great Britain by I.C.I. and a number of other firms. In 1926 a company called Charles E. Bedaux Ltd. was registered in London with the object of supplying technical consultants to companies in this country. In 1931 some two hundred men had been trained in the original Bedaux methods and had applied these methods to some five hundred plants.

A certain amount of resentment towards the Bedaux consultants arose owing to the fact that the introduction of the system coincided with the general depression of 1929 and the early thirties, when employers appeared to be largely concerned with economies in labour. There is no question that certain employers brought the Bedaux system into disrepute by adopting the extremely bad practice of cutting properly established values after the Bedaux consultants had completed the application.

Just as World War I provided the circumstances for the first step towards work study, so World War II saw a second step—organized support by the Government. Although most people recognize the name of Sir Stafford Cripps as that of the founder of the Anglo-American Productivity Council, it is not generally realized that it was under his aegis at the Ministry of Aircraft Production that a Production Efficiency Board was set up which ran the first Government-sponsored courses in motion study based on Gilbreth's teaching. Parallel with this, and brought about by the need for the rapid development of supervisors, was the sponsorship by the Ministry of Labour and National Service of a " Training Within Industry " Programme on similar lines to that which had long been carried on in the United States. T.W.I. as it is familiarly called, is divided into three parts; Job Instruction, Job Relations and Job Methods; the last-named, which has recently been revised to strengthen its effectiveness, has been brought into line with method study, and has helped junior supervision to become more aware of the benefits of critical examination of the facts.

The British contribution of recent years has been along three special lines—

(*a*) The systematic attempt to humanize and co-ordinate techniques and to emphasize that work study is an integral part of management's job and not an expert system superimposed upon them and those for whom they are responsible. This is coupled with a more intensive theoretical and practical training for work study practitioners.

(*b*) The successful extension of method study to far beyond the individual work-place and covering the whole existing department or works and increasingly to the development and design of new processes and products and layout of factories. Particularly notable has been the development of the more highly organized critical examination of proposed as well as existing processes and procedures.

(c) The development of work measurement to cover non-repetitive work such as engineering maintenance and construction much more effectively than heretofore and to establish data from which work values for this type of work can be synthesized.

To all these developments the well-known consultant firms have contributed in substantial fashion and with a high standard of professional knowledge and integrity.

It has been a typically British story of a large number of unrelated efforts all tending the same way and finally combining in a coherent attitude to work study based on the national need for higher productive efficiency; and of great importance in this general development has been the increasing interest and action taken by the British Trade Union Movement to investigate, teach and encourage the use of work study.

2

Productivity and Work Study

In the last ten years increasing realization is evident of the true meaning of productive efficiency. This is coupled with a growing understanding that only through the economic health of all industrial organizations great and small can come the progressive rational prosperity which will vitally affect the standard of living of the whole nation.

Productivity in its broadest sense is the quantitative relationship between what we produce and the resources which we use. There is a clear and distinct difference between production and productivity. It is quite possible to increase the actual volume of production and yet decrease productivity. In seeking higher productive efficiency, therefore, we are concerned, not simply with increasing output, but with increasing output from the same or smaller use of our resources of all kinds.

Productivity is an overall conception which is difficult to express or to measure. It is, however, possible to consider productivity in terms of various basic resources used in industry. Thus it is sometimes expressed in terms of the output from labour, or from services, or from the capital invested. Whilst these partial expressions do not necessarily give an accurate picture of the overall position, they may be very useful in that they show trends and broad movements.

In the long term it is only through advance in productivity that employees can hope to obtain an increase in real wages, shareholders an increase in the purchasing power of their dividends, and customers lower real prices. It is equally true that the future economic strength of the nation in a competitive world depends on management's success in achieving this aim, wherever the provision of goods or services is involved. With the increase in scientific knowledge and the development of better management techniques this advance should not only be continuous, but should take place at an ever-increasing pace. Here it is as well to remind ourselves of a well-known definition of management: the organization and control of human activity directed to specific ends.

Factors Affecting Productivity

Since national problems may be considered as the sum of individual problems, the best way of improving the national level of productivity would seem to lie in improving that of the individual concern. Clearly, if one can devise ways of improving the productivity of the individual concern, one has gone a long way towards solving the problem on a national level. The starting-point is to consider the factors affecting productivity.

Nature and Quality of Raw Materials

In Britain we have heard too much in the past about our disadvantages in the relative lack of many raw materials and far too little of the compensations we enjoy by the " short hauls " which permit economic internal and coastal transport services to get our materials where we need them.

Both factors demand better methods to eliminate the woeful waste which is evident in the use of our natural resources and to provide for their efficient handling.

Basic Nature of Processes Employed

In respect of scientific research to improve the processes and procedures we use this country has almost unequalled resources in the brain-power of its chemists, engineers, physicists, accountants, etc. Here the drive for better methods in using what is possibly the most valuable of any nation's resources demands that our technologists should be used to the best advantage in constantly improving our processes. Too often in the research and development fields we find our technologists—and we are dangerously short of them—doing all sorts of pedestrian work which could be done by less qualified people or by machines.

Amount of Plant and Equipment Employed

It should be remembered that the physical effort a man himself can give is only about $\frac{1}{8}$ h.p. whereas the average power used in industry per man today is 10 h.p. in Britain ,and 30 h.p. in U.S.A. Broadly speaking, therefore, it is highly uneconomical from a productivity point of view for a man to do any physical work at all which could reasonably be done by mechanical equipment. Far too much of the country's plant equipment and buildings is obsolete and ill-designed. This is due to a failure to plough back enough capital for modern equipment for future profit. Many whole industries stand indicted on this. It must also be remembered that even when there are plenty of funds to invest in new plant and equipment, it is still necessary to ensure that capital resources are used to the best advantage for productive efficiency.

Efficiency of the Plant and Equipment Employed

This factor partly depends on an adequate supply of technologists; but equally it demands eagerness and action at all levels in a firm to obtain the best from existing resources. To make this eagerness effective, information on production, performance and cost must be available to all concerned.

Volume, Continuity and Uniformity of Production

Standardization of products, resulting in longer and more economical runs, depends upon finding out the best and most simple product to fill the market's needs and the best method of making it. Some " customer education " may be necessary, but this should not be difficult if the product offered is cheap and satisfying.

Utilization of Manpower

Manpower—brain as well as brawn—is the fundamental resource. Britain is not at any disadvantage in quality at any level and, hence, there is real need to see that both general planning and detailed methods of work are not wasteful of effort and productive of avoidable fatigue and frustration.

" The Six Lines of Attack "

At this stage, now that the major influences at work have been very broadly examined, it is possible to formulate positive lines of action. These can be summarized under six headings which have come to be known as " the six lines of attack " to improve productive efficiency ; and since they were first enunciated by I.C.I. they have proved their value on the national scale as well as on the basis of the individual firm—

1. Improve basic processes by research and development.
2. Improve existing, and provide better, plant, equipment and buildings.
} Long-term—will require capital.

3. Improve and simplify the product, reduce and standardize the range.
} Intermediate—may require capital.

4. Improve methods of operating existing material resources.
5. Improve the planning of work and the use of manpower.
6. Increase the effectiveness of all employees.
} Short-term—will require little or no capital.

1. *Improve Basic Processes by Research and Development*

2. *Improve Existing and Provide Better Plant, Equipment and Buildings*

There is an essential difference between the first two lines of attack and the others. These two will require considerable capital expenditure and are necessarily long-term projects. They entail investment in highly trained technical staff and in buildings, plant and equipment, as well they demand all those facilities which go with technical and engineering research and development especially as applied to the creation of new products and the design of new plants. Work study is now making a significant contribution here; a modern trend is for all technical staff to be given appreciation in the principles and to have well-trained work study specialists in development and design teams.

3. *Improve and Simplify the Product, Reduce and Standardize the Range*

The third line of attack may be considered an intermediate-term policy which may or may not require the expenditure of capital, to improve technical efficiency or make other changes; but the significance of expenditure will depend on the particular circumstances of each case. In most cases, however, a great deal of negotiation and co-operation will be required, and the planned changes will take time. There are great economic benefits to be gained from standardization and the reduction of range of products to a reasonable minimum. In all these ways work study techniques have their part to play, in simplifying the problem and in assessing the economics of various alternatives.

The remaining three lines of attack represent the short-term campaign which is essentially concentrated in the operational field where work study can be widely and immediately applied. Little or no capital expenditure is required, but again progress can be handicapped unless there is an appreciation of the potentialities of work study and the trained staff to put these potentialities to work. Either from a national or individual point of view it is important to remember that it is from the savings resulting from these lines of attack that the capital becomes available for the long-term measures mentioned above.

4. *Improve Methods of Operating Existing Material Resources*

By an analytical and intensive study of the details of operation of existing plant, many firms great and small have found unexpected and still growing fields for improvement. The general approach and the techniques of work study are essential to success in such an approach provided they are adequately integrated with technical considerations.

5. *Improve the Planning of Work and the Use of Manpower*

To suggest improvements in planning and organization sounds obvious and elementary and there are few readers of this book who would not claim to be able to do somebody else's job better. The work study attitude of mind turns this critical attitude towards one's own organization. Who would claim his job could not be better planned? How many fully realize that manpower is the most valuable of all our resources and that the cost of human effort is increasing relatively faster than any other? The fundamental facts revealed by work study have been proved beyond a doubt to be a far better basis for executive judgement than inspiration or misguided experience.

6. *Increase the Effectiveness of all Employees*

This last line of attack should be considered in the broadest possible terms and should include everybody from the most exalted executive to the most recently joined apprentice. As a senior director of a large company has said—

> Whatever thinking may have been in the past, we have found the impact of work study travelling steadily away from the shop floor to the Board Room. We now regard it as symbolizing the analytical and progressive attitude of mind which is mainly concerned with making management manage better, rather than getting the workman to work harder.

In each of the foregoing fields, then, work study has obvious applications.

In regard to the last three factors referred to, work study can play a major role. For some years now it has been widely recognized that work study applied to an existing plant and to proposals for its modernization or extension can reduce the amount of capital required, or perhaps even postpone the necessity for such expenditure; and because short-term improvements are always desirable, and are normally within the scope of all sizes and types of organization, work study has come into favour particularly as an attractive and useful means of improving productivity during and between changes of more far-reaching nature. Recent trends in the application of work study to activities on the larger scale are discussed in Chapter 19.

Purpose of Work Study

The agreed definition of work study issued by the British Standards Institute is that it is a generic term for those techniques, particularly method study and work measurement, which are used in the examination of human work in all its contexts, and which lead systematically to the investigation of all the factors which affect the efficiency and economy of the situation being reviewed, in order to effect improvement.

The objective of work study is to assist management to obtain the optimum use of the human and material resources available to an organization for the accomplishment of the work upon which it is engaged. Fundamentally, this objective has three aspects—

1. the most effective use of plant and equipment;
2. the most effective use of human effort; and
3. the evaluation of human work.

Too often it has been the practice, wherever human activities have been organized, to accept opinion in place of fact, with the result that decisions have tended to be based upon what was believed to be true rather than upon what was known to be true. The function of work study is to obtain facts, and then to use those facts as a means of improvement. Consequently, work study may be regarded principally as a procedure for determining the truth about the activities of existing people and existing plant and equipment as a means to the improvement of those activities. It will provide the means of achieving higher productive efficiency under prevailing circumstances.

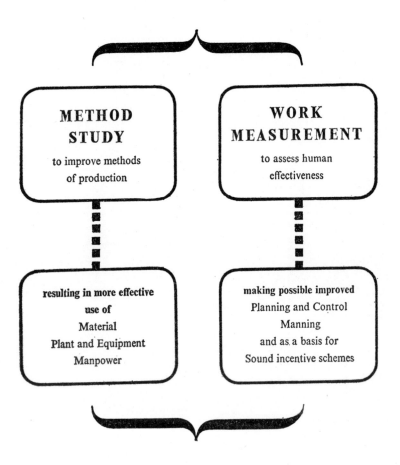

FIG. 1. THE TECHNIQUES OF WORK STUDY

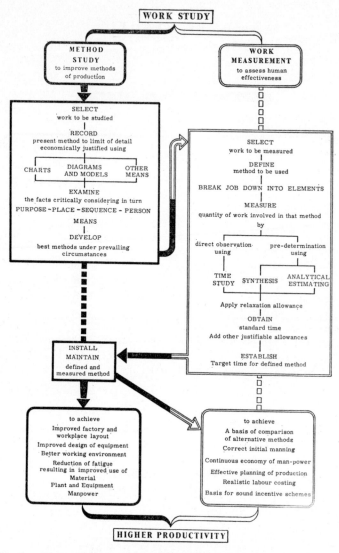

FIG. 2. METHOD STUDY AND WORK MEASUREMENT : CO-ORDINATED
PROCEDURE

Work Study Procedure

Work study, as the name implies, is the study of work; of human work in the deepest sense and dignity of the word, and not merely in the special and more restricted meaning used in the physical sciences. Even today it is not sufficiently realized that work study is not limited to the shop floor, nor even to manufacturing industry. In one form or another it can be used in any situation where human work is performed.

The term *work study* itself is used to associate two distinct yet completely interdependent groups of techniques. These groups have been subtitled method study and work measurement respectively, as shown in Fig. 1. As this diagram suggests, the techniques to which they refer are concerned on the one hand with the way in which work is done (i.e. the *method*), and, on the other, with the value or *work content* of the task itself. The distinction, although convenient for instructional purposes, should be carried no further, for while in practice individual specialists may spend the majority of their time in one or other field, from the point of view of an organization as a whole a major portion of the benefits of work study will be lost if attempts are made to use either group of techniques without adequate use of the other.

The co-ordinated procedure has been set out as a chart in Fig. 2. From this it will be seen that method study, supported by work measurement, is aimed principally at the first two of the three objectives referred to earlier in this chapter—the most effective use of plant and equipment, and the most effective use of human effort after proper method study has been carried out. The work measurement techniques, having as their purpose the evaluation of human work, provide information which can be used to increase the effectiveness of work planning and day-to-day control, as well as in the manning of plant, and for soundly based financial incentive schemes and other purposes.

Basic Principles

The techniques of work study in each field are primarily means of recording in convenient form the use to which an organization's resources are being or may be put in the provision of goods or services. These records are subsequently analysed along specified lines to ascertain where unnecessary effort and waste of all kinds occur, so that steps can be taken with a view to eliminating them.

A feature of work study is the valuable variation in degree of analysis permitted by the different techniques. Whether a task is performed entirely in one location or necessitates a person moving about continuously; whether it takes seconds or weeks to complete; or whether it is continuously repetitive or seldom, if ever, follows the same pattern of operations more than once; whatever the situation techniques have been developed to study the method and measure the work involved. The choice as to which techniques to use is normally governed by the economics of each individual situation as well as the particular type of activity concerned.

The Human Context of Work Study

IT has been said that there is nothing new in work study and that it is largely common sense. In work study, however, an attempt is made so to order common sense that it becomes more a matter of routine and less a product of inspiration. The fact that the techniques have been co-ordinated, codified and extended by constant research has meant that work study has become a specialist function in industry and in other fields, and it is now regarded as an essential service within the management team. Since, however, the main object is to improve the existing way of doing things by effecting change, regard must be paid to the reactions of all employees of any status whatsoever who experience these effects.

To be effective, work study must be integrated into the normal process of management and must not be left to specialists alone; this is especially important since work study is not something which can be started and applied haphazardly; it should be continuous. In many progressive companies it is regarded as essential that all likely candidates for higher management spend a period of two or three years specializing in work study, so that they may appreciate its values and recognize opportunities for its use. Also, where this is not possible, it is regarded as essential nowadays that managers should be given sufficient knowledge of work study to ensure that they have proper executive control over its application and a full appreciation of its potentialities. Readers of this book have the advantage that they have accepted this necessity. They will thus be in a good position to make use of the breadth and variety of the techniques outlined in Chapters 4 to 18.

For the manager versed in work study and for the specialist himself, there is the danger that having themselves accepted the need for change they may overlook that the majority of people have a natural resistance to it. Every person, whether manager, or employee, is to a greater or less extent interested in his own job. The fact that the job has been done in a certain way for what appear to have been good and sufficient reasons invests the existing method with a certain sanctity. Unless work study is properly applied, one must, therefore, expect to meet with considerable resistance at all levels in an organization. In other chapters it has been pointed out that at various important stages of method study and work measurement then, if at no other time, human reactions must be fully considered. But the firms who have most successfully applied work study are those who maintain a continuous watch over the human issues; whence the work study aphorism that the application of it is " 10 per cent technical, 90 per cent psychological."

Trade Union Reactions

The most highly organized industries tend to have the highest degree of trade unionism among their employees; and since trade unions exist to concern themselves with the hours and conditions, including financial conditions, governing the work of their members, it is natural that they should pay particular attention to any changes in those hours and conditions that are proposed by managements. That is why many firms go to great trouble to make sure that, at the outset of the application of work study, the trades unions are brought into the picture at the earliest possible moment. In such consultations there must be no hesitation in discussing honestly all the problems involved, and the possible repercussions and effects. Since the basic principle of work study is to find and state the facts fearlessly the same attitude must inspire discussions with the trades unions, otherwise there can be no real understanding or permanent confidence. This is a stage which cannot be left out, or even shortened, and hence adequate time must be found for it. As described later it is important to run appreciation courses in work study for management and supervision at all levels as part of the campaign for creating the setting in which work study can succeed. The same is true of key trade union personalities, whether the course is provided by the firm or, as is increasingly the case, by the union concerned.

Most unions now appreciate the immediate benefits which work study can give their members by cutting out drudgery, frustration and unhealthy working conditions, by providing an opportunity for higher earnings, and indirectly by strengthening the economy of the company concerned and the nation as a whole.

There are likely to be three points in particular upon which the unions will wish to be satisfied—

1. That there should be adequate consultation before the introduction of any scheme which affects their members.

2. That there should be a definite policy in respect of those people who might become redundant as a result of work study and incentive schemes.

3. That the procedure for dealing with changes in the method of work and for the re-measuring of work should be clearly laid down and should not omit the necessary consultation.

On the question of consultation there are two ways in which workers can be informed about the nature of work study and the purposes of the firm in introducing it. In addition to the formal negotiations which take place on those matters which are decided by Trade Unions and Employers' Organizations as such, most firms have some kind of internal Council or Committee at which matters of concern to the staff and payroll come up for consideration. The opportunity should be taken for work study people to address these bodies and answer questions at an early stage. At the same time, useful work in support of this effort can be done by the employee newspaper or magazine and through any system of notice boards or information leaflets used for such general purposes. Work study films are available for showing to general audiences, and some firms have issued explanatory booklets for distribution among employees in advance of work study activities. No existing method of communication should be ignored.

The question of a redundancy policy is one for the individual firm to decide. An important feature, however, of any redundancy policy must be that it is communicated promptly to all concerned, so that the adverse effects of rumours on the " grape-vine " are kept to a minimum. As a background to any general explanation it may be pointed out that redundancy does not normally arise—

1. Where rising demand will absorb greater production, as has happened in firms where price reductions due to higher productive efficiency resulted in an increased demand for the product.

2. Where a firm has a vigorous programme for the development of new products, so that workers redundant in one section may be employed in another.

3. Where recruitment can be adjusted or excessive working hours reduced. This means taking on no new employees to replace those retiring from or leaving the section concerned. Alternatively recruitment may be stopped for some time before the changes are made so that the department or section is run down to the lower strength that will be needed after the change.

As far as changes of method are concerned, with their implications in respect of incentive payments, it will be obvious that so long as a tradition of full consultation and explanation has been created such difficulties should not occur; if they do occur they should be easily dealt with in an atmosphere of mutual confidence.

Management Reactions

Although there is no possibility of organized opposition on the part of management, the situation is essentially the same, since existing practices are to be changed. The assumption must be that men have been doing their jobs as well as they know how. On this assumption any proposed change must necessarily at first sight appear to be a criticism and hence in all probability a threat to the prestige or future prospects of the person concerned. It follows also that this kind of reaction will be the more intense the longer the service with the Company and the more entrenched the man's position.

Apart from this manifestation of the general conservatism of human beings, any change in existing methods and practices is an interruption of a comfortable situation in which well-established routines have been set up.

Another possible source of difficulty is that when a work study specialist or team is active in a plant or office, it sometimes for the time being appears to take on a management role; so that the sitting managers are likely, unless the situation is handled with tact, to feel that their position has been usurped.

Here it is necessary to invoke the support of top management, without which, indeed, any effort to initiate work study is fore-doomed to failure. If there is any danger of the existing management being made to feel incompetent or threatened by obvious improvements that can be made as a result of work study, some senior person should explain that it is a principle that there will be no recrimina-tions or fault-finding as a result of the facts that have emerged from the study. After all this is perfectly reasonable, since the techniques of finding and weighing the facts might not have been available previously, or if available might not have been used.

The second difficulty will not occur if all concerned are clear that the position of work study in the organization is that it is a tool of management in much the same way as mathematics is a tool of science.

It is of the greatest importance that lower management—supervision, by which is meant foremen and chargehands—should be put in possession of the fullest information. This management echelon is closest to the workers, and here is where the work study specialist can obtain the greatest degree of day-to-day co-operation and information as he pursues his task. Supervision is responsible for passing on to employees the details of what management requires to be done; for implementing to a great extent the programme of work on a monthly or weekly or daily basis; for output and quality of production and the proper utilization of labour and raw materials; for the necessary standards of safety; for the methods used to carry out the work; and for the training of new workers and the retraining of existing workers to new practices. Work study can result in considerable modifications both in the nature of these responsibilities and the way in which they are discharged. Hence any course or conference intended to introduce work study to supervision should concentrate on the following points—

1. the economic necessity of reducing manufacturing costs;
2. the advantages of systematic method study over occasional and haphazard attempts at method improvement;
3. the advantages of measuring work rather than relying on labour requirements sanctioned by custom and established possibly many years ago;
4. the fairness and advantages to the workers of additional payment for additional work;
5. the basis of incentive schemes and the way in which the bonuses are worked out.

Quality of Work

An argument sometimes raised against the introduction of work measurement, particularly when the results form the basis of an incentive scheme, is that it may have an adverse effect on the quality of the product or service provided.

There is, of course, no guarantee that quality will not decline if management and supervision do not keep a proper check on the maintenance of quality standards, and this applies whether work study is in force or not. In one leading British company, however, an independent committee of investigation found no evidence at all that the quality of work had suffered as a result of work measurement, or as a result of the subsequent introduction of incentive schemes covering 40,000 workers.

In many cases quality is actually improved, since standard times are normally specified as being applicable only to a particular standard of quality; consequently, supervision retains the right to return or reject substandard work, and this may result in the loss of bonus earnings. In effect, the introduction of work-measured incentive schemes means that the foreman or supervisor is able to take a much more active part in ensuring that an agreed level of quality is maintained in all the work for which he is responsible.

Individual Reactions to Work Study

Behind the foregoing recommendations lies the experience of managers and work study specialists gained in actual application of the techniques both in industry and elsewhere. Their experience is backed up by knowledge of the nature of human beings derived from other fields. Both social and individual psychologists have something to contribute to understanding of how people are likely to react to the impact of work study.

One of the earliest social researches in industry was the famous Hawthorne project conducted by Elton Mayo at the Western Electric Company in Chicago. Since then, especially in Great Britain, a great deal of valuable work has been done, and there is by now a fairly general consensus of view, summed up by Professor E. Wight Bakke of Yale University. In answer to the general question: "What are the goals to which a man works, and the fulfilment of which he may regard as successful living?" Professor Bakke summarized the following points—

(a) the society and respect of other people,
(b) the degree of creature comforts and economic security possessed by the most favoured of his customary associates,
(c) independence in and control over his own affairs,
(d) understanding of the forces and factors at work in his world,
(e) integrity.

Most researchers have observed that foremost among the expressed needs of people at work is money, but this is interpreted as meaning that they go to work to earn things they need at home for those dependent upon them. One common conclusion is that once the reasonable financial needs are satisfied, other needs become more prominent. But these do not always emerge in the same order, and the main influences here seem to be connected with the position a person occupies at work. The hourly paid worker, given an adequate wage, wants security in that wage. The salaried worker, for whom a greater degree of job security exists, tends to go for increased status. Such points are worth remembering in considering the human context of work study; it will be useful if the five basic needs outlined above are considered in terms of how work study is likely to minister to them or leave them unsatisfied.

The Society and Respect of Other People

One of the bases of mutual respect in a working group is that there should be some balance of fairness in the distribution of work and responsibility and that each member should feel that the others attach some meaning and value to his job. Since this is one of the objectives of applying work study to the activities of teams, it provides a useful basis for explaining what it is proposed to do.

The Degree of Creature Comforts and Economic Security Possessed by the Most Favoured of Customary Associates

As explained later, incentive schemes based on work study demonstrate a clear link between extra effort and extra reward. Hence a man may feel that the creature comforts are within his capacity to obtain. On broader levels, one of the purposes of using work study to decide the initial manning of new plants is, to put it simply, to provide regular work. Hence properly organized working teams have security "built in."

Independence in and Control over his own Affairs

Complete independence is not enjoyed by anybody at work and perhaps independence for the man at the bench is difficult to visualize. In practice it may be taken as training him to do a job, telling him exactly what is expected of him, and then letting him get on with it. Here the value of work study introducing a clear description of a job and the detailed duties involved in it should be stressed. Furthermore, if a man knows what he has to do he will obviously have more control over the way he does it; and where work measurement information about his performance is regularly obtained and provided for him, he has a clear indication of whether or no his performance is up to standard. Knowledge of results has been proved to be a great spur to better performance.

Understanding of the Forces and Factors at Work in his World

Irrespective of any efforts a firm may make through works magazines and other channels to convince employees of the national need for higher productivity, it is obvious that such information will not answer the individual worker's curiosity about what is happening in his immediate environment. When somebody comes to look at his job and the way it is done, he naturally wants to know what is proposed and why, so that he can think about how it is going to affect him and discuss it with somebody who can give him the answers. If work study is properly conducted, these answers are available and, where possible, they are given in advance.

Integrity

The fact that work study enables a man to do " a fair day's work for a fair day's pay " will certainly help him to feel that his working situation is fundamentally an honest one. The significance here of integrity, however, is in its meaning of " wholeness " and hence the work study specialist when he is being trained is continually urged to keep in mind " the whole man."

Reactions of the Group to Work Study

But while the individual reaction is important, much of the fear and even opposition to productivity techniques in the past has been demonstrated by groups, organized or otherwise. Those responsible for introducing work study do well to remember that the work study specialist is a person from outside the working group which he studies and may therefore be regarded—until the appropriate explanations have been made—as a threat to the equilibrium of the group. From this it follows that, if the effect of work study is to break up or rearrange working groups, every effort must be made by patient, and perhaps even individual, consultation and detailed information to explain the reasons for the change and to gain acceptance for it.

Since people have been put to work together in groups, it is reasonable that they will assume first that what they have been told to do is what the management wants to be done. To the extent that they may have developed working habits of their own, they will feel that the present way of doing things is the one that suits everybody best. All bodies of people who live and work together for a long time develop common traditions and establish customs; but by its very nature work study is a challenge to tradition and custom, and seeks to replace for these aspects of work a closer discipline relating to the facts.

When the facts are ascertained, they may be very different from what people believed was happening. Obvious inefficiencies, waste of time, material and effort, may become apparent which were not at all obvious before the study was made. Hence it is a principle of work study that whatever emerges in the way of pointers to possible improvement must not be used as a means of reproaching those who have been doing their best with insufficient information. They should not be reproached with not having thought of the desirable changes; instead they should receive patient and clear exposition of why the changes are desirable.

The points raised in this chapter should only be regarded as very general. The pioneers of scientific management, however much they may have differed in the practices they recommended, all agreed (*see* Chapter 1) that concern for the people involved was necessary if the improvements were to be really effective.

4 ▰▰▰▰▰▰▰▰▰▰▰▰▰▰▰▰▰▰▰▰▰▰▰▰▰▰▰▰▰▰▰▰▰▰▰

Method Study : Introduction

THE old concept of method study as applying only to light repetitive work did scant justice to its potentialities. Method study can, in fact, be applied anywhere, since any type of process or procedure is open to improvement.

Fundamentally, method study involves the breakdown of an operation (or procedure) into its component elements and their subsequent systematic analysis. Thence, those elements which cannot withstand the tests of interrogation are eliminated or improved. In applying method study the governing considerations are, on the one hand, economy of operation and, on the other, the maintenance of accepted good practice as laid down by management (e.g. safety and quality standards).

In carrying out a method study investigation, the right attitude of mind is as important as a knowledge of the techniques. It is therefore essential that anyone responsible for method study should possess—

1. the desire and the determination to produce results;
2. the ability to produce results; and
3. an understanding of the human factors involved.

When considering the desirability of method study investigation of a particular job, it is essential to keep certain factors in mind—

1. economic considerations;
2. technical considerations; and
3. human reactions.

Economic considerations will be paramount at all stages, since it is obviously a waste of time to embark upon, or to continue, an elaborate investigation if the economic importance of the subject is slight. Technical considerations will normally be self-evident. Human reactions, on the other hand, will usually be the most unpredictable factor, involving as they do mental and emotional reaction to investigation and to subsequent changes in method. Knowledge of local personnel, however, and experience of local conditions should help to resolve these problems (*see* Chapter 3).

By approaching method study analytically, a basic procedure has been evolved. This follows the *select-record-examine-develop-install-maintain* sequence set out in Fig. 3, and represents the six essential stages in the application of method study. None of these stages can be omitted, and strict adherence to their sequence as well as to their content is essential to the success of an investigation.

It is necessary to guard against being deceived by the simplicity of this procedure into thinking that method study is easy and therefore unimportant. On the contrary, method study can sometimes be extremely complex and call for considerable skill and knowledge on the part of the work study officer making the investigation.

The merit of the basic procedure is that, whatever the size and nature of the problem, it can be approached and dealt with on a common pattern.

The *record* step in the procedure justifies special mention: the degree of accuracy achieved in recording what is taking place on the job determines the success of the whole procedure, because the records provide the subsequent basis of both the critical examination and the development of the improved method.

The recording techniques employed vary according to the nature of the activity being studied, the principal types used being charts, diagrams and models (more than one type may be necessary adequately to portray some activities). Photographic aids are sometimes used.

Charts are used primarily for sequence and time records. The former are known as *process charts* in which use is made of symbols, not only to speed up the work of investigation but also to enable the overall picture of a situation to be obtained much more quickly than would be possible from an equally detailed written description. Time records are frequently of the " bar chart " type.

A diagram or model of a plant layout or of a work-place may be prepared as a space record of the path of movement of men, materials or equipment (or, for fine detail studies, workers' body movements) in relation to their surroundings.

The more detailed recording techniques call for appreciable time and effort on the part of the work study officer, and should only be embarked upon when the return expected shows them to be justified.

With a detailed record of a particular task available, it becomes possible to apply what is really the heart of the method study procedure: the critical examination. This takes the form of a systematic analysis of the purpose, place, sequence, person and means involved *at every stage of the operation*, satisfactory answers being required in turn to each of the following questions—

(i)	(*a*) What	(is achieved)?	(*b*)	Why	(is it necessary)?
(ii)	(*a*) Where	(is it done)?	(*b*)	Why	(there)?
(iii)	(*a*) When	(is it done)?	(*b*)	Why	(then)?
(iv)	(*a*) By whom	(is it done)?	(*b*)	Why	(that person)?
(v)	(*a*) How	(is it done)?	(*b*)	Why	(that way)?

A satisfactory answer to the query " why?" leads in each case to consideration of alternatives which might also be acceptable, and finally to a decision having to be made as to which, if any, of these alternatives should apply. For instance, the apparent necessity for an activity taking place in a particular location having been satisfactorily established, line (ii) above would be developed to consider in turn (*c*) where else could it be done?; and finally, (*d*) where else should it be done?

At any stage at which a practice cannot be justified in the light of this examination, it is either eliminated altogether from the job or superseded by one which can.

Conducting the critical examination and developing the new method are processes in which the work study officer will make full use of the specialist advice available, both inside and outside his organization. In this way methods will be adopted in which there can be complete assurance that they are not only economically sound and technically correct, but are based on sound physiological and psychological principles, and, above all, make a positive contribution to the value of the product or service provided.

In subsequent sections, the preceding outline of method study is filled in in detail. Students are advised, however, to commit to memory the " six essential stages " and the basic questions of the " critical examination " stage, and apply them to the actual business of study, or to other forms of work in which they may be involved in everyday life.

Method Study Objectives

The first step in work study procedure should be the carrying out of a method study of the work under consideration. Method study is the systematic recording, analysis and critical examination of the methods and movements involved in the performance of existing or proposed ways of doing work, as a means of developing easier and more productive methods. The general procedure is shown in Fig. 3. During this procedure, work measurement will frequently have to be used as a means of helping to get at the facts.

Method study is essentially concerned with finding better ways of doing things, and it contributes to improved efficiency by getting rid of unnecessary work, avoidable delays, and other forms of waste. This it achieves through—

1. Improved layout and design of factory, plant and work-place.
2. Improved working procedures.
3. Improved use of material, plant and equipment, and man-power.
4. Improved working environment.
5. Improved design or specification of the end product.

The techniques of method study aim at doing three things—

1. To reveal and analyse the true facts concerning the situation.
2. To examine those facts critically.
3. To develop from the examination of the facts the best answer possible under the circumstances.

When a method study is done, it may be found that the traditional way of doing work has no longer any sense under present conditions. There is the example of the canteen which, because of regulations made in pre-refrigerator days, prepared none of the food overnight, with the result that an unnecessarily large staff had to be used to cope with the midday rush; there are many examples of unit loads retained at the size designed to suit manhandling, even though mechanical equipment capable of handling many times the load has been adopted, and other constantly recurring instances where traditional habits have become outdated.

Basic Procedure

Much of the value of method study is due to the flexibility with which the techniques may be used in so many different situations.

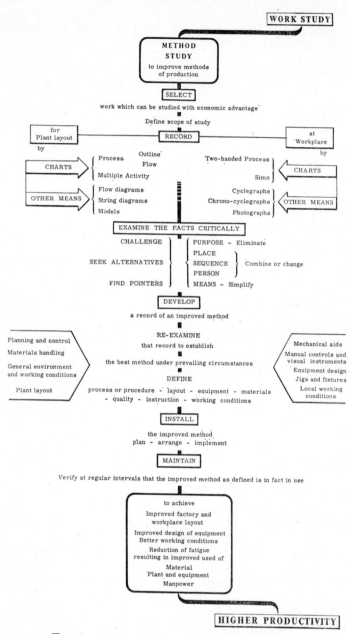

FIG. 3. METHOD STUDY: GENERAL PROCEDURE

There is, however, a simple framework for their application in any circumstances—

Select—the work to be studied.

Record—all the relevant facts of the present (or proposed) method.

Examine—those facts critically and in sequence.

Develop—the most practical, economic and effective method, having due regard to all contingent circumstances.

Install—that method as standard practice.

Maintain—that standard practice by regular routine checks.

The Function of Method Study

Method study does not replace the ability to make the best use of available information, the inventive genius or the organizing ability necessary to develop new methods. What the analytical approach of method study does, by its carefully planned sequence of analysis, is to show where change is likely to be most effective by highlighting unnecessary activities and showing where improvements are possible. In this way thoughts are directed into channels likely to be profitable, and any inherent flair for improvements the members of the work study team may possess stands the best chance of finding full expression. Thus, method study enables the ordinary man to improve methods and at the same time avoid the dangers of taking " short cuts." It must, however, always be remembered that success will very much depend on avoiding any suggestion of censure of past methods and those responsible for them. In any case, the very basis of success is the knowledge obtained from others while following out the formal procedures laid down.

5

Method Study : Select and Record

COST is the usual basis for the selection of operations, sections or departments likely to benefit from method study. It should nevertheless be remembered that it is not necessarily the work with the obvious faults that offers the most valuable improvements. The following defects in an organization indicate where method study is likely to bring worth-while savings—

1. Poor use of materials, labour or machine capacity, resulting in high scrap and re-processing costs.

2. Bad layout or operation planning, resulting in unnecessary movement of materials.

3. Existence of bottlenecks.

4. Inconsistencies in quality.

5. Highly fatiguing work.

6. Excessive overtime.

7. Complaints from employees about their work without logical reasons.

The question then arises whether a change in methods is likely to achieve the following results in sufficient degree to make the cost of method study worth while—

1. Increase production and reduce costs.

2. Maintain production but use less labour, materials or equipment.

3. Improve quality without additional labour or equipment.

4. Improve safety conditions.
5. Improve standards of cleanliness and housekeeping.
6. Reduce scrap.

When all these matters have been weighed up in the light of the economic importance of a task and its expected life, the manager should be able to select the work he is going to have investigated. He should also be able to list the objectives for study in order of priority or importance, although the danger of going too far and carrying the study to uneconomic limits must be avoided. Both in selecting objectives on the larger scale (e.g. a whole company or plant) and in choosing the economically appropriate methods, the mathematical techniques grouped under the heading of " operations research " or " operational analysis " are used hand in hand with method study.

Since the study to be carried out affects the work of managers, supervisors and employees, the need for full consultation and explanation should be borne in mind at this stage (*see* Chapter 3).

The Need for Records

In order that the activities selected for investigation may be visualized in their entirety, with a view to improving them by subsequent critical analysis, it is essential to have some means of placing on record all the necessary facts of the existing method. A record is also essential if a " before and after " comparison is to be made to assess the effectiveness of the investigation and the subsequent installation of the new method.

The techniques listed below have been designed to simplify and standardize this work. It will later be shown that these techniques differ not only in the type of information they can be used to record, but also in the degree of detail they are capable of recording. The principle is to use the simplest and most economical technique which will serve the purpose and is capable of producing full and accurate records of procedures in the method under review. These records will need inspection on the highest level of management available.

Recording Techniques

According to the nature of the job being studied, and the purpose for which the record is required, the technique chosen will fall into one or other of the following categories—

1. Charts (for process and time records).
2. Diagrams and models (for path of movement records).

The manner in which the appropriate techniques are applied is described in the subsequent sections of this and following chapters.

Sometimes more than one technique may have to be used to provide all the necessary information. This information may be obtained by visual observation, by calculation, or by means of a photographic technique. In the case of very detailed (micromotion) studies, elaborate equipment and specialized knowledge may be necessary.

The following are the most generally used techniques, by means of one or more of which every normal type of activity can be recorded in the appropriate degree of detail required—

Charts

Outline process chart	— principal operations and inspections.
Flow process chart	— activities of men, material or equipment.
Two-handed process chart	— activities of a worker's two hands.
Multiple activity chart	— activities of men and/or machines on a common time scale.
Simultaneous motion cycle (simo) chart	— activities of a worker's hands, legs, and other body movements on a common time scale.

Diagrams and models

Flow and string diagrams	— paths of movement of men, materials or equipment.
Two- and three-dimensional models	— layout of work-place or plant.
Cyclegraphs and chrono-cyclegraphs	— high speed, short-cycle operations.

Process Chart Construction

The construction and interpretation of process charts are simplified by the use of two or more of the following symbols[1] which divide the task selected into five functions; all activities can be so divided—

Symbol	Activity	Predominant result
◯	OPERATION	Produces, accomplishes, furthers the process.
⇨	TRANSPORT	Travels.
▽	STORAGE	Holds, keeps or retains.
⃔	DELAY	Interferes or delays.
☐	INSPECTION	Verifies quantity and/or quality.

[1] As recommended by the American Society of Mechanical Engineers. In the original symbols introduced by Gilbreth, from which these developed, the distinction is also drawn between inspection for quality and inspection for quantity.

In the case of outline and flow process charts, these symbols are used to represent steps in the procedure or manufacturing process. In two-handed process charts they represent the elements of the work cycle.

When the investigation warrants it, the *operation* activity can frequently be subjected to more detailed analysis, and a distinction made between *make ready, put away* and *do* operations in the following manner—

    (*a*) *"Make ready" and " put away " operations.* These are concerned with the preparation of material, plant or equipment, to enable *do* operations or *inspections* to be performed, and with the placing aside or clearing up after the *do* operation or *inspection.*

    (*b*) *"Do " operations.* These represent the actual performance of work on the material or work with plant and equipment, and they result in a change in the properties or characteristics of the material.

To emphasize the classification, the *do* operation symbols on the chart can be shaded to facilitate subsequent examination in order of their importance to the overall process.

Time Chart Construction

Time charts are of the bar type, where shading is used on a time scale to represent the activities in two or more synchronizing work cycles. As used in method study, these are called multiple activity charts. More elaborate types, used in planning, are often termed Gantt charts after their originator. It is possible merely to indicate periods of work and idleness by shading a bar or leaving it blank, and this may be found sufficient for many purposes. For subsequent analysis, however, it is sometimes convenient to be able to distinguish between the nature of the activities recorded, in which case various colours or shadings can be used to make certain features stand out, e.g. different types of activity and inactivity, team working, and so on.

Basic Information

Whatever type of chart or diagram is prepared, great care should be taken to ensure that the information it portrays is easily understood and recognized. The following information should always be provided—

    1. An adequate description of all the activities or movements entailed in the method.

    2. Whether the present or proposed method is shown.

3. The specific reference to where activities begin and end.
4. The time and distance scales used, where applicable.
5. An explanation of any abbreviations or special devices.
6. The date of construction of the chart or diagram.

Micromotion Studies

Two-handed process charts, simo charts, cyclegraphs and chrono-cyclegraphs are used for the study of operations at the work-place. The last three of these are the main techniques of what is known as micromotion analysis, which is concerned with the most detailed aspects of methods improvement.

Micromotion analysis is expensive to conduct, and should be undertaken, if it appears economically justifiable, only after large-scale improvements have been fully investigated as a result of using the other recording techniques listed.

Outline Process Charts

The outline process chart gives an overall view of a process, from which it can be decided whether a further and more detailed record is needed. It is a graphic representation of the points at which materials are introduced into a process, and of the sequence of all operations and inspections associated with the process.

The chart does not show where work takes place, or who performs it, and since it is concerned only with operations and inspections, only two of the five recording symbols are used.

In the design stage, where it is increasingly the practice to use work study, outline process charts are often used to assist in the layout of plant, and in the design of the product or of the machinery for making that product. The charts can be made to record the basic data, which can then be subjected to the complete method study procedure while still on the drawing board. Features in the design of a product which are wasteful of material or labour can often be eliminated, and it is frequently the case that expensive equipment, which otherwise might have been bought, proves unnecessary in the light of the investigation.

Construction of the Chart

As a preliminary it must be decided in what detail operations are to be recorded, and consistency must be shown throughout the chart.

As shown in Fig. 4, a start is made by drawing an arrow to show the entry of the main material or component, writing above the line a description of the component, and below the line a description of

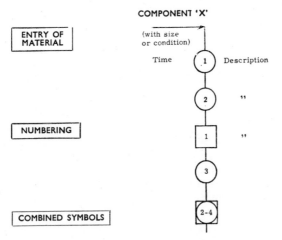

COMPONENT 'X'

ENTRY OF MATERIAL

(with size or condition)

Time

1 Description

2 "

NUMBERING

1 "

3

COMBINED SYMBOLS

2-4

FIG. 4. SIMPLE OUTLINE PROCESS CHART

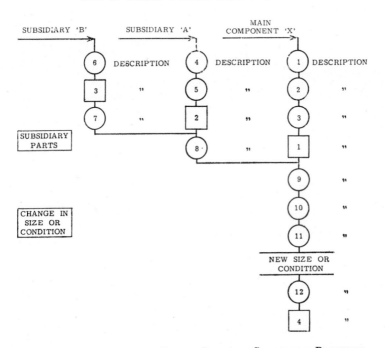

SUBSIDIARY 'B'   SUBSIDIARY 'A'   MAIN COMPONENT 'X'

6 DESCRIPTION   4 DESCRIPTION   1 DESCRIPTION

3 "   5 "   2 "

7 "   2 "   3 "

SUBSIDIARY PARTS

8 "   1 "

9 "

CHANGE IN SIZE OR CONDITION

10 "

11 "

NEW SIZE OR CONDITION

12 "

4 "

FIG. 5. OUTLINE PROCESS CHART, SHOWING SUBSIDIARY PROCESSES

its condition. As each operation or inspection takes place, the appropriate symbol is entered and numbered in sequence, with a brief description to the right, and, if required, a note of the time taken on the left. Where an operation and an inspection take place simultaneously the symbols will be combined.

Fig. 5 shows how a final product is assembled from several subsidiary components or materials, which join the major process during its progress. The major process is charted towards the right-hand side of the chart, and subsidiary processes are charted to its left. These subsidiary processes are joined to each other and to the main trunk at the place of entry of the materials or sub-assemblies.

Operations and inspections are numbered in the normal way commencing with the major process and continuing until a point of entry of a subsidiary process is reached. The sequence of numbering is then continued from the start of the subsidiary process, and proceeds

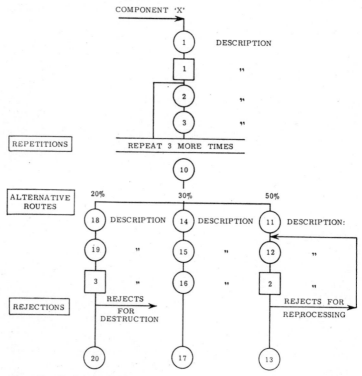

FIG. 6. OUTLINE PROCESS CHART, SHOWING DIVISION OF PROCESS

down that subsidiary process, and the main trunk if necessary, until the next point of entry of a subsidiary process is reached, when the procedure is repeated.

Where the shape, size or nature of a material being processed is so changed that its handling properties from then on are altered, the change is shown on the chart by breaking the chart line and inserting a brief legend describing the changed nature of the material.

Similarly, when an operation divides a material into several parts, which from then on receive separate treatment, the main trunk is divided into the appropriate number of branches, as shown in Fig. 6. The right-hand branch will normally represent the major flow and other flows will be drawn successively toward the left of the chart in order of importance. The way of dealing with repeat operations and rejects is also shown. If required, the proportion of original material in each branch may be shown above the branch.

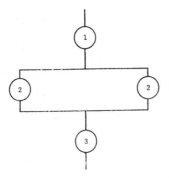

FIG. 7. SYMBOLS SHOWING DUPLICATED OPERATION

When it is necessary, in order to balance the flow of work, to carry out the same operation at more than one place, or by more than one worker, the chart can be split into two or more paths, each of which represents a duplication of the operation, as shown in Fig. 7. This can be done to show that some material may follow alternative but complementary routes during a process.

When simultaneous operations have to be carried out on the main part of a unit and an assembled component, a partial dismantling may sometimes be unavoidable. In the example in Fig. 8, a dismantling operation has occurred after the second operation. One operation has then been carried out on the main assembly and another on the dismantled portion. The two parts have then been reassembled.

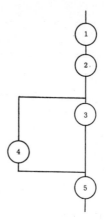

FIG. 8. SYMBOLS SHOWING DISMANTLING AND REASSEMBLY

Summary

When the chart is complete it must be summarized. Operations are totalled, and also inspections—

Operations .	.	.	.	.	x
Inspections .	.	.	.	.	y
Total time (min and sec)		.	.	z

The chart is now ready for the *examine* and *develop* stages of the basic procedure, described in Chapters 6 and 7.

Example

The example shows an outline process chart (Fig. 9) used to record manufacture of a rocker arm. A diagram of the arm (Fig. 10) and a written description of the procedure shown on the chart are also given.

The drawing shows the rocker assembly for the valve mechanism of an oil engine. It consists of a drop forging, a phosphor bronze bush, a hardened steel tappet, an adjusting screw and a locknut.

The rocker itself is made from steel bar of rectangular section $1\frac{1}{2}$ in. × $\frac{3}{4}$ in. The first operation is to punch the drop forging blank on a 40-ton press. The blank is then heated in a muffle furnace to 950° C, and formed in one operation on a 1-ton drop forge. The spoil is trimmed off in a blanking press, and the forging passes to the inspection section, where it is electrically tested for flaws and cracks. It is then routed to the drilling section where it is mounted in a drilling

OUTLINE PROCESS CHART

Task: Manufacture and assembly of rocker arm (present method)

Chart begins: Raw material for each component

Chart ends: Completed assembly inspected

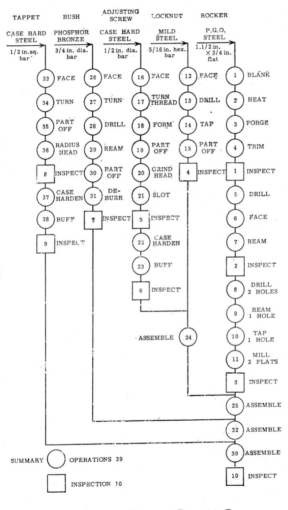

FIG. 9. SPECIMEN OUTLINE PROCESS CHART

fixture, the boss is drilled, the cheeks are faced using a counterbore, and the rocker bearing is reamed. A multi-spindle drilling machine is used for this operation. The machined forgings are inspected

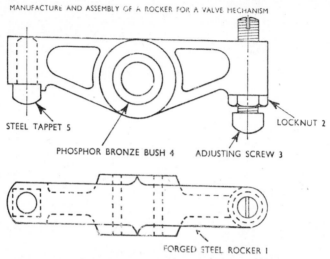

MANUFACTURE AND ASSEMBLY OF A ROCKER FOR A VALVE MECHANISM

STEEL TAPPET 5

LOCKNUT 2

PHOSPHOR BRONZE BUSH 4 ADJUSTING SCREW 3

FORGED STEEL ROCKER 1

FIG. 10. ROCKER ARM (ASSEMBLY SHOWN IN FIG. 9)

before the second drilling operation is carried out. For this the forging is mounted in another drilling fixture which locates in the rocker bearing, and the two holes at the ends of the rocker are drilled. One hole is reamed to size, the other being tapped $\frac{3}{8}$ in. B.S.F. The operation of " drill two holes, ream one, tap one " is also carried out on a multi-spindle machine. The forging is then passed to the milling section where the two flats are milled on a vertical milling machine.

The completed rocker is routed to the inspection department where a final inspection is carried out. It then proceeds to the finished part stores to await an assembly order.

The hardened steel tappet is made from case-hardening steel using $\frac{1}{2}$-in. square bright bar stock. The machining operation " face, turn and part off " is carried out on a capstan lathe. The head is radiused on a grinding machine, using a special fixture, after which it is inspected and passed to the heat treatment section for the head to be case-hardened. The head is then buffed and a final inspection made. The part is then dispatched to the finished part stores.

The bush is made from phosphor bronze using $\frac{3}{4}$-in. diameter bar stock. The machining operation " face, turn, drill, ream and part off " is done on a capstan lathe. The parting burr is removed by finishing. The part is then inspected and passed to the finished part stores.

The adjusting screw is made from case-hardening steel using $\frac{1}{2}$-in. diameter bright bar stock. The machining operation " face, turn thread, form and part off " is carried out on a capstan lathe. The ball head is then ground by means of a special grinding attachment, and the screwdriver slot cut using a slotting saw on a horizontal milling machine. After inspection the part is passed to the heat treatment section for the head to be case-hardened. The head is then buffed and a final inspection made before the screw is sent to the finished part store.

The locknut is made from $\frac{5}{16}$-in. Whitworth hexagonal bright mild steel bar stock in one operation on an automatic screw machine. The part is inspected and sent to the finished part store.

Assembly is performed in four operations. The first and second of these consist of running the locknut up to the head of the adjusting screw and screwing the complete sub-assembly into the rocker. The third operation is to insert the phosphor bronze bush into the rocker forging. This is done on a small bench press. The last operation is the assembly of the hardened steel tappet to the rocker arm, which is also done on a small bench press. The rocker assembly is finally inspected and passed to the finished part stores to await a further assembly order.

Flow Process Chart

The flow process chart is an amplification of the outline process chart, in that it shows *transports, delays* and *storage* as well as operations and inspections. It can express the process in terms of the events as they affect the material being processed, or it can express the process in terms of the activities of the man or the use of certain types of equipment.

Flow process charts recording simultaneous activities of two or more subjects can be presented alongside each other on the same sheet of paper to indicate more clearly their interdependence. *It is essential, however, that only the activities of the particular subject to which it refers, either man, material or equipment, are recorded on any single chart.*

Construction of the Chart

The conventions used in the construction of the chart and the method of construction are the same as for the outline process chart, except that all five symbols are used. It is usual for distance to be recorded on the left of the symbol for transport in the same way as time can be recorded against operations. The total distance can then be entered at the foot of the chart in the manner shown in Fig. 11.

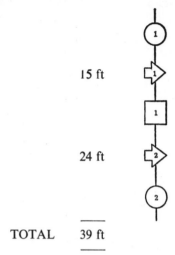

15 ft

24 ft

TOTAL   39 ft

FIG. 11.   SECTION OF FLOW PROCESS CHART SHOWING " TRANSPORTS " AND DISTANCES

Amplifying the Chart

The value of a flow process chart as a record may be increased by making full use of colouring and hatching in order to show up some particular aspect of a process. The transport symbol may be used to show movement in one direction or another by altering the way it faces.

When a particular activity extends over a large area covering different work-places, a clearer understanding of what is done at each is obtained if they are separated on the chart. The movement between the sections concerned is also brought out.

Examples

(i) Fig. 12 shows a *material* type chart recording the flow process of a drum during a packing operation.

(ii) Fig. 13 shows flow process charts recording on the same sheet the activities of *man* and *material* for the job of writing a letter by shorthand-typist.

Fig. 14 shows the same *man* type chart amplified to bring out the process at each work-place and the distance the shorthand-typist travels in writing the letter.

FLOW PROCESS CHART—" MATERIAL " TYPE

Job: Inspection, stencilling and filling 5 cwt drums
(present method).
Chart begins: Empty 5 cwt drum in stock.
Chart ends: Filled 5 cwt drum in stock.
1 Empty 5 cwt drum

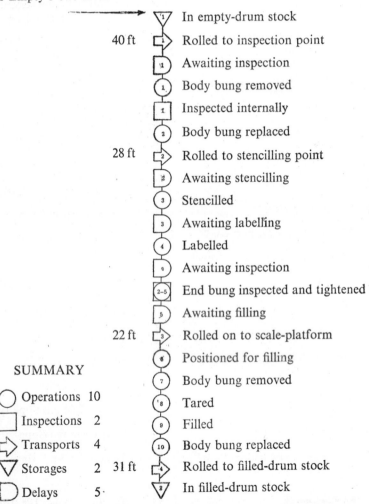

40 ft — In empty-drum stock

Rolled to inspection point

Awaiting inspection

Body bung removed

Inspected internally

Body bung replaced

28 ft — Rolled to stencilling point

Awaiting stencilling

Stencilled

Awaiting labelling

Labelled

Awaiting inspection

End bung inspected and tightened

Awaiting filling

22 ft — Rolled on to scale-platform

Positioned for filling

SUMMARY

Body bung removed

○ Operations 10 — Tared

□ Inspections 2 — Filled

⇨ Transports 4 — Body bung replaced

▽ Storages 2 — 31 ft — Rolled to filled-drum stock

◗ Delays 5· — In filled-drum stock

FIG. 12. FLOW PROCESS CHART SHOWING PROCESS OF " MATERIAL "
THROUGH A PROCESS

FLOW PROCESS CHARTS—"MAN" TYPE AND "MATERIAL" TYPE

Job: Writing a letter using a shorthand-typist (present method).

Chart begins: Typist in own office awaiting dictation.	*Chart begins:* Contents awaiting dictation by author.
Chart ends: Typist puts letter in "out" tray.	*Chart ends:* Contents of letter to "out" tray.

Man
(Typist)

- To author's office
- ① Take dictation
- To own office
- ② Prepare typing set
- ③ Typist types letter and copy
- ④ From m/c and separate copies
- ▢1 Check
- ⑤ Place in book for signature
- To author's office
- ① During checking and signing
- To own office
- ⑥ Type envelope
- ⑦ Letter to envelope
- ⑧ Letter and copy aside to "out" tray

Material
(Contents of Letter)

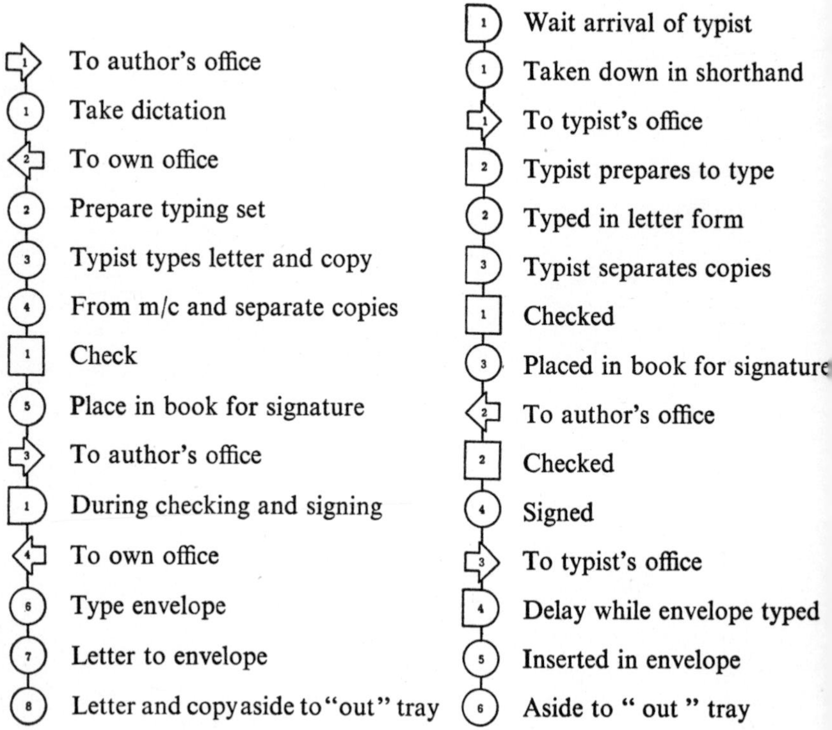

- ① Wait arrival of typist
- ① Taken down in shorthand
- To typist's office
- ② Typist prepares to type
- ② Typed in letter form
- ③ Typist separates copies
- ▢1 Checked
- ③ Placed in book for signature
- To author's office
- ▢2 Checked
- ④ Signed
- To typist's office
- ④ Delay while envelope typed
- ⑤ Inserted in envelope
- ⑥ Aside to "out" tray

FIG. 13. FLOW PROCESS CHARTS, "MAN" AND "MATERIAL," FOR THE SAME JOB

FLOW PROCESS CHART (AMPLIFIED)—
"MAN" TYPE

Job: Writing a letter using a shorthand-typist (present method).

Chart begins: Typist in own office awaiting dictation.

Chart ends: Typist puts letter and copy in out tray.

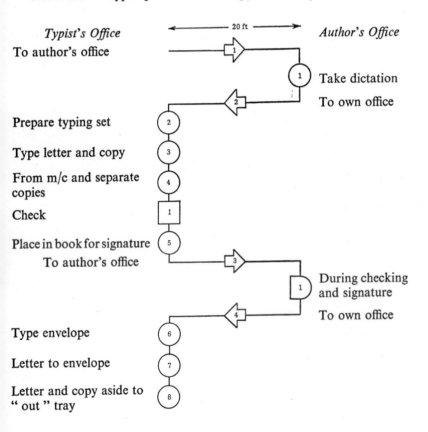

Fig. 14. "Man" Type Flow Process Chart from Fig. 13, Amplified to Emphasize Distances Travelled

Two-handed Process Charts

Work confined to a single work-place often consists of the use of hands and arms only, and the two-handed process chart has been devised to give a synchronized and graphical representation of the sequence of manual activities of the worker. Recording is made by the ordinary symbols with the omission of the inspection symbol, since inspections will be shown as movements of the hands. They can be labelled as inspections by bracketing such movements and writing the word in. The triangle symbol implies *hold* instead of *storage.*

A two-handed process chart is made up of two columns in which are recorded the symbols representing the activities of the left hand and the right hand respectively. They are interrelated by aligning the symbols on the chart so that simultaneous movements by both hands appear opposite each other. A brief description of the activities represented by the symbols should be inserted.

Movements of the two feet can be recorded by making two additional columns.

The use of two-handed process charts is limited by the comparatively broad meaning of the symbols, and the fact that neither paths of movement, nor detailed movements of hands and arms are shown. They do, however, help to assess whether the expense of detailed micromotion analysis is justified.

Two-handed Process Chart—Operations Only

Where only an overall picture of the activities at the work-place is required, the activities of the hands will be described solely in terms of operations. The example given in Fig. 15 gives an overall picture of the assembly of two washers and a nut to a bolt. It will be seen that only the first operation is carried out by both hands simultaneously.

Two-handed Process Chart in Full Detail

If more detail is required for the study, then the symbols for transport, delay and hold will also be used as shown in Fig. 16.

Pre-printed Form for Two-handed Process Charting

Fig. 17 illustrates a suitable design of form for simplifying the construction of two-handed process charts when the volume of work makes such an innovation justifiable.

The Five Gilbreth Classifications of Movement

It may appear that there is excessive body movement in carrying out the operation. If this is the case, the appropriate classification of movement can be placed alongside the symbol to which it refers on the chart. Necessity for the use of these five classifications is usually an indication that the entire operation needs detailed micromotion study.

1. Fingers only I
2. Fingers and wrist II
3. Fingers, wrist and lower arm III
4. Fingers, wrist, lower and upper arm IV
5. Fingers, wrist, lower and upper arm and shoulder . V

TWO-HANDED PROCESS CHART

Job: Assemble two washers and nut to bolt (present method).

Chart begins: Hands empty: material in boxes.

Chart ends: Completed assembly aside to box.

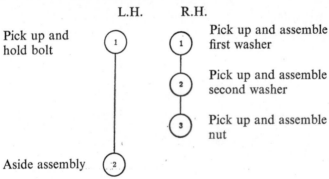

L.H.   R.H.

Pick up and hold bolt ① ① Pick up and assemble first washer

② Pick up and assemble second washer

③ Pick up and assemble nut

Aside assembly ②

FIG. 15. TWO-HANDED PROCESS CHART SHOWING " OPERATIONS " ONLY

Multiple Activity Charts and Simo Charts

The multiple activity chart is used whenever it is necessary to consider on the same document the activities of a subject in relation to one or more others. By allotting separate bars, placed against a common time scale, to represent the activities of each worker or machine during a process, the multiple activity time chart shows

TWO-HANDED PROCESS CHART

Job: Assemble two washers and nut to bolt
(present method).

Chart begins: Hands empty: material in boxes.

Chart ends: Completed assembly aside to box.

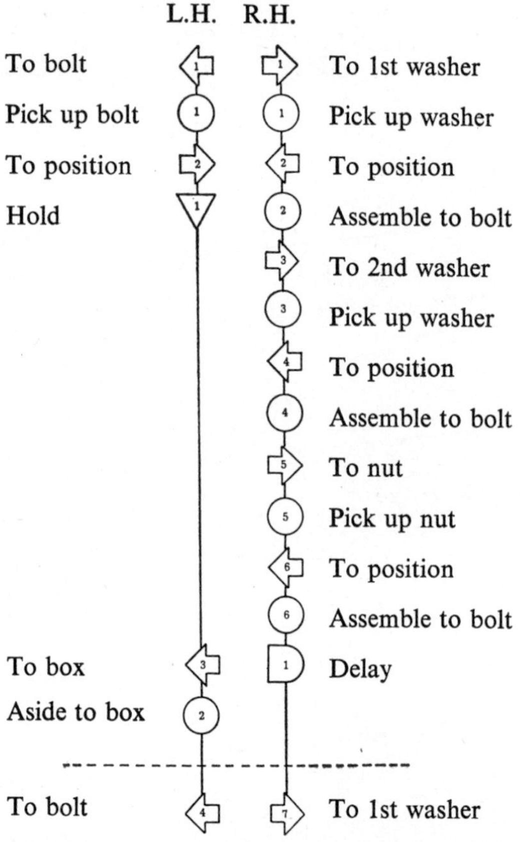

L.H. R.H.

L.H.			R.H.
To bolt	⟨1	1⟩	To 1st washer
Pick up bolt	(1)	(1)	Pick up washer
To position	2⟩	⟨2	To position
Hold	▽1	(2)	Assemble to bolt
		3⟩	To 2nd washer
		(3)	Pick up washer
		⟨4	To position
		(4)	Assemble to bolt
		5⟩	To nut
		(5)	Pick up nut
		⟨6	To position
		(6)	Assemble to bolt
To box	⟨3	(1)	Delay
Aside to box	(2)		
To bolt	⟨4	7⟩	To 1st washer

FIG. 16. TWO-HANDED PROCESS CHART SHOWING FULLER USE OF SYMBOLS

up clearly periods of ineffective time within the process. This makes
the avoidance of such time by rearrangement of work a very much
easier task. It is often useful to construct the chart so that the most
important subject from the aspect of costs receives the major emphasis.

TWO-HANDED CHART

PRESENT
PROPOSED METHOD

REF NO
PAGE ____ OF ____

	SUMMARY		
	PRESENT	PROPOSED	DIFFERENCE
	L.H.	R.H.	L.H.	R.H.	L.H.	R.H.

JOB

CHART BEGINS

CHART ENDS

CHARTED BY ____ DATE ____

OPERATOR

LAYOUT

PARTS SKETCH

LEFT HAND	MOVEMENT CLASS	OPERATION	TRANSPORT	HOLD	DELAY	OPERATION	TRANSPORT	HOLD	DELAY	MOVEMENT CLASS	RIGHT HAND
		○	☐	▽	D	○	☐	▽	D		
		○	☐	▽	D	○	☐	▽	D		
		○	☐	▽	D	○	☐	▽	D		
		○	☐	▽	D	○	☐	▽	D		
		○	☐	▽	D	○	☐	▽	D		
		○	☐	▽	D	○	☐	▽	D		
		○	☐	▽	D	○	☐	▽	D		
		○	☐	▽	D	○	☐	▽	D		
		○	☐	▽	D	○	☐	▽	D		
		○	☐	▽	D	○	☐	▽	D		
		○	☐	▽	D	○	☐	▽	D		

FIG. 17. PRE-PRINTED FORM FOR TWO-HANDED PROCESS CHART

This type of chart is particularly useful for enabling maintenance and similar work to be organized so that the time expensive equipment is out of commission is reduced to a minimum (*see* Fig. 20). It is also a useful means, when organizing team work, of deciding the number of machines workers should look after, and for other similar purposes. It enables complex processes to be recorded in a simple way for study at leisure.

Construction of the Chart

Worker and machine activities are normally recorded by shading the respective bars. The timings, which can be built up from previous measurements or by direct timing, need only be sufficiently accurate to ensure the chart will be as effective as possible. Timings by clock or wristwatch are sometimes adequate; frequently however, it will be necessary to ascertain times by one of the techniques of work measurement. The activities are then plotted in sequence against the time scale within their own particular bar on the chart.

Fig. 18 is an example of a multiple activity chart of the job of writing a letter using a shorthand-typist described in Fig. 13.

Summary

A concise summary of the present and proposed methods, showing the times and percentage use of all subjects should be made. An illustration of a possible form is shown in Fig. 19.

MULTIPLE ACTIVITY CHART

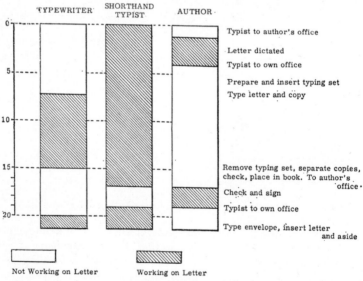

FIG. 18. MULTIPLE ACTIVITY CHART OF JOB SHOWN IN FIG. 13

	PRESENT				PROPOSED				DIFFERENCE			
	Subject A		Subject B		Subject A		Subject B		Subject A		Subject B	
	Time	%	Time	%	Time	%	Time	%	Time	%	Time	%
WORK												
IDLE												

FIG. 19. SUGGESTED FORMAT FOR SUMMARY OF MULTIPLE ACTIVITY CHART

MULTIPLE ACTIVITY CHARTS

Job: Inspection of catalyst in converter.

Chart begins: Converter ready for opening for inspection of catalyst.

Chart ends: Converter ready for operation again.

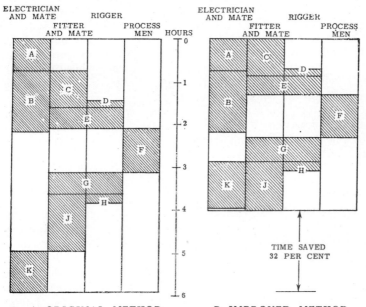

A ORIGINAL METHOD   B IMPROVED METHOD

A	Remove heaters	F	Inspect or adjust catalyst
B	Workshop repairs	G	Replace top
C	Release vessel top	H	Remove tackle
D	Fix tackle	J	Secure vessel top
E	Remove top	K	Replace heaters

FIG. 20. MULTIPLE ACTIVITY CHART COVERING MEMBERS OF A TEAM

Example

Multiple activity charts have many important uses and a further example may help in understanding them. Fig. 20 shows the charts for a team engaged in the operation of inspecting the catalyst in a converter.

During the " running-in " period of a new catalytic converter in an organic chemical plant, it was necessary to make frequent checks of the condition of the catalyst, and to make such adjustments to the catalyst as were then found to be necessary. It was desired to ensure that the time the converter was open for inspection, and, therefore, out of service, was as short as possible. The task was studied in order to find the best sequence of carrying out the various parts of the work.

In the original method the removal of the vessel top was not started until the heaters had been removed, and replacement of the heaters was not started until the top had been completely fixed.

It was found unnecessary for the removal or replacement of the heaters to be done entirely independently of the other work. It was accordingly arranged for the top to be unfastened while the heaters were being removed, and for the heaters to be replaced during the time the top was being secured in place.

The saving: nearly two hours' reduction in the time the converter was out of service on each occasion. The importance of reducing the time that a major unit of expensive plant of this nature is out of service needs no emphasis.

Therbligs

When there is justification for studying work in much greater detail than is possible with the two-handed process chart, it is necessary to use a technique which will enable an accurate record to be made of the events taking place during very short periods of time. This is done by making the record in terms of *therbligs*, which is the name Gilbreth gave to the seventeen elementary movements or groups of movements into which he divided all types of human activity. (Since his time the number has been increased to eighteen.) As some of the therbligs refer to activities requiring a somewhat lengthy description, a series of symbols and colours has been developed to facilitate their use for charting purposes.

After establishing these therbligs from a detailed analysis of many varying types of work, Gilbreth considered that further subdivision was impracticable. For a description of the different categories of

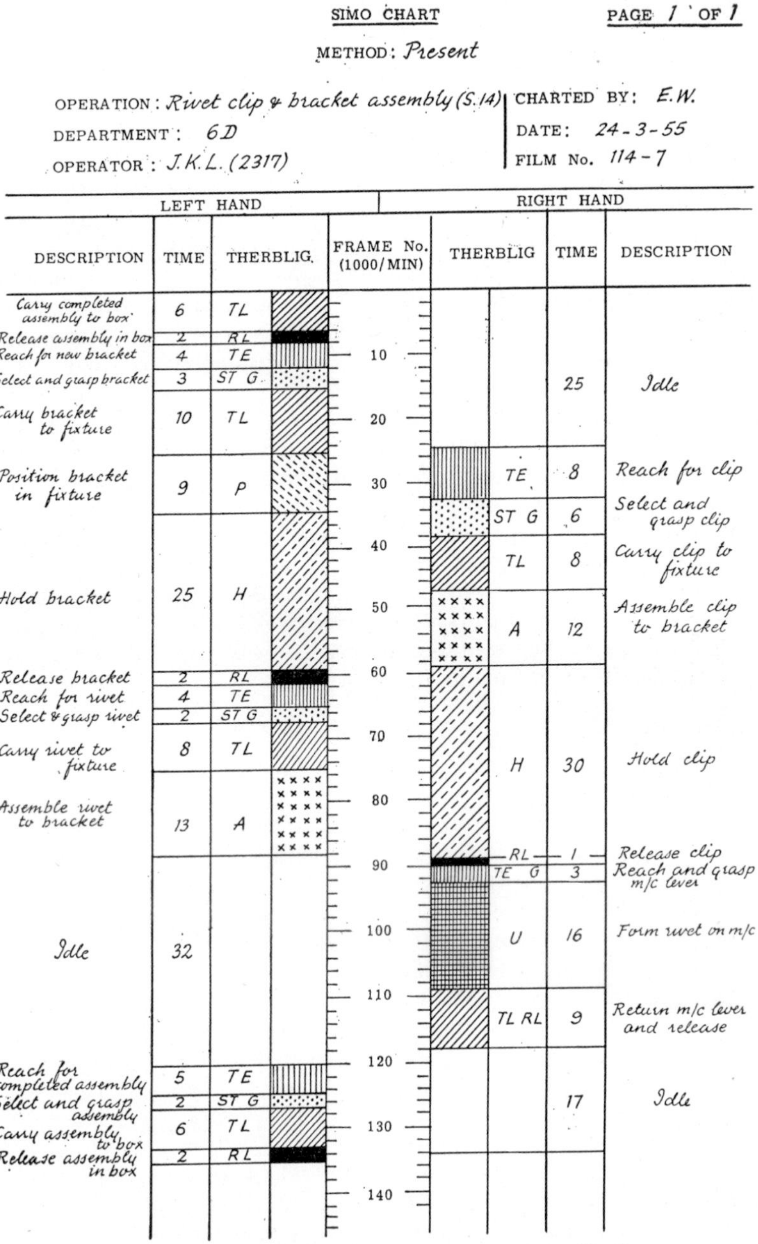

METHOD: *Present*

OPERATION: *Rivet clip & bracket assembly (S.14)*   CHARTED BY: *E.W.*

DEPARTMENT: *6D*   DATE: *24-3-55*

OPERATOR: *J.K.L. (2317)*   FILM No. *114-7*

LEFT HAND			FRAME No. (1000/MIN)	RIGHT HAND		
DESCRIPTION	TIME	THERBLIG.		THERBLIG	TIME	DESCRIPTION
Carry completed assembly to box	6	TL				
Release assembly in box	2	RL				
Reach for new bracket	4	TE	10			
Select and grasp bracket	3	ST G			25	Idle
Carry bracket to fixture	10	TL	20			
Position bracket in fixture	9	P	30	TE	8	Reach for clip
				ST G	6	Select and grasp clip
			40	TL	8	Carry clip to fixture
Hold bracket	25	H	50	A	12	Assemble clip to bracket
Release bracket	2	RL	60			
Reach for rivet	4	TE				
Select & grasp rivet	2	ST G				
Carry rivet to fixture	8	TL	70			
				H	30	Hold clip
Assemble rivet to bracket	13	A	80			
			90	RL	1	Release clip
				TE G	3	Reach and grasp m/c lever
			100	U	16	Form rivet on m/c
Idle	32		110			
				TL RL	9	Return m/c lever and release
			120		17	Idle
Reach for completed assembly	5	TE				
Select and grasp assembly	2	ST G				
Carry assembly to box	6	TL	130			
Release assembly in box	2	RL				
			140			

FIG. 21. SIMULTANEOUS MOTION CYCLE (" SIMO ") CHART

The shaded areas against each therblig in this example represent the different colours which would be used in practice.

movement to which they refer the reader is referred to one of the authoritative textbooks on micromotion analysis.

Simultaneous Motion Cycle (Simo) Chart

The simultaneous motion cycle or simo chart is used to record simultaneously on a common time scale the activities of the two hands, or other parts of the worker's body during the performance of a single cycle of the operation being investigated. From the accompanying example, Fig. 21, it will be noticed that the record is made in therbligs, and that the time scale is exceptionally large. A record of this type is usually made from a frame-by-frame analysis of a cine film of the operation.

The scope and limitations of micromotion analysis can be gauged from this example, where the complete operation cycle recorded is of only a few seconds' duration. Within this short period, appreciable idle time and unbalance of work have been detected. To prepare such a chart, however, an elaborate procedure and the use of expensive equipment is required. Investigation in this degree of detail is only justified, therefore, when the repetitiveness of the operation and the period for which it is likely to run are such that the savings resulting from an improved method will defray the cost of the work involved.

Diagrams and Models

Although the flow process chart shows the sequence and nature of movements, it does not show clearly the paths of movement. In the paths of movement there are often undesirable features such as backtracking, congestion and unnecessarily long movements. To record these undesirable features, representations of the working area, in the form of flow diagrams, string diagrams or two- and three-dimensional models can be made.

The clarity of these techniques makes them particularly useful when considering problems of plant layout and design, and they can be used effectively to demonstrate proposed improvements both to management and workers. Colouring may further enhance their value.

Flow Diagrams

The flow diagram is a drawing, substantially to scale, of the working area, showing the location of the various activities identified by their numbered symbols, and is associated with a particular flow process chart, either *man* or *material* or *equipment* type.

The routes followed in transport are shown by joining the symbols in sequence by a line which represents as nearly as possible the paths of movement of the subject concerned. The direction of movement is shown by the numbered transport symbols which form part of the flow line.

Example (I). Fig. 22 shows a simple flow diagram, recording the work performed by a shorthand-typist in writing a letter. The corresponding man type flow process chart to which the symbols refer appears on page 51.

Example (II). Fig. 23 (page 62) shows a flow diagram for the job of drum packing, originally charted on page 49.

Flow Diagram Elevations. As distances moved on the vertical plane can be just as significant as those on the horizontal plane, flow diagrams can be prepared to show an elevation as well as a plan of the area concerned.

Three-dimensional Flow Diagrams. When a subject covers several floor levels as well as different parts of the factory, a three-dimensional flow diagram is particularly useful.

Example (III). The illustration in Fig. 24 shows the unloading of goods and their removal to storage on the first floor.

String Diagrams

The string diagram is a scale layout drawing on which a length of string is used to record the extent as well as the pattern of movement of a worker or piece of equipment working within a limited area

FLOW DIAGRAM

Operation. Writing a letter using a shorthand-typist.

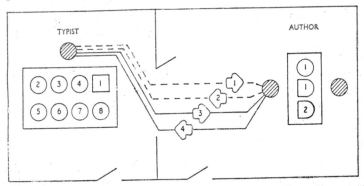

FIG. 22. FLOW DIAGRAM RELATING TO JOB SHOWN IN FIGS. 13 AND 18

FLOW DIAGRAM (DRUM PACKING)

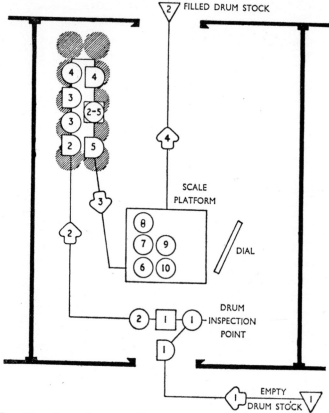

Fig. 23. Flow Diagram Relating to Job Shown in Fig. 12

during a certain period of time. Although it can be used in places where the movement is a simple backward and forward one between two or three fixed points, it is of most value where the journeys are so irregular in distance and frequency that it would otherwise be difficult to see exactly what is happening.

Construction

Once the need for a string diagram has been established, the first step is to make a study of the movements in the task concerned. This should take the form of a continuous half- or whole-day, or other

THREE-DIMENSIONAL FLOW DIAGRAM

Job: Unloading goods and removal to storage on first floor (present method).

Chart begins: Goods on lorry arriving at goods entrance.

Chart ends: Goods in store.

Flow Diagram

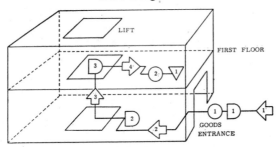

FLOW PROCESS CHART
(Material Type)

Goods to building on lorry

Await unloading

Unloaded to hand trolley

To goods lift on trolley

Await arrival of lift

Enter lift on trolley and to 1st floor

Await removal of trolley from lift

From lift and to store on trolley

Unloaded from trolley

In storage

FIG. 24. FLOW DIAGRAM, WITH FLOW PROCESS CHART OF ACTIVITIES ON TWO FLOOR LEVELS

appropriate period, of observation, during which every journey involved in the performance of the work should be recorded on the study sheet.

The form of study sheet required is extremely simple. The first page should contain sufficient data to ensure that the information recorded is readily identifiable. A suggested form of heading is illustrated below.

STRING DIAGRAM STUDY

Man/material/equipment/studied................   Study No...........
....   Sheet No. 1 of.......
Department................................   Date...............
Section....................................   Time started........
Worker's name....................No......   Time finished........
Cross reference............................   Study taken by.......

1 Time Dep.	2 Time Arr.	3 Time Elapsed	4 Destination	5 Notes

All this information, with the exception of the study and sheet numbers, and column headings, could be omitted from succeeding pages.

When the study has been completed, a scale layout drawing is prepared of the area in which the recorded moves have taken place. The scale used should be as large as possible: half an inch or quarter of an inch to the foot are excellent if they can be accommodated on the paper. Care should be taken to include in this drawing not only building features, such as walls and doorways, but also block plans of machinery and other equipment installed in the immediate vicinity of the route, whether or not it is actually concerned with the job or equipment being studied.

The completed drawing should then be attached to a sheet of plywood or composition board and panel pins driven into it at each of the terminal points observed during the study; it will also be necessary for additional pins to be inserted where the direction of moves between these points changes. Pins should be driven in until only about half an inch of their shanks protrude, so that they do not work loose as construction of the diagram proceeds. Terminal points will correspond to machines, storage racks, stacked materials, loading docks and other similar places between which journeys are made.

A strong thread is then tied to the starting point pin, and by reference to the study, taken round each of the other terminal points on the drawing in the sequence in which they were visited; the pins placed at corners along the route enable the thread to follow on the diagram a course very similar to that actually taken while the study was being made.

In this way it is possible to record on the diagram any number of journeys between any number of points. Because thread is used instead of drawing in lines to represent each trip, there is no risk that obliteration will take place along the most frequented portions of the route. Also, if it is required to make several studies of the same task or equipment on different occasions, each diagram may be photographed as soon as it is completed. After other relevant information has been obtained, the string can then be removed and the layout is ready for use with the next study.

By using different coloured threads, diagrams can be prepared on which the movement of several different workers or pieces of equipment working within the same general area are represented. Thread of a single colour can also be used to indicate movement under different circumstances, such as whether a truck is travelling empty or full, by attaching clips or flags or otherwise marking the lengths between certain terminal points.

Use

The primary function of a string diagram is to produce a record of an existing set of conditions so that the job of seeing what is actually taking place is made as simple as possible. Like other recording techniques, the string diagram is not an end in itself, and if it is to justify the time spent in its preparation it is important that it should be correctly interpreted and used.

As soon as it has been completed, the diagram should be carefully examined to see what facts it brings to light. In the normal way it will be known what type of information is being looked for and whether, for instance, an excessive amount of movement appears to be involved as a result of the arrangement of certain machines or the location of material storage points, or whether there is congestion in some areas. This knowledge will be of great help in interpreting the diagram.

One of the most valuable features of the string diagram is the way it enables the actual distance travelled during the period of the study to be calculated by relating the length of the thread used to the scale of the drawing. Thus it is possible to make a very effective comparison between different layouts or methods of doing a job in terms of the amount of travelling involved.

If changes in operation rather than in layout are indicated, it may be a better proposition actually to introduce such changes on a temporary basis. A study of the new method in use can then be made and the resulting string diagram compared with data obtained from the original. When changes in layout appear inevitable, a considerable amount of experimental work can often be performed on the original diagram itself before the expense of altering doorways, moving machinery, etc., need be incurred. For instance, the use of cardboard templets to represent machines, stacks of materials, etc., will enable different arrangements to be tried out quite easily on the scale drawing. The routes between the new terminal points can then be re-strung and measured until the most satisfactory movements have been found. These can then be translated on to the shop floor, and, if necessary, another study made to check performance with that provided for.

Apart from the measured information it provides, especially if the study included a time record, the general appearance of a string diagram can sometimes repay careful study. A diagram for a single worker or piece of equipment will give a good idea whether an excessive amount of backtracking is taking place or whether the movement pattern is orderly and consistent. If the movements of two or more workers or pieces of equipment have been plotted on the same diagram, a realistic picture of what is happening may be obtained if the studies are made simultaneously. (This will mean a different observer being detailed to make each study, although the diagram itself could afterwards have been compiled by a single individual.) The result is then a much truer picture of the way in which movements overlap or interfere with each other than if the studies were made at different times. In this manner bottlenecks and other unprofitable activities, such as duplicated or unnecessary journeys, may be located.

Summary

Preparation of the string diagram from a study of the type indicated enables a convenient form of summary to be prepared showing the likely effect on transport of changes in either the existing layout, the nature of existing operations, or their sequence. As far as proposals for changes in layout are concerned they can be assessed for their probable advantages by preparing string diagrams of them on which are reproduced the new routes of the journeys recorded in the original study. In the same way, the effect on transport requirements of alterations to certain operations can sometimes be gauged, and the result incorporated in a string diagram to enable its significance to be seen.

SUMMARY

Total clocked time (duration of study)...........

Unproductive time noted.......................

Method	Movement			Loading and unloading time		Total saving as % of clocked time	Total saving in distance travelled
	Distance (feet)	Time					
		Min	% of clocked time	Min	% of clocked time		
1. Present							
2. Proposed (alternative 1)							
3. Proposed (alternative 2)							

It may sometimes also be useful to include in the study some notes on the work performed at each terminal point between different journeys, and to give some indication of this on the string diagram. In practice the amount of additional detail recorded depends very much on individual requirements, but care should be taken not to complicate the diagram by attempting to include too much information on it. Construction and interpretation will be simpler if the purpose for which it is being prepared is constantly borne in mind.

To summarize. The principal uses of string diagrams are to investigate movement in the following circumstances—

1. When a team is working.
2. When one worker is tending several machines.
3. In processes where several sub-assemblies have to be moved to another assembly.
4. Where the process necessitates the worker moving from one work-place to another.
5. For testing the relative values of different layouts. (In this case the alternative routes for achieving the same ends are measured and compared on each layout.)

Example. Fig. 25 shows the appearance of a string diagram, recording the path of movement of a laboratory assistant in performing a
day's work.

STRING   DIAGRAM

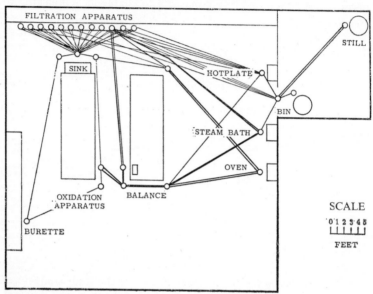

FILTRATION APPARATUS

SINK

STILL

HOTPLATE

BIN

STEAM BATH

OVEN

OXIDATION
APPARATUS

BALANCE

BURETTE

SCALE

0 1 2 3 4 5

FEET

FIG. 25. STRING DIAGRAM. (HEAVY LINES SHOW FREQUENT JOURNEYS)

Two-dimensional Models (Templets)

Loose templets can be used to represent machinery, furniture, and
fittings, in developing new methods. Templets made from thin card
will suffice for most purposes. If frequent re-layout is essential,
heavy card or plywood will prove more satisfactory. To prevent
them moving about while the layout is being prepared, templets
may be backed with coarse emery or glass paper, and the arrangement tried out on a piece of baize cloth.

If the layout has to be arranged in a vertical position, pressure-
adhesive or magnetic templets may have to be used upon an appropriate material.

When positioning templets care must be taken to see that the areas
required for maintenance and cleaning, safe clearance, loading and
satisfactory operation, are included. These areas can be coloured
distinctively to give greater clarity. To eliminate drawing and trac-
ing, the final layout can be photographed.

Three-dimensional Models

A scale model of a working area has similar uses to a three-dimensional flow diagram. It also enables questions of environment, lighting, heating, ventilation, maintenance and safety to be visualized. Being easily understood by employees, it is useful in obtaining their practical advice on changes in method and layout, and can be of great value in demonstrating the advantages of the proposed changes to all concerned. Because of the cost of their preparation, however, three-dimensional models should not be resorted to unless it is felt that their use is essential to portray satisfactorily a certain set of conditions.

Photographic Aids

In those techniques of method study concerned with investigation on a plant- or factory-wide basis, nearly all the observations are carried out using the naked eye. In the case of more detailed investigation at a work-place where the operations may be of very short duration, or performed at a high speed, or where several different jobs are being carried out simultaneously, the observer is frequently unable to perceive movements accurately enough for recording purposes. In such circumstances photography can be used to make the record on which the examination is based.

Both still and cine photography are employed for this work, and while the provision of equipment and processing facilities can be a major item, where there is frequent opportunity for their use the cost of the materials is usually a minor consideration.

New applications for photography are still being found in the field of work study. The following are some of the more obvious benefits made possible by one or other of the techniques—

1. A permanent record is obtained of the work being studied.
2. The record can be referred to at any time, in any place, and by any number of people.
3. An excellent means is obtained of demonstrating differences in methods. This is a particularly valuable aid to training.
4. Reproduction of the original method is possible at any time after the improved method has been installed. This is a useful feature when the degree of improvement achieved may be disputed.
5. Repeated study of a worker's activities can be made without disturbing him at frequent intervals.
6. The examination of intermittent work can proceed when the work itself is not actually in progress.

Use of Cine Films

Cine films possess a number of features which are of particular value for method study purposes—

1. They can be projected at any required speed and can be stopped at any convenient point.

2. They can be run backwards, which sometimes enables clumsy or awkward movements to be more easily detected.

3. The fact that movement is confined within the limits of the film enables absolute concentration to be focused on the activities without the noise and distraction of the normal surroundings in which the work is carried out.

It will be appreciated that special equipment, both for making the films and projecting them, may be necessary to take advantage of these features. When this is available the following are the main ways in which films are employed—

Micromotion. The therbligs referred to in Chapter 5 can often be determined only from a frame-by-frame analysis of a cine film record. When a film is made for this purpose an exposure speed of 1,000 frames per minute is sometimes employed which enables a decimal minute scale to be used for charting purposes. Alternatively a time indicator is placed in the field of view of the camera during exposure, which enables the duration of each element to be established irrespective of the frame speed used.

Normal Records. Cine photography at normal substandard speed (960 frames per minute) is particularly useful for obtaining a record of an existing method, including layout of the work-place. Because it can be carried out with the cheapest type of camera and material available (8 mm), it is frequently a proposition to use it as a means of recording a complete cycle of every operation involved in a process. Before filming the cycle itself, a " shot " of a card or blackboard upon which details of the operation are written ensures subsequent identification.

Memomotion. It is possible to couple to a cine camera a timing device which permits the exposure of a single frame of the film at predetermined regular intervals. The interval period usually lies between a half and four seconds, and can be varied according to the nature of the activity being studied. By employing this device it is possible continuously to record the activities within the working area over a lengthy period. The resultant series of still shots can be analysed and used as the basis for the construction of the appropriate charts.

This method of recording is likely to be most useful when it is desired to examine the simultaneous activities of a team of workers. Without this technique several observers would probably have to be employed to record the activities and their individual records would be difficult to co-ordinate.

Memomotion is economical in film consumption, as, assuming a rate of exposure of one frame per second, activities extending over a period of an hour can be recorded on 100 ft of 16 mm film.

Cyclegraphs and Chronocyclegraphs

In addition to the straightforward use of still photography to make permanent records of work-place layouts, string diagrams and models, etc., a technique was originated by Gilbreth to enable comparatively short motion patterns to be recorded on a photograph of the work-place itself. The record can be made as a continuous or dotted white line, known as a cyclegraph or chronocyclegraph, respectively.

A cyclegraph is a record of path of movement, usually traced by a continuous source of light on a photograph. It is produced by attaching small lights to the worker's wrists (or whatever member it is desired to observe) and making a time exposure (on a small lens stop) while a single cycle or portion of a cycle is performed. The camera shutter is then closed after which a normal instantaneous exposure is made on the same film.

A similar photographic procedure is used to make a chronocyclegraph in which the light source is suitably interrupted so that the path appears as a series of pear-shaped spots. This enables both the direction of movement and the speed at any point along the path to be recorded. This is achieved in the following way—

1. The interruption of the light source is arranged to take place at carefully controlled regular intervals (usually 10, 20 or 30 times per second).
2. The method of interruption is such that, when the light is being recorded on the film, the movement of the subject results in a pear-shaped dot being produced, distinctly tapering off at one end. This is achieved either by means of suitable equipment in the lighting circuit operating at the required frequency, or by exposing the film through a disc rotating at the appropriate speed and of suitably graduated density.

When the frequency of the interruptions is known, the speed and direction of movement at any point along the path can be easily calculated from the number and shape of dots recorded.

The main value of cyclegraphs and chronocyclegraphs, however, lies in the convenience with which different motion patterns can be compared for variations in the method of performing a particular operation.

Although still photography is simpler and cheaper to carry out than cine photography, it usually involves some interruption of the work being studied. This can sometimes be minimized, even when making cyclegraphs and chronocyclegraphs, by using equipment which will enable exposures to be developed before the apparatus is taken away. In this manner the necessity to go back and repeat the procedure because of an unsatisfactory record is eliminated.

6

Method Study : Examine

THE critical examination is the crux of the basic procedure. Consequently it is sometimes more effective to have two people working on it together. The object of critically examining the recorded facts of an existing or proposed method is to determine the true reasons underlying each event, and to draw up a systematic list of all the possible improvements for later development into a new and improved method. The whole examination procedure requires exhaustive collaboration with everyone in a position to offer information which may prove useful, and also full use of all available sources of technical information.

The recording techniques used should have been chosen so that all the essential facts concerning the process are exposed for this thorough examination. In practice, after the examination starts, it is often found that more information is wanted on some aspect of the process. It is then necessary to have further consultation with those best suited to provide this, and, if required, to make additional records. Frequently the approximate timings originally recorded on process charts are found to be insufficiently accurate, and further timings have to be obtained by one of the techniques of work measurement.

When examining the recorded facts of a process it is important to keep to a set plan. The set examination begins by focusing attention in turn on individual aspects of activities. Only after full consultation with those concerned has established the true facts and reasons underlying one aspect of a procedure should the next aspect be investigated. When he has this full knowledge of the underlying reasons, the work study officer is in a position to review the process as a whole, and, using the same system of full consultation with those who may be able to offer him useful knowledge and ideas, seek the alternatives which are available.

Approach

The results which the set form of critical examination can achieve will naturally be influenced by the attitude of mind of the work study officer, and by his ability to elicit relevant information from all the many available sources. It is perhaps worth mentioning a few points which should be borne in mind—

1. Facts must be examined as they are, not as they appear to be, or should be, or are said to be.

2. Preconceived ideas, which often colour the interpretation of facts, must be allowed no play.

3. All aspects of the problem must be approached with a challenging and sceptical attitude. Every detail must be examined logically and no answer accepted until it has been proved correct.

4. Hasty judgements must be avoided.

5. Detail must have persistent and close attention.

6. Experiment resulting from " hunches," which should have been immediately committed to paper as they occurred, should be reserved to the appropriate place in the investigation.

7. New methods should not even be considered until all the undesirable features of the existing method have been exposed by systematic examination.

The objectives of the method study as outlined in Chapter 4 should at all times be remembered. The results of improvements in the fields referred to will be the elimination of waste of both materials and time.

Classification of Operations

Although transports and delays may superficially appear to give the greatest scope for improvement, it may be possible to reduce work by eliminating certain operations, or by changing their sequence, and this will automatically affect transports and delays. An examination of the operations in a process should therefore first be made in order of their importance to the overall process. If they have been divided into *make ready, do* and *put away* classifications on the lines indicated in Chapter 5, elimination of any of the do operations will enable any make ready and put away operations connected with them automatically to be eliminated, as well as corresponding transports and delays.

Examination Procedure

The examination is achieved by means of two sets of detailed questions: the primary questions to indicate the facts and the reasons underlying them, and the secondary questions to indicate the alternatives and consequently the means of improvement. The questions are asked under five headings which inquire into the purpose of the operation, the place where it is carried out, and the means by which it is carried out. Both primary and secondary questions are asked for each aspect before passing on to the next. Obviously, if the detailed questioning by both primary and secondary questions does not establish a purpose for an operation, there is no need to waste time inquiring into any other aspect of it.

Other activities which still appear to be necessary after the full examination of the operations can then be subjected to the same procedure.

The Primary Questions

The following are the primary questions under their respective headings—

1. *Purpose*. The questions " What is *achieved?* " and " Is it *necessary?* " and " Why? " challenge the existence of the activity. The answers to these questions determine whether the particular activity will be included in the new method.

2. *Place*. The questions asked under this heading are " *Where* is it done? " and, " Why *there?* "

3. *Sequence*. The sequence of the activity in relation to other activities is challenged by asking " *When* is it done? " and " Why *then?* "

4. *Person*. The next questions refer to the person performing the activity. They are " *Who* does it? " and " Why *that person?* "

6. *Means*. Finally the means of carrying out the activity are challenged by asking " *How* is it done? " and " Why *that way?* "

The first question, " What is achieved? " ensures that whatever is written as the description against the symbol on a chart is accurately phrased and, more important still, properly understood. In this way the real achievement of the activity is established. The answer to this first question indicates the form which succeeding questions should take, and ensures that the correct details of the activity are considered in those questions, and that questions which are inapplicable to the circumstances are not asked.

Since the object of the primary questions is to ensure that every facet of an existing method is clearly understood, it is important not to confuse the questions and answers relating to " purpose " and " means." For instance, when considering the operation of tying a parcel with string, the question under purpose, " What is achieved? ", would receive the answer, " The parcel is fastened," and *not*, " The parcel is tied with string." Similarly, in applying the questioning sequence to the operation of planing a certain length of timber to $\frac{1}{2}$-in. thickness, the question under purpose, " What is achieved? " should receive an answer such as " A length of timber, 3 ft. × 6 in., is reduced to $\frac{1}{2}$-in. thickness." The question " How is it done? " might then be answered " By planing with a rotating cutter block on a 9-in. Wadkin surface planing machine."

The primary questions fill in the background of events and establish whether existing procedures are based on sound reasoning. They should clearly indicate any part of the work which is unnecessary or inefficient in respect of place, sequence, person or means.

The Secondary Questions

The secondary questions seek to establish suitable alternatives to existing, or previously proposed methods.

Under—
    Purpose, it is asked—What else *could* be done?
    Place, it is asked—Where else *could* it be?
    Sequence, it is asked—When else *could* it be?
    Person, it is asked—Who else *could* do it?
    Means, it is asked—How else *could* it be?

When each of the above questions is applied to any event it may suggest a number of possibilities. When these have been established it may be necessary to ask—

    What *should* be done?
    Where *should* it be done?
    When *should* it be done?
    Who *should* do it?
    How *should* it be done?

The answers to these last five questions indicate the lines along which a new method for the overall process should be developed,

Reference . . . .
Page . . . .
Date . . . .

DESCRIPTION OF ELEMENT

	The Present Facts	Alternatives	Selected Alternative for Development
Purpose—WHAT is achieved?	IS IT NECESSARY? YES / NO. If YES—Why?	What ELSE could be done?	What?
Place—WHERE is it done?	WHY THERE?	Where ELSE could it be done?	Where?
Sequence—WHEN is it done?	WHY THEN?	When ELSE could it be done?	When?
Person—WHO does it?	WHY THAT PERSON?	Who ELSE could do it?	Who?
Means—HOW is it done?	WHY THAT WAY?	How ELSE could it be done?	How?

FIG. 26. CRITICAL EXAMINATION SHEET

though it is possible that adequate decisions cannot be made at this stage and further inquiries may have to be made when developing the new method.

In obtaining the answers to these secondary questions, which will be the pointers to improvement, the following considerations are of first importance—

1. When the purpose of the activity is challenged, the main object is to see whether it can be *eliminated* entirely.

2. If the activity proves to be essential, then the object must be to see whether it can be modified by *changing* it or *combining* it with other activities. In some cases it is, of course, possible to obtain improvements by separating and redistributing the work content of particular activities. In this way improvements are often obtained by combining or changing the *place* where work is done, the *sequence* in which activities are performed, or the *persons* performing the activities.

3. Finally, and this is particularly important when the "means" of doing a job are being considered, attention is given to see how an activity can be *simplified*.

Creative Thinking

Creative thinking or brainstorming first came into prominence in pre-war days in America in the advertising field and was credited with startling successes. In practice, however, the technique is nothing new. It is applied by most people in varying degrees of intensity; but since imagination is often suppressed from childhood onwards, a premium is placed on sound and reasoned judgement. Many ideas may thereby be stifled at birth. The specialized technique of the creative thinking session has been used to ensure that, at the stage of method study concerned with seeking alternative methods, a greater flow of new ideas is generated.

A group of people are gathered together, presented with a specific problem and asked to fire off the first ideas that come into their heads for solving it. All criticism both by word and implication is ruled out. The wilder the ideas that emerge the better, and quantity of ideas is sought rather than quality. Ideas suggested by one member of the group are built on and improved by the other members. The result of the session is a mass of ideas, most of them admittedly completely impractical, but a few worthy of closer attention. It is argued that these few are far more likely to produce " a bunch of keys " for solving the problem than would have been achieved by exclusively conventional methods.

There is no standard practice for running a session. The following points, however, will always well repay attention—

(*a*) Careful definition of the problem. If the problem is of a general nature, better results are likely to be achieved if it can be divided into parts.

(*b*) Careful selection of the team. The group should be of roughly the same managerial or intellectual level and have a background knowledge of the type of problem under discussion.

(*c*) Inhibitions must be broken down. Careful selection of the team helps, and better results may be achieved if they have had an opportunity to make each other's acquaintance in a relaxed atmosphere.

(*d*) The team should be kept informed of what happens after the session and where possible should be present when the ideas are critically examined.

Summary

The sequence of the examination to which each activity is subjected can be summarized as follows—

Purpose	— What is achieved?
	Is it necessary? Why?
	What else could be done?
	What should be done?
Place	— Where is it done?
	Why there?
	Where else could it be?
	Where should it?
Sequence	— When is it done?
	Why then?
	When else could it be?
	When should it?
Person	— Who does it?
	Why that person?
	Who else could do it?
	Who should?
Means	— How is it done?
	Why that way?
	How else could it be?
	How should it?

This questioning pattern ensures that every aspect of the activity is examined and that all alternatives are considered fully. From this

DESCRIPTION OF ELEMENT ....

A selected "Do" Operation

Reference.........................
Page...............................
Date..............................

The Present Facts	Alternatives	Selected for Alternative Development
Purpose—WHAT is achieved? Consider this operation in isolation (bear in mind the subject of the chart). NOTE *What is ACHIEVED, not what or how it is DONE.* **IS IT NECESSARY?** YES NO **If YES—Why?** *Reason given may not be valid. True reason must be uncovered.*	**What ELSE could be done?** Can the achievement be ELIMINATED? Can the achievement be MODIFIED? *All alternatives to the purpose should be stated including those which may require long-term investigation. The answer to this section is never "nothing"; there is always an alternative even if only the non-achievement.*	**What?** *Helpful to divide into short-term and long-term. Under long-term can go suggestions for future research and development.*
Place—WHERE is it done? The location with reference to (a) Geographical position (b) Position within the factory, plant or area (c) Detailed position under (b) *When appropriate, give reference to location and distance from preceding and succeeding activities.* **WHY THERE?** *The reason for siting the operation there.*	**Where ELSE could it be done?** *Consider alternatives under each heading. Can working areas be combined or distances reduced?*	**Where?** *Where appears to be most suitable situation with present knowledge? Answer may be in relation to some other operation. Consider limitations of building design and services (steam, air) etc.*
Sequence—WHEN is it done? *What are the previous and subsequent significant activities and what are the time factors involved?* **WHY THEN?** *The reason for the present sequence and time factor in the present process.*	**When ELSE could it be done?** Can it be done either earlier or later in the process? *If the sequence is fixed, can it be moved back to the previous operation? For example "Immediately after."*	**When?** *As soon as possible in the process or immediately after the previous activity.*
Person—WHO does it? (a) Grade, e.g. unskilled male (b) Employment, e.g. day worker (c) Name/s **WHY THAT PERSON?** *Reasons for choice under each heading.*	**Who ELSE could do it?** *All alternatives under each heading. Can a disabled person be employed?*	**Who?** *It may not be possible to select the individual without Work Measurement.*
Means—HOW is it done? *All relevant details are required of Material, Equipment and Operator engaged in the operation. Information should be tabulated as simply as possible under the following main headings.* (a) Materials Employed. (b) Equipment Employed. (c) Operator's Method. **WHY THAT WAY?** *The reason should be investigated for each of the tabulated items under each main heading.*	**How ELSE could it be done?** *Investigate all alternatives for each heading.*	**How?** *Decide the alternative for each item separately and knit together at development stage. Consider safety. Consider posture and environment operator.*

FIG. 27. GUIDE TO THE USE OF THE CRITICAL EXAMINATION SHEET

point logical deduction indicates the most effective means of improvement. The next stage is to use the information now available as a basis for developing an improved method.

Pre-printed Form

Some people find it useful to have a pre-printed form for the critical examination. Fig. 26 illustrates such a form. It is of particular use when making a critical examination for the first time. The form is the most suitable for all types of work in general and great experience should be gained before endeavouring to change it in any way. A guide to its use is given in Fig. 27.

7

Method Study : Develop and Submit

WHEN planning the new method, the human factors should be carefully considered. Everything economically reasonable should be done to ensure comfortable working conditions, and the following " contingent considerations " are typical of those that should be borne in mind, in addition to the human factors discussed in Chapter 3.

Sight and Lighting

While sight is largely the concern of the medical officer, the work study specialist should be aware of certain elementary principles concerning sight so as to be in a position to seek the medical officer's expert advice over any aspect of a proposed method where problems of sight are accentuated. Output depends in very large degree on the comfort with which eyes are able to perform their task. The eyes demand satisfactory conditions of environment, for on the visual impression of environment will largely depend the contentment of the employees. An adequate standard of general illumination should be provided, together with supplementary local lighting correctly positioned for tasks requiring close attention. Specialist advice is essential.

The normally proportioned eye is said to be at rest when looking at objects more than 20 ft away. At lesser distances the muscles of the eye will have to be used. Like other muscles these are liable to fatigue, and become markedly less efficient with increasing age. For fine work, near-sighted people are particularly suitable as they will require to use the eye muscles less than normal-sighted or long-sighted people. Further general points are that the performance of those doing fine work is likely to be improved more if the size of the object they are working on can be increased than if they are given extra light. Another way in which performance can often be improved is by raising the contrast between the object being worked on and the background against which it is worked.

Colour

Colour has other functional uses besides increasing contrast for purposes of better visual acuity. For instance, colour can be used to differentiate between the contents of different pipe lines by painting bands of a particular colour on them at convenient intervals. It is also commonly accepted practice to paint certain machine controls so that the attention of the worker is drawn to them, while white lines are often used to mark out storage and communication areas on factory floors.

When it comes to applying colour to give a sense of pleasure and well-being to the employees in any particular department, this is best left to an interior decorator accustomed to the special problems of factories, which include the elimination of glare. Scale models coloured variously could be shown to employees so that they might express their preference for any particular scheme, but a pleasing overall effect likely to give the full benefits which a well-planned colour scheme can bring, is not likely to be obtained by consulting employee preference alone. Where it is not desired to employ a specialist, study of an authoritative colour reference system and the colours advised is probably the next best thing.

Ventilation and Heating

The health and comfort of employees are directly affected by the ventilation and heating of the buildings in which they work. Humid and stagnant air and uneven temperature are often causes of inefficient working as well as ill-health, and can be remedied by installing proper heating and ventilating systems. These should be so designed that people in all parts of a building are supplied with fresh air in such a way that an even temperature is maintained. A normal working temperature would be between 60° and 65° F, although this will vary according to the type of work being carried out. Sedentary work will require higher temperatures, and heavy manual work lower temperatures. Where abnormally high or low temperatures are necessitated by, or result from, the process a worker's energy and dexterity are sometimes seriously affected. The effects of these conditions must be anticipated, and consideration should be given to reducing them by the provision of more adequate local ventilation, by special clothing, or by other protective measures.

One of the most important effects of constantly changing air is to minimize the risk of infection among people working together. While an even air-flow creates a feeling of freshness, it must not be allowed to cause draughts. In some cases elaborate systems will have to be installed to rid the atmosphere of fumes and dust; these will certainly require expert knowledge.

Noise

As yet, little reliable information is available on the effect of noise on output. It is generally accepted that noise is a distraction, but that one can become accustomed to it, and it is true that under noisy conditions a normal rate of output can be maintained. It has been found, however, that this is usually at the expense of increased fatigue. Intermittent noise or noise of a sudden shrill nature is particularly disturbing.

A partial solution to the problem may be to isolate the noisy work in a separate room. Where this is impossible it may be feasible to dampen the sound by using sound-absorbent materials on roofs and walls. In extreme cases such as some crushing plants, ear-plugs may be helpful.

Seating

Properly designed seating is of great importance. There are many kinds available which are intended for different types of work. The general principle governing the choice of seats is that, when seated, an employee should be able to work in a comfortable and natural position with adequate support for the back and feet.

Whenever possible people working at benches should be provided with seats of such a height that they can work sitting or standing, as they feel inclined. Plenty of leg room should be available between each bench and seat, while the provision of adjustable foot rests is occasionally beneficial.

Where normal seating proves to be impracticable it may be possible to provide padded back rests against which employees can lean from time to time.

Amenities

This heading covers a variety of factors which help to achieve satisfactory working conditions—

1. The safety of personal belongings and the provision of lockers.
2. Good toilet facilities.
3. Facilities for drying wet clothes.
4. Provision of canteens, tea and drinking water.
6. Rest rooms.
6. Provision of protective hand creams.
7. Adequate first aid and fire precautions.
8. Transport to and from work.
9. Cleanliness in the factory.
10. Convenient location of clocking stations.

The Improved Method

Examination of the existing method provides a comprehensive statement of what is being done at present, and shows in which direction improvements may be made. With the results of the examination as a guide, the work study officer next proceeds to develop the improved method, taking into account those factors listed under contingent considerations. He must be particularly sure to seek advice from any source which may help.

The Framework of the Improved Method

When the existing method is examined, certain " do operations " and " inspections " are found to be essential parts of the task. These operations and inspections form the framework of the improved method.

Scope for Improvements

In Chapter 4, five directions were referred to in which method study can contribute to improved efficiency. At this stage it is useful to give more detailed consideration to the opportunities afforded in each of these directions.

1. *Layout and Design of Factory, Plant and Work-place.* In many industries the time and effort expended in handling materials and in the movement of workers amount to as much as, and often more than, that involved in the processing operations themselves. This is frequently a direct result of restrictions imposed by factory layout and plant design. In a large-scale investigation this fact may soon

be brought to light and indicate the need for a rearrangement of machines or their controls, the re-location of storage and working areas, the provision of suitable mechanical handling equipment and transport facilities, etc.

In the case of more detailed investigations the flow or two-handed process chart may reveal that, even at the work-place itself, the time spent loading and unloading a fixture or machine (make ready and put away operations) appreciably exceeds that required to perform the actual process (the do operation). When elimination and combination of operations have been taken as far as possible, recourse may be had to such devices as hopper and bin feeds, drop disposal chutes, better locating points, and so on, to reduce the proportion of time spent on handling and ineffective movement within the normal operation cycle.

2. *Working Procedures.* The fact that an established system of working has never appeared to be particularly inefficient should not prevent the work study officer from subjecting every aspect of it to a critical examination when the opportunity arises. The outcome of such an examination may show the need for changes in the way in which operations are planned and work is initiated and progressed; the manner in which materials are ordered, received and stored may be unnecessarily restricting the capacity of the departments concerned; alterations in batch sizes, or a change over from batch to flow type production may be indicated, while a preponderance of work dominated by " know-how " or quasi-scientific theories may be covering up inefficiencies of a very high order.

3. *Use of Materials, Plant and Equipment, and Manpower.* While material utilization is primarily determined by the product and tool designers or the production technologists, it sometimes happens that the examination stage of a method study investigation reveals factors which have not normally received consideration. As a result of applying his questioning procedure to the purpose of a job and the means by which it is performed, the work study officer may be able to suggest the use of a cheaper material or a more economical method of using the existing material, or even the means of completely eliminating certain operations and the material required for them.

In the direction of plant, equipment and labour utilization, a method study investigation is frequently the only satisfactory means of seeing what is actually taking place and enabling a valid comparison to be made with a proposed improvement. The number of semi-automatic machines which can be attended by one worker, the advantages and disadvantages of shift working, the extent to which mechanization of operations is an economical proposition, means by which advantage may be taken of different human skills and abilities, and the balancing of operations, particularly on mechanized assembly lines, are typical examples of the way in which improved utilization of a firm's resources may be arranged when method study is applied.

4. *Working Environment.* Although it is not usually difficult to see directions in which working conditions may be having an adverse effect on output, it is a job of systematic analysis and examination to determine to what extent and in which directions improvements will yield a most satisfactory return. Heating, ventilation, lighting, noise level and personal comfort all have limits between which working conditions are most satisfactory, and these can vary according to the type of work being done.

In the matter of amenities, it frequently happens that these cannot be directly associated with any particular level of productivity. Consequently it is not always possible, nor even desirable, to allow output considerations entirely to govern the degree of improvement introduced. Nevertheless, it is an established fact that, within reason, the provision of better amenities of all types can, in the long run, have a marked effect on the standard of output of those who benefit. In this connexion the following types of amenities are most likely to occupy the attention of the work study officer—

1. The convenience and adequacy of cloakroom and toilet facilities.

2. The times at which refreshment breaks occur, as well as their duration.

3. The reliability and adequacy of safety precautions and first-aid services.

4. The suitability of washing facilities for the type of job involved.

5. Customary allowances for starting and finishing work.

5. *Design or Specification of the End-product.* It is often possible to incorporate minor changes in the design or specification of a product, which make the work of handling and processing it appreciably easier without detracting from its saleability or functional efficiency. Such changes might take the form of clamping lugs or carrying holes being incorporated in awkwardly shaped parts, of simple sub-assemblies being redesigned to permit the use of components formed as far as possible in one piece from continuously-fed stock material, of greater accessibility being provided for assembly work, and similar innovations.

Package designs may be changed in size or shape to facilitate filling and closure, or to enable the use of standard containers for internal or external transport.

The advantages of using preferred materials and of standardization of products or components should be continuously borne in mind, particularly when they enable the range of articles produced to be cut down and additional plant capacity made available. The quality standards worked to should also not be allowed to escape attention; it may be found that in some cases they are unnecessarily high, while in others the limits are set too wide with the result that an undue amount of sorting, correcting or selective assembly has to be carried out towards the end of the process.

Characteristics of Easy Movement

The possible merits of any " hunches," which were noted down earlier in the study, can now be examined. Work-places can be " mocked up " with improvised equipment and various ideas tried out. The help and advice of the experts in the fields affected should be constantly sought. In particular, what are termed the " characteristics of easy movement " or " principles of motion economy " should be considered whenever the type of job being studied lends itself to their application.

To assist in the critical examination of a worker's movements and to decide on the most effective work-place layout, it is helpful to know the principles on which easy and economic movement patterns are built. Equally it is necessary to be able to identify types of movement which are wasteful and fatiguing.

During his early motion study investigations, Gilbreth recognized that there were certain principles that were common to all skilled movements. As a result of a close study of many different activities, he isolated these and put them forward as a basis upon which all movement patterns should be constructed.

Wide violation of these principles often provides a pointer to a possible improvement. They should, however, be used only as a guide to efficient movement, and not as a series of inflexible rules to be applied rigidly on all occasions. In motion study, as with all method study, there are variable factors in every situation, and it may be necessary to modify the application of the principles to meet the prevailing circumstances.

Application of the " Characteristics "

As motion study examinations are mostly concerned with the movements of the hands and arms, the principles apply more generally to those limbs, though many can be applied also to the legs and feet.

Any survey of the characteristics of easy movement must necessarily include consideration of the work-place where the movements take place and of the equipment used. For this reason, some authorities separate them into those affecting hand movements, work-place layout and tool or equipment design. A variety of systems has been evolved, and individual textbooks differ in their presentation. Generally speaking, however, most of the variations are special applications of one or more of six basic principles which are described in succeeding paragraphs.

The Six Basic Characteristics

Each of the principles has as its basis one of the six characteristic classifications into which human movements can be conveniently divided.

1. *Minimum Movements.* This principle requires that tools, material supply and equipment should be positioned so that they can be used with minimum of movement by the worker, and at the same time ensure that the movement classification used is of the lowest practicable group in the circumstances.

If distances moved are to be kept to a practical minimum, a knowledge of working areas is required. When a worker is seated at a work-place there is an area in front of him which can be called his normal working area. The normal working area in the horizontal plane is bounded by arcs drawn by the right and left hands with the lower arms pivoting from the elbows which are held naturally by the side of the body.

If the various tools, material and equipment are positioned in or around the normal working area, they can be reached without undue use of the worker's upper arm and shoulder muscles. The area immediately in front of the worker, where the arcs overlap, is called the immediate working area, and is the most suitable area for bi-manual operation. Where all the equipment cannot be located in or around the immediate and normal working areas, it should be placed within the maximum working area. This area in the horizontal plane is bounded by arcs drawn by the right and left hands, with the arms pivoting from the shoulders. Objects placed between the normal and maximum working area can be reached by the worker with a Class IV movement. Anything placed outside the maximum working area can only be reached by a Class V movement involving body stretching or bending. There are corresponding normal and maximum working areas in the vertical as well as the horizontal planes. These working areas are illustrated in Fig. 28.

When considering the movement classifications used, it must be remembered that the principle is intended to eliminate body and shoulder movements as far as possible, substituting for these Class III and Class IV movements. It is not intended that wherever possible Class I movements *must* be used for in many cases this would mean that the fingers were overloaded and working beyond their natural capacity.

The application of this principle of minimum movement has resulted in the use of semicircular work-places as instanced by the design of cinema organ consoles and manual telephone boards. In industry, the design of effective work-places in assembly processes makes use of this principle.

When considering layouts within the working area, it is obvious that movements will be kept at a minimum if the most frequently used equipment is nearest to hand. The principle also indicates the use of gravity fed containers and drop- or spring-ejection to avoid stretching unnecessarily. Obviously, it is advantageous to plan the work-place layout so that each movement cycle starts and finishes in the same locality.

2. *Simultaneous Movements.*

3. *Symmetrical Movements.*

These two characteristics are best taken together: they suggest that movements of the arms and hands should be balanced by being simultaneous and/or symmetrical. The anatomy of human beings is such that if movements are unbalanced excessive fatigue is caused.

As an example of this, consider a man walking with a heavy load in his right hand. His body is thrown off balance by the weight and muscular exertion caused by his endeavour to balance himself. If he divided the weight equally between his left and right hands, his balance would be restored, and less total exertion would be necessary. It is also true that if the right hand is moving, the left hand tries to move in a similar fashion. Experiments have proved that usually more fatigue is induced when one hand is kept inactive while the other hand moves, than is the case when both hands move simultaneously and symmetrically. One result of this is that workers will sometimes introduce extra movements which are unproductive but serve to maintain balance.

Symmetry and simultaneity are best achieved when the hands move to and fro along the natural area of movement. As far as it is possible both hands should be given tasks which are the

" mirror-image " of each other. As an example, consider the difficulty of trying to draw a circle with the right hand while the left hand is drawing a triangle. It is much easier for both hands to operate simultaneously and symmetrically drawing two circles or two triangles. Swinging Indian clubs is another excellent example.

The application of this principle often requires the duplication of

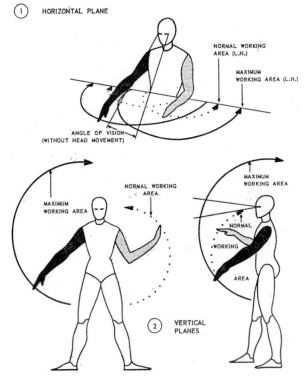

FIG. 28. NORMAL AND MAXIMUM WORKING AREAS: HORIZONTAL AND VERTICAL PLANES

fixtures and tools, so that both hands can work at similar tasks at the same time.

4. *Natural Movements.* This principle requires that the movements used should be those which can be performed most naturally by the body. The application of the principle includes the use of other limbs, fingers, etc., so that the work load is spread over those parts of the body best fitted to the work. To relieve the hands it is often

practicable to use foot operation. In many cases the third and fourth fingers may be employed to hold small parts or tools while the other fingers are usefully employed.

The principle is also concerned with the correct use of muscles and posture when weight lifting. All designs of tools, seating and equipment are influenced by this principle.

5. *Rhythmical Movements.* This principle states that rhythm should be present in movements. Rhythm may be described as the regular repetition of a movement pattern. It is often characterized by the accentuation of a part of the cycle. It is one of the prime factors on which speed is developed. When rhythm is established, hesitations are eliminated and movements are carried out at higher speeds with less fatigue. The acquisition of rhythm is particularly stressed when training workers in new movements. When the movements are established, the maintenance of rhythm eliminates much of the mental exertion. The provision of music to maintain a suitable rhythm is a well known practice.

6. *Habitual Movements.* This principle states that the movement pattern should be arranged so that it becomes habitual. Human beings possess a natural ability to form habits. When a set of movements is performed habitually, fatigue is at a minimum and the movements are carried out almost as a reflex action. However, it must be remembered that incorrect movements can also become habitual, and that a habit is difficult to eradicate. This principle has, therefore, a considerable bearing when workers are being trained in new movements.

Application of this principle requires that tools and equipment should be located always in the same position relative to the worker in each successive cycle. Containers must also be designed so that supplies can always be obtained from the same position easily without searching and fumbling, and without demanding excessive eye movement.

7. *Continuous Movements.* This principle is based on the fact that smooth, curved and continuous movements are generally preferable to straight movements involving sharp changes of direction. This is because before a hand changes its direction it must slow down and stop and subsequently accelerate again to its normal pace. If the hand has to do this frequently there is a constant state of controlled tension of the muscles, which induces fatigue. Smooth, continuous movements which employ natural momentum do not involve such pronounced muscle tension.

Tools and material must be positioned at the work-place so that objects can be picked up without undue changes of direction.

The Field of Vision

In considering the characteristics of easy movement, the field of vision is an important factor which is all too frequently ignored. Where inspection work is involved it must take place within the field of vision of the worker and, as will be seen from Fig. 28, this is a relatively limited area. It follows that material located in a number of well-designed bins at different points around the perimeter of the normal working area can only be seen by moving the eyes. As excessive eye movements cause considerable fatigue, it may be necessary to adopt multi-tiered bins which can be located well within the field of vision.

General Considerations

The characteristics of easy movement must be applied with common sense. Where they appear to conflict they should be applied in the manner most appropriate to the prevailing circumstances. For instance, the principles of rhythmical and habitual movements may, in certain circumstances, indicate the desirability of longer movement paths than would be indicated by applying the principle of minimum movements. Equally, the principle of natural movements sets limits to the movement classifications used in any given movement, irrespective of the principle of minimum movements.

Finally, it must be remembered that the movements must be carried out by human beings, and there must be sufficient flexibility in any set of movements to ensure that adequate relaxation is given to the worker. On occasion it may be necessary to introduce movements which in themselves are less economic for the sole purpose of using one set of muscles to rest another set which is in danger of being overworked. For example, workers who are employed in repetitive assembly work are often given the added responsibility of servicing their own work-place so that their arm muscles are rested while leg and body muscles are brought into use.

Work Measurement

In assessing economic manning of a job, two questions require answers which can only be provided by using work measurement—

1. Are workers fully occupied, or are they limited in their operating time by layout, machines or equipment?

2. Are all workers occupied to the same extent, or does their operating time vary so that some are less occupied than others?

If work measurement reveals deficiencies in either of these two respects the new method must be reconsidered.

Chart of the Improved Method

When the improved method has been finally evolved, it is constructed in chart form. This is subjected, activity by activity, to the same analysis as that applied to the records of the existing method. This ensures that the improved method is a logical one which will withstand any future analysis that may be made.

Submitting the Proposals

When an improved method has been worked out with the help of the specialist departments concerned, managers, supervisors, and where possible the workers who will be affected, the method can be submitted to higher management. Getting wide support for the new method before it is submitted is essential. If it is felt by management that those who will be responsible for working it are prepared to give it a fair trial, they are likely to be influenced in its favour.

As important is a clear statement of the benefits to be expected of the new method, and how it is to achieve these benefits. A compelling argument is that of the savings anticipated, and figures of these should be presented clearly, along with the details of the estimated costs of installing and operating the new scheme. If this statement is not made clear and forceful, it is likely the proposals will be rejected.

It is of paramount importance in presenting the figures referred to that they take into account everything which is affected by the proposals. This can be done by establishing the initial cost of the installation and its annual operating cost, including maintenance, depreciation and insurance where applicable, for each of the following items—

Land and buildings	Ancillary equipment
Power services	Office equipment
Plant and machinery	Personnel

The Report

Many organizations have their own procedure for writing reports, but there are a number of specific points to consider.

People do not like being told bluntly they have been wrong. The proposals for the new method may make some former procedure appear wasteful. Any tendency to recriminate is likely to antagonize management and defeat the purpose, which is simply to get the new method accepted.

Unless the report is very short, it should always commence with a summary which should show with utmost brevity—

1. Recommendations.
2. Reasons for recommendations.
3. Results expected from recommendations.

When a summary is included, it provides a convenient opportunity for outlining the purpose of the study and its conclusion and proposals.

The report itself, which should be clearly written and self-supporting, should generally follow the order of presentation given above.

Recommendations. All means of presenting information more vividly should be used; charts, photographs, diagrams and figures. These can be incorporated in the body of the text to help to enliven the reading matter and to explain points more clearly. Any that are of a more elaborate nature and require prolonged study, should be included in an appendix.

Reasons for Recommendations. An explanation should be included as to how the new method was devised and a reference made to all the alternatives which were considered, including the reasons for their rejection. Any experimental work carried out in order to reach the final decision should also be described in the report.

Results Expected from Recommendations. The way in which the various parts of the organization are likely to be affected and any repercussions which may occur, should be shown in the report. It is particularly important to make clear to management the effect the new method will have on the input/output ratio of the undertaking, and that their approval will be required for the changes which will be necessary in other directions to accommodate this. Operating instructions for the new method, at least in general form, should be included for the approval of management at the same time that the report is accepted.

A forecast should also be made of any difficulties which may be encountered when the new method is being installed or operated. If installation is likely to be a prolonged procedure, or something which, for personal or technical reasons, has to be done in several stages, a description of these and a time-table, not necessarily related to any particular period, should be included.

The following factors should be borne in mind when this time-table is drawn up—

1. Attitude of workers.
2. Production levels.
3. Levels of existing stocks of material affected by the changes.
4. Delivery of supplies, new material and equipment.
5. Normal maintenance shut downs and stock-taking periods.
6. Coincidence with costing periods.
7. Periods when staff are depleted through holidays.

Detailed and exact dates may not be necessary, nor even desirable, but management should be given a clear idea of what is involved if time is a significant factor.

The report should always include a full acknowledgement to the various people who have assisted in the investigation.

Subsequent Action

After the report has been adjusted and agreed by management, alterations are recorded. A separate note should be made of any proposals which were rejected, together with the reasons. On some future occasion, the method may be reviewed again and proposals which were previously rejected may then prove to be acceptable in the light of changed conditions.

Operating Instructions

Before introducing the new method, the operating instructions approved by management in the report are issued to all concerned. In this way everyone will know their responsibility and subsequent misunderstanding will be avoided.

In presenting operating instructions to employees in particular, use has been successfully made of flow process charts, which denote clearly the nature of each successive activity, and obviate the need for pages of lengthy verbal description.

8

Method Study: Install and Maintain

As a result of following the basic procedure of method study, the stage is eventually reached at which the agreed method is ready to be put into practice. Installation will require the active support of everyone concerned, and is by no means simple. An opportune moment must be chosen for installing the method, and no attempt should be made to introduce the changes until adequate preparation has been made. This includes finding alternative work for any workers who may be displaced as a result of the new method.

Operating instructions covering every detail of the new method will have been issued. As a consequence, everybody will have had ample opportunity to read them, and all should understand how they will be affected by the changes, and the part they have to play in their introduction.

Throughout the course of the study, the opportunity should have been taken to establish good working relationships at all levels, so that all who have taken part in the discussions leading to the improvements can feel that they have themselves contributed to the scheme. It is just as important for people less intimately concerned with the scheme—for instance, other employees who may be working near at hand—to be brought into the picture so that they too realize the need for and purpose of the change. Reference has been made to these aspects, generally, in Chapter 3.

The new method can now be installed in the knowledge that people have confidence in it, and will support it.

The installation should be made in two stages—

1. Preparation.
2. Installation.

There are many considerations under both these headings. The extent to which they will apply in particular cases will depend on the nature and scope of the changes to be made.

For some of the work involved the work study department will always be actively responsible. For the remainder, in which executive action has to be taken by one or more of the service or operating departments concerned, the work study officer's role becomes one of advisor and co-ordinator. From the very nature of the considerations listed in Chapter 7 it will be clear that the work of installation must always be a co-operative affair. The work study department performs the function of ensuring that the scheme is implemented according to the recommendations made and accepted in the report. The confidence of management in the possibilities of work study and in the competence of its practitioners is an essential prerequisite for success.

Preparation

Detailed preparation must be made before the actual installation takes place. This preparation can be broken down into three stages—

1. Plan.
2. Arrange.
3. Rehearse.

Plan

A general programme for the installation should be drawn up—

1. One person only should have responsibility during installation of the method, and all should know who that person is. He may need to delegate his authority, but everyone should know in whom final responsibility and authority rest.

2. If the installation is to take place in stages, and they have not already been announced before preparation of the report, actual dates should be fixed for each stage. These should be selected so that they are convenient both for the people responsible for or affected by the installations and for the process itself.

3. Copies of any time-table drawn up to cover the installation

should be brought into line with the dates selected for each stage. It may be advisable for this to be in much more detail than the form in which it appeared in the report.

Arrange

The necessary detailed arrangements should be made—

1. Check all layouts in detail to ensure that all the necessary plant, tools and equipment are available, and that services are laid on. Ensure that anything which has to be specially made has been ordered, and that everything will be ready when required.

2. Arrange for the running-down of old stocks and the building-up of necessary new stocks of materials in advance of the installation.

3. Check the availability and continuity of all supplies and services.

4. Set up any additional or new clerical records which may be required for purposes of control and comparison.

5. If changes in hours of working are involved, e.g. from day to shift work—make sure that warning is given to auxiliary services such as transport, canteens, etc.

6. Select the number and ability of the workers for the new method carefully. This is particularly important when team-work is involved. Try to avoid any difficulties which may arise between those selected for the new method and any who may remain on the old.

7. Provide the necessary training. This must not be skimped and needs to be very thorough, especially where team-work is required. Where practicable, training should take place away from the production line, preferably in an independent training department.

8. Anticipate wage and payment problems and settle them well in advance. Be sure that the wages and costing departments know when the new method is to be installed.

9. Advise every one concerned of the plans and time-table for the installation.

Rehearse

It is frequently beneficial to give the improved method a trial run—

1. The rehearsal should usually take place while the old method is still operating, and may have to be conducted outside normal working hours so that there is no interference with normal production.

2. Ensure that all inspections have been allowed for, so that proper quality standards will be maintained.

3. All departments affected by the change should be represented at the rehearsal.

Installation

When all detailed preparations have been made and a successful rehearsal has been held, the actual installation can take place—

1. The physical aspect of the changeover of methods can generally be made outside normal working hours. Often a week-end or holiday is a suitable opportunity, because there will be sufficient time to alter layouts and install plant and equipment without affecting regular production.

2. The first few days of operating the new method are critical. During this time very intimate supervision will be necessary. This extra supervision should be continued until all workers are thoroughly familiar with their job. It is advisable to hold meetings each day with the supervisors concerned so that progress can be discussed.

3. In spite of every effort to ensure that the method is the best and most practical, there may be some part of it which does not turn out as well in practice as had been anticipated. In these cases some modification may have to be made. If alterations are made to the method, the operating instructions should be modified accordingly.

4. During the initial period after installation a close watch should be kept for any prejudice against parts of the method among workers, and the reasons should be sought immediately.

5. Weak links should be bolstered by extra training. It may be necessary to replace unsuitable personnel, or to increase temporarily the labour allotted to parts of the method.

6. A close watch should be kept of the effect which the new method is having on stocks.

7. Tact and restraint are required throughout the period of the installation. Ample credit should be given where deserved.

When the heads of the departments concerned are satisfied that the new method is running smoothly, and are prepared to accept it as a going concern, the installation can be considered complete.

Maintaining the New Method

After an improved method has been installed and is operating satisfactorily, it does not necessarily follow that its benefits can be maintained without further effort. The conditions are liable to change from time to time, and this may mean that some of the assumptions upon which the improved method was built up are no longer valid. The labour for manning the improved method will have been allotted on the basis of the work content of the method as set out in the operating instructions. Consequently any changes may alter the balance between the work content and the labour allotted for carrying out the method. The method should be reviewed at intervals to make allowances for any changes.

Changes can arise from three main sources—

1. There can be deliberate and discernible alterations and improvements to method for good reason.

2. Changes may take place as a result of suggestion schemes.

3. Minor innovations may be introduced by the worker or by immediate supervision.

Where changes in method are introduced deliberately by management, the work study officer must be notified in advance so that he can make the necessary allowances for the effect which they will have on the operation of the method. This should not present difficulties providing liaison exists between the sections concerned and the work study section. A copy of the operating instructions should always be available in the section concerned.

Changes of a minor nature are liable to creep into the method from time to time, causing a gradual drift away from the authorized method of operation. The most effective means of revealing these changes of method is to institute a regular review of current practice.

Reviewing the Method

The frequency with which a method should be reviewed will depend on the nature of the work. The main purpose of the review is to discover whether there are any discrepancies between the authorized procedure as defined in the operating instructions and current practice at the time of the review.

Reasons for any variations in the method must be investigated. Any changes that have occurred for valid reasons should be accepted and the operating instructions amended accordingly. If operating instructions are to remain " live " documents and show current practice they must be amended as soon as authorized changes in the method are revealed. In accepting any change in the method the work study officer should ensure that credit for the improvement is given where it is due.

Where the review reveals that there are undesirable variations in the method, measures should be taken, through supervision, to ensure that the method reverts to the authorized procedure. Changes which are made unofficially often cause inefficiency, such as deterioration in quality and safety standards, and duplication of work. It is particularly important in the period immediately following the installation to see that the defects of the old method are not revived by habit in the new method.

A further aspect which should be noted in the periodic review of the method is the long-term reaction to the improvements, both on the part of the workers using the method and on the part of other sections who were affected by the changes when they were made. Much useful experience can be gained from their reactions to the improvements which have been introduced, and these reactions may provide clues which will disclose still further possibilities of improvement.

Finally, when methods are reviewed an excellent opportunity exists for making the organization " method-conscious." When the benefits to be obtained from method study are fully appreciated it can be applied on a much wider scale within the organization, with the active support and co-operation of all concerned.

Cumulative Effects of Method Study

The fact that management are taking active steps in promoting method study means that within a short space of time the whole organization becomes method study conscious. The systematic approach of method study can be applied almost anywhere within the enterprise. Almost any task can be improved, provided that it is systematically analysed and thoroughly examined, yet it is surprising how often a worker comes to feel that management is not really interested in improvements he may suggest for his own job, with the result that all too frequently he loses the inclination to view it critically. He allows the routine of the job to obscure his search for all those little improvements, the sum of which make up the big improvements. By integrating method study into the normal process of management, the search for improvement becomes a matter of accepted and normal routine throughout an organization.

9

Work Measurement : Introduction

THE measurement of human work has always been a problem for management, as plans for the provision of goods or services to a reliable programme and at a predetermined cost are often dependent on the accuracy with which the amount and type of human work involved can be forecast and organized. While it has commonly been the practice to make estimates and set targets based on past experience, these too frequently prove a rough and unsatisfactory guide.

Work measurement, by enabling target times to be set, into which are incorporated rest allowances appropriate to the type of work involved, provides a far more satisfactory basis on which to plan. It has been defined by the British Standards Institution as—

> The application of techniques designed to establish the time for a qualified worker to carry out a specified job at a defined level of performance.

In this sense it includes those aspects of work study which are outside the province of method study (see Chapters 4 to 8). This separation of techniques, as illustrated diagrammatically in Fig. 1 is, however, purely for convenience of description. In practice the most satisfactory results are achieved only when the appropriate techniques from each field are applied to problems as complementary activities.

Even though absolute accuracy cannot be claimed for values arrived at by using the techniques of work measurement, properly trained observers can obtain a high degree of consistency in their results and are able to measure acceptably many different types of work. As use of the techniques extends, it is being found that they can be successfully applied to certain routine operations with a high content of mental work, such as reading gauges, sorting parts, etc. Work of a completely mental nature or which is purely creative, however, has not so far been measured on a practical basis.

The Objectives

Using as a target the times established for jobs at the defined level of performance, work measurement will be found to have the following uses—

1. To assist in method study by comparison of times for alternative methods, and for allocating labour to jobs in proportion to the work involved so that the labour on a job is properly balanced.

2. To enable realistic schedules of work to be prepared by relating reasonably accurate assessments of human work to plant capacity.

3. As the basis of realistic and fair incentive schemes.

4. To assist in the organization of labour by enabling a daily comparison to be made between actual times and target times.

5. As a basis for labour budgeting and budgetary control systems.

6. To enable estimates to be prepared of future labour requirements and costs.

Work Measurement Techniques

For the purpose of work measurement, work may be regarded as *repetitive* or *non-repetitive*. By repetitive is meant that type of work in which the main operation or group of operations recurs continuously during the time spent at the job. This applies equally to work cycles of extremely short duration as, for instance, light press-work jobs, and to those of several minutes' or even hours' duration.

Non-repetitive work includes some types of maintenance and construction work, where the work cycle itself is hardly ever repeated identically. Even in such work, however, as will be shown later, many of the same small movements and groups of movements occur repeatedly, and are often common to quite different jobs, such as painting and bricklaying. It is this fact which has made it possible to apply certain work measurement techniques to this type of work.

The techniques which are in general use, and which are described in this book are as follow—

1. Time study
2. Synthesis from element times or synthetic data
3. Analytical estimating

} Applicable to repetitive work.

} Applicable to non-repetitive work.

The general procedure is shown in Fig. 32.

Rate of Working

The actual time taken to do a job depends on the rate of working maintained by the individual concerned. In practice variations in this rate result from a variety of different causes. To facilitate calculation, work measurement values, unless otherwise stated, are always related to what is termed *standard performance.*

By standard performance is meant the optimum rate of output that can be achieved by a qualified worker as an average for a working day or shift, due allowance being made for the necessary time required for rest. (An idea of what this means in practice can usually be obtained by observing the performance of workers whose output is paid for on a piece-work basis.)

A qualified worker is one who is physically and mentally suited to the job he is given, and who has acquired the necessary skill and knowledge to carry out the work it involves to satisfactory standards of safety, quantity and quality.

The Unit of Work

The unit of work is founded on the notion that the human work content of many different types of job can be expressed quantitatively in terms of a common unit. In this unit provision is made both for the effort called for by the job and for an appropriate rest allowance. In order to achieve consistency in its application, this allowance is always related to the concept of a standard rate of working. In practice this is represented by the average effectiveness at which a qualified worker will naturally work on a job when he knows and adheres to a specified method and is suitably motivated. If a worker maintains the standard rate of working as an average over the day or shift after taking whatever relaxation allowance is due to him, the principle is that he will average a fixed number of units of work per hour irrespective of the type of work upon which he has been engaged. This particular number of units of work per hour will depend upon the scale of measurement adopted by an organization (60 per hour is convenient for many purposes). Whatever it is, this number is taken to represent what is termed standard performance and provides a datum against which subsequent applications of the results of work measurement are made. Additional allowances outside the work content are made as necessary to cover additional plant or machine running times to enable overall times to be set.

When expressed in units of work the work content of any job should be related to its most suitable characteristic for planning, control, costing, payment, and other purposes (i.e., per part handled, per ton processed, per dozen packed, etc.); and in this form may be compared directly with any other job on a quantitative basis.

Comparison by Units of Work

An allowance for rest, which varies according to the mental and physical effort involved in each job, is included in human work values assessed by the techniques of work measurement. The observed working times for different parts of a job are first each adjusted to allow for the extent to which the worker under scrutiny is deemed to have varied from what is termed the standard rate of working (a description of which is given in Chapter 10). After addition of the relaxation allowance (R.A.) appropriate to the work, the resultant values are totalled to give a value for the complete job in composite units, each of which represents an equivalent amount of effort by the worker. These composite units are referred to as units of work, a constant number of which is produced in one hour when a job is carried out at standard performance, irrespective of the nature of the work involved.

Definition

In making the above points clear the following definition of a unit of work and the accompanying diagram may be of assistance—

A unit of work consists partly of effort and partly of rest, the proportion of rest varying with the nature of the job.

Units of work for light, medium and heavy jobs having relaxation allowances of 10 per cent, 20 per cent and 30 per cent respectively, might thus be represented as illustrated in Fig. 29.

Since the value of the unit of work itself does not depend upon the *type* of job, and, consequently, the proportion of rest allowed, different jobs can be directly compared with each other on the quantitative basis of their work contents: for instance, a job valued at 4 units of work may be considered as having half the work content of one valued at 8 units and twice that of one valued at 2 units, irrespective of the fact that the proportion of relaxation may be different in each case.

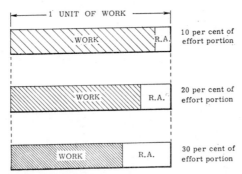

FIG. 29.   REPRESENTATION OF UNITS OF WORK

Duration of the Unit of Work

Because it is intended to represent a certain amount of work, together with an appropriate period of relaxation, the unit of work as such has no absolute time value; other things being equal, one worker may take more or less time than another to perform a job containing the same number of units of work simply because he works at a different level of performance. In order to establish and use work contents, therefore, it is necessary to associate the rate at which units of work are accomplished with a definite level of working performance.

For the purpose of the examples given in this book a basis of 60 units of work per hour at standard performance has been adopted as a datum, and units of such value denoted as standard minutes (SM). The SM will thus have a time-equivalent of $\frac{1}{60}$ of an hour or 1 minute when a man works exactly at standard performance.

(Some other systems of evaluation in use have as their basis 1, 80 or 133 units of work per hour at standard performance.)

10

Time Study : Principles and Procedure

TIME study is the basic technique of work measurement since it is concerned with the direct observation of work while it is being performed. As one object of work measurement is to enable target times to be set with which to compare the results subsequently achieved, and thereby exercise control, direct time study is only of use for repetitive work, that is to say, for any job which is subsequently going to be repeated under the circumstances which applied and by the method used while the study was being taken.

An important feature of time study is the way in which the accuracy of the results obtained improves as the number of occasions upon which the operation is observed increases. It is a matter of economics as to whether time study is merited on jobs which are likely to be of short duration or in which the repetitive element is small. It is possible to establish formulae relating estimated job duration to average cost of production time study, which will be of assistance in making the decision in the case of border-line examples.

The following are the four essentials for the time study of any job—

1. An accurate specification of where the job begins and where it ends, and of the method by which it is to be carried out, including details of material, equipment, conditions, etc.

2. A system of recording the observed (actual) times taken by workers to do the job while under observation.

3. A clear concept of what is meant by *standard rating*, which is described later in this chapter.

4. A means of assessing the amount of rest which should be associated with the job.

Time Scales

Much of the value of the ordered work study approach lies in the speed with which it enables results to be obtained. It follows, therefore, that anything which affects the time required for *working up* a study, as the process of calculation is termed, should be understood by anyone who has administrative responsibility for work measurement in an organization. For this reason the choice of time scale to be used should not be looked upon only as a matter of detail. Although the same answer will be obtained with each of the scales commonly employed, the work involved in arriving at this answer will vary according to which is actually used and the purpose for which the information is required.

Decimal-minutes

The decimal-minute system as used in this book, where observations are recorded in centiminutes (CM) and, thereafter, times are expressed in minutes and decimal fractions of a minute, will be found perfectly satisfactory for most applications. Stop-watches having a dial calibrated 0–100 over which the sweep hand revolves once per minute are readily available. The system has the advantage of simplifying both recording and calculation, and gives a slightly more accurate result than is achieved by using seconds as basic time units.

Seconds

Although the second is an established unit or time for many purposes, the significance of which is easily appreciated, its use for work measurement makes recording and calculation somewhat clumsy. While this does not affect the accuracy of the results, it is a marked disadvantage in the case of long studies, and there is a tendency among many firms who have been using second-type watches for work measurement to convert them to decimal-minute watches by having the dials changed.

Decimal-hours

Decimal-hour stop-watches, in which the sweep hand makes 100 revolutions per hour or 1 every 36 seconds, are available as standard equipment (*see* Fig. 30). One hundredth of an hour can be described as a decimal-hour unit and abbreviated to CH. Incomplete revolutions of the sweep hand will represent decimal fractions of a CH, e.g. in Fig. 30, 0·67 CH is indicated.

The use of the decimal-hour system is considered to be convenient for long cycle work, particularly in conjunction with the concept of standard performance as either 1 or 100 units of work per hour, instead of 60 units of work per hour as used in the illustrations in

Fig. 30.   Decimal-hour Stop Watch

this book. Two objections are frequently raised to the use of decimal-hour systems for work measurement purposes, namely—

1. The recording of observed times to four places of decimals (in accordance with the calibration of the decimal-hour dial) is not convenient, while times expressed in this way are difficult to handle during calculation.

2. Even though it is desirable for estimating, loading and other purposes to have operation times expressed in hours and decimal fractions of an hour, the significance of such times is difficult to explain to the workers concerned.

For recording purposes, however, the decimal points can be omitted (for instance 67 would be recorded in the case of Fig. 30). Similarly 1¼ units, for instance, would be recorded as 125. Decimal points can be inserted at the stage of deriving the selected basic element times on the time study analysis sheet (Fig. 46) in the same way as with decimal-minutes. Thereafter all calculations can be performed according to the procedure outlined in the main text of this book but in terms of CH instead of minutes.

The necessity for workers to be able to understand clearly the significance of work measurement is of prime importance, and no attempt to introduce any system should be made until it is clear that this requirement can be met. Where times are issued in terms of hours and decimal hours, it may be helpful to provide some form of conversion table, similar to that given in Fig. 31.

Some examples in the use of the table will illustrate the procedure—

1. To convert 3·47 CH to minutes and seconds—
   In the table 3·47 appears in minute column 2 and second line 5
   ∴ 3·47 CH = 2 min 5 sec
2. To convert 5·28 min to CH—
   Read off the CH value which is 8·80
   ∴ 5·28 min = 8·80 CH.
3. To express 13 min 7 sec as decimal fraction of an hour—
   First from the table, 7 sec is equivalent to 0·12 min ∴ value to be converted to 13·12 min.

   Since the table gives values directly only up to 9·98 min, read off CH value for 1·312 min (or 1·31, to two decimal places) and multiply by 10—
   1·31 min is equivalent to 2·18 CH
   ∴ 13·12 min is equivalent to 21·8 CH or 0·218 hours

From the foregoing examples it will be apparent that a table of the type given can be made use of in several ways. In addition to enabling job times to be expressed in any desired form for planning and other purposes in places where an incentive scheme based on work study is in operation, because it is so simple to use, it may be advantageous to have a copy of the table displayed in a prominent position so that workers can make their own reference to it.

Using the Decimal-hour Watch

Competence in the use of the decimal-hour stop-watch is easily acquired by observers (some practice is necessary to become used to the greater speed of the sweep hand), but as it is not feasible to convert minute watches for this purpose, decimal-hour watches will

SECONDS	MINUTES										DECIMAL MINUTES (MINUTES÷100)
	0	1	2	3	4	5	6	7	8	9	
0	—	1·66	3·33	5·00	6·66	8·33	10·00	11·66	13·33	15·00	0·00
1	0·03	1·69	3·36	5·03	6·69	8·36	10·03	11·69	13·36	15·03	0·02
2	0·06	1·72	3·39	5·06	6·72	8·39	10·06	11·72	13·39	15·06	0·03
3	0·08	1·75	3·42	5·08	6·75	8·42	10·08	11·75	13·42	15·08	0·05
4	0·11	1·78	3·44	5·11	6·78	8·44	10·11	11·78	13·44	15·11	0·07
5	0·14	1·80	3·47	5·14	6·80	8·47	10·14	11·80	13·47	15·14	0·08
6	0·17	1·83	3·50	5·17	6·83	8·50	10·17	11·83	13·50	15·17	0·10
7	0·19	1·86	3·53	5·19	6·86	8·53	10·19	11·86	13·53	15·19	0·12
8	0·22	1·89	3·56	5·22	6·89	8·56	10·22	11·89	13·56	15·22	0·13
9	0·25	1·92	3·58	5·25	6·92	8·58	10·25	11·92	13·58	15·25	0 15
10	0·28	1·94	3·61	5·28	6·94	8·61	10·28	11·94	13·61	15·28	0·17
11	0·31	1·97	3·64	5·31	6·97	8·64	10·31	11·97	13·64	15·31	0·18
12	0·33	2·00	3·66	5·33	7·00	8·66	10·33	12·00	13·66	15·33	0·20
13	0·36	2·03	3·69	5·36	7·03	8·69	10·36	12·03	13·69	15·36	0·22
14	0·39	2·06	3·72	5·39	7·06	8·72	10·39	12·06	13·72	15·39	0·23
15	0·42	2·08	3·75	5·42	7·08	8·75	10·42	12·08	13·75	15·42	0·25
16	0·44	2·11	3·78	5·44	7·11	8·78	10·44	12·11	13·78	15·44	0·27
17	0·47	2·14	3·80	5·47	7·14	8·80	10·47	12·14	13·80	15·47	0·28
18	0·50	2·17	3·83	5·50	7·17	8·83	10·50	12·17	13·83	15·50	0·30
19	0·53	2·19	3·86	5·53	7·19	8·86	10·53	12·19	13·86	15·53	0·32
20	0·56	2·22	3·89	5·56	7·22	8·89	10·56	12·22	13·89	15·56	0·33
21	0·58	2·25	3·92	5·58	7·25	8·92	10·58	12·25	13·92	15·58	0·35
22	0·61	2·28	3·94	5·61	7·28	8·94	10·61	12·28	13·94	15·61	0·37
23	0·64	2·31	3·97	5·64	7·31	8·97	10·64	12·31	13·97	15·64	0·38
24	0·66	2·33	4·00	5·66	7·33	9·00	10·66	12·33	14·00	15·66	0·40
25	0·69	2·36	4·03	5·69	7·36	9·03	10·69	12·36	14·03	15·69	0·42
26	0·72	2·39	4·06	5·72	7·39	9·06	10·72	12·39	14·06	15·72	0·43
27	0·75	2·42	4·08	5·75	7·42	9·08	10·75	12·42	14·08	15·75	0·45
28	0·78	2·44	4·11	5·78	7·44	9·11	10·78	12·44	14·11	15·78	0·47
29	0·80	2·47	4·14	5·80	7·47	9·14	10·80	12·47	14·14	15·80	0·48
30	0·83	2·50	4·17	5·83	7·50	9·17	10·83	12·50	14·17	15·83	0·50
31	0·86	2·53	4·19	5·86	7·53	9·19	10·86	12·53	14·19	15·86	0·52
32	0·89	2·56	4·22	5·89	7·56	9·22	10·89	12·56	14·22	15·89	0·53
33	0·92	2·58	4·25	5·92	7·58	9·25	10·92	12·58	14·25	15·92	0·55
34	0·94	2·61	4·28	5·94	7·61	9·28	10·94	12·61	14·28	15·94	0·57
35	0·97	2·64	4·31	5·97	7·64	9·31	10·97	12·64	14·31	15·97	0·58
36	1·00	2·66	4·33	6·00	7·66	9·33	11·00	12·66	14·33	16·00	0·60
37	1·03	2·69	4·36	6·03	7·69	9·36	11·03	12·69	14·36	16·03	0·62
38	1·06	2·72	4·39	6·06	7·72	9·39	11·06	12·72	14·39	16·06	0·63
39	1·08	2·75	4·42	6·08	7·75	9·42	11·08	12·75	14·42	16·08	0·65
40	1·11	2·78	4·44	6·11	7·78	9·44	11·11	12·78	14·44	16·11	0·67
41	1·14	2·80	4·47	6·14	7·80	9·47	11·14	12·80	14·47	16·14	0·68
42	1·17	2·83	4·50	6·17	7·83	9·50	11·17	12·83	14·50	16·17	0·70
43	1·19	2·86	4·53	6·19	7·86	9·53	11·19	12·86	14·53	16·19	0·72
44	1·22	2·89	4·56	6·22	7·89	9·56	11·22	12·89	14·56	16·22	0·73
45	1·25	2·92	4·58	6·25	7·92	9·58	11·25	12·92	14·58	16·25	0·75
46	1·28	2·94	4·61	6·28	7·94	9·61	11·28	12·94	14·61	16·28	0·77
47	1·31	2·97	4·64	6·31	7·97	9·64	11·31	12·97	14·64	16·31	0·78
48	1·33	3·00	4·66	6·33	8·00	9·66	11·33	13·00	14·66	16·33	0·80
49	1·36	3·03	4·69	6·36	8·03	9·69	11·36	13·03	14·69	16·36	0·82
50	1·39	3·06	4·72	6·39	8·06	9·72	11·39	13·06	14·72	16·39	0·83
51	1·42	3·08	4·75	6·42	8·08	9·75	11·42	13·08	14·75	16·42	0·85
52	1·44	3·11	4·78	6·44	8·11	9·78	11·44	13·11	14·78	16·44	0·87
53	1·47	3·14	4·80	6·47	8·14	9·80	11·47	13·14	14·80	16·47	0·88
54	1·50	3·17	4·83	6·50	8·17	9·83	11·50	13·17	14·83	16·50	0·90
55	1·53	3·19	4·86	6·53	8·19	9·86	11·53	13·19	14·86	16·53	0·92
56	1·56	3·22	4·89	6·56	8·22	9·89	11·56	13·22	14·89	16·56	0·93
57	1·58	3·25	4·92	6·58	8·25	9·92	11·58	13·25	14·92	16·58	0·95
58	1·61	3·28	4·94	6·61	8·28	9·94	11·61	13·28	14·94	16·61	0·97
59	1·64	3·31	4·97	6·64	8·31	9·97	11·64	13·31	14·97	16·64	0·98

DECIMAL-HOUR UNITS (HOURS÷100)

FIG. 31. TIME CONVERSION TABLE

have to be provided. Thus, although the decision to use a decimal-hour time scale is comparatively straightforward when made at the time of introduction of work measurement, in the case of companies already using other systems the cost of replacement of watches will have to be carefully weighed against the benefits expected.

It will be clear that, depending on the type of work, e.g., work involving long or short time cycles, the most appropriate and convenient time scales and stop watches should be selected. In general, for most industrial work, the decimal-minute scale, with the related watch, is in widest use.

The Concept of Standard Rating

Time study is based on a record of the observed times for doing a job together with an assessment of the effectiveness of working of the worker in relation to a concept combining, separately or together, one or more factors necessary to the carrying out of the job, such as speed of movement, effort, dexterity, consistency. Assuming that the worker also takes the proportion of rest allotted to the job he is doing, this optimum effectiveness applied to the " effort " portion of the job will enable him to produce, without becoming more than healthily tired, standard performance over the working period, i.e. one standard hour per hour or 60 standard minutes per hour. For the purposes of this book, all references to units of work are in standard minutes (SM).

Thus, standard performance results when the work in a job is done at ideal degree of effectiveness and the appropriate relaxation allowance is taken in full. While neither the worker nor the amount of work which will make him no more than reasonably tired are definable in a strictly scientific sense, it has been found that, in the long run, standard performance can be maintained throughout the year without over-exertion and consequent detriment to health.

A scale has therefore been fixed giving this ideal of effectiveness a value of 100, and this is designated as the standard rating. Observers are trained to be able to recognize the conditions of standard rating, and to assess to the nearest five points the degree to which a worker's observed speed and effectiveness vary from the " 100 " concept. The procedure in which this assessment is noted simultaneously with the observed time is known as *rating*.

Although his preliminary training will have included rating exercises and training with rating films, to be able satisfactorily to make ratings in practice the observer must on each occasion, before commencing a study, acquire a thorough understanding of the job to be studied. Before he is called in to make a time study, the job should

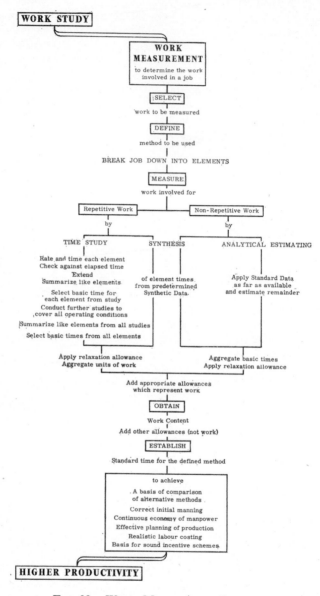

FIG. 32. WORK MEASUREMENT PROCEDURE

114

have been method studied and the worker allowed sufficient time to become used to the layout and system of working which have been approved. If, however, the same operation is being performed by more than one worker it is advisable for the observer to see how each is managing before commencing, to make sure that all reasonable variations in materials and conditions have been taken into account. The exact amount of time which will have to be spent in this way will depend on the complexity of the operations being studied and the period for which the job is expected to run.

Rating Scales

While the 100 scale is used throughout this book, some organizations make use of others; and those in most general use are demonstrated diagrammatically in Fig. 33.

The general procedure outlined is applicable irrespective of the actual scale employed. In this respect the situation is akin to that of indicating temperature where, for instance, the boiling point of water at normal atmospheric pressure may be expressed as 100°, 212° or 80° according to whether the Centigrade, Fahrenheit or Réaumur scale is used.

The changeover from one scale to another can usually be very easily made, since it is only in the recording of the study and the

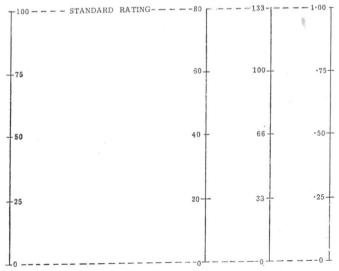

FIG. 33. COMPARISON OF RATING SCALES

calculations of standardized times that rating plays an essential part. Observers experienced in the use of a particular scale may, of course, feel it convenient to continue using their own scale. It is more satisfactory, however, to provide opportunities for observers to become competent in the use of the company's official rating scale, whatever it is, since this will reduce the possibility of misunderstandings between the various persons concerned.

Breaking the Task into Elements

It is found in practice that a worker's ratings may vary not only from cycle to cycle of a job, but frequently also within each cycle itself. As this would make it difficult to make an overall rating for the period of the study, or even a separate rating for each cycle, it is customary before starting a time study to break down into what are called *elements* all jobs but those having a very short cycle time. These elements, each of which should preferably be between 10 and 50 centiminutes' (6 and 30 seconds) duration for direct time study purposes, represent the parts or phases into which an operation can be conveniently divided for timing and rating purposes.

When breaking the job down into elements it is essential that they should each be clearly distinguishable. Observation of the following principles will be of assistance—

1. Separate elements which are identical from those which are variable in the work they comprise.
2. Separate heavy work from light work.
3. When convenient use audible points in the work, such as the snap of a switch or the sound of an article dropping into a container, as element break-points.

Long Cycle Repetitive Work

Sometimes elements occupying considerably longer than 50 centiminutes ($\frac{1}{2}$ minute) are unavoidable because no break-point can be established within that time. Break-points are then arbitrarily made every $\frac{1}{2}$ minute and a rating recorded. The rating for the whole element will be the weighted average value of the ratings for the portions of the elements.

Short Cycle Repetitive Work

In some types of work, such as labelling bottles, metal press work, filling containers, etc., many elements and sometimes complete cycle times will be of less than 10 centiminutes' duration. This presents problems both in taking the actual times of the elements and in the rating. There are two usual ways in which such problems are overcome—

1. The overall time of a number of cycles of exactly similar elements occurring in succession is taken and an overall rating is made. The observed time for one of the cycles or elements can then be obtained by dividing this overall time by the number of cycles or elements observed.

2. The element is observed in isolation, that is to say, a number of separate rated times are recorded at convenient moments without any attempt to include them in the main continuous study of the job.

Rating and Standardized Time

Rating the speed, effort and effectiveness of a man's work on each element against a concept of standard is done so that observed times can be converted into *basic times*. Basic times are those which would have been taken had the work been done at 100 rating, without any relaxation allowance being taken.

Thus, if we require the basic time for an element which has been observed to take 20 centiminutes (12 seconds), and has been rated at 110, this would be

$$\frac{20 \times 110}{100} = 22 \text{ centiminutes (or 13 seconds)}$$

Motion Pattern

To improve accuracy of rating in highly repetitive work, it may pay to study the basic motion pattern by the micromotion analysis techniques, and then train workers in the best pattern for each element of the work.

For most time study work, however, such studies will be found too expensive and the work study officer must appreciate from his knowledge of the work being done what movements are necessary and how those movements should be made. For instance, the size, weight, shape and position of an object will determine how best to pick it up. If a heavy hammer is used to nail a small packing case the motion pattern will be different from that used when driving a long nail into a fence. If a worker has to wear gloves to handle sharp-sided iron sheets, his motion pattern will be clumsy in comparison with his pattern when moving smooth-edged sheets with bare hands. If, when sawing wood, there is a decrease in driving pressure on the saw, it will be necessary to use more strokes to complete the job, and so a change in the overall motion pattern will have occurred.

Requirements for Satisfactory Ratings

1. An ample supply of work must be available.

2. Ratings must not be influenced by restrictions imposed by the nature of the work, such as the time required for an automatically-controlled item of plant to function or a process reaction to take place, or by the fixed rate of achievement demanded by a conveyor line: these are recorded separately.

3. Ratings should refer to the attainment of the minimum acceptable quality specifications; no credit should be given for attaining a quality higher than this minimum. (There are occasions when best possible quality may be required and any improvement above the minimum acceptable may be of real value. In such cases, each change in quality is essentially a change in the specification of the work and should be treated as such.)

Factors Affecting Ratings

It may be that, because of adverse conditions beyond his control, a worker takes longer to perform an element on one occasion than on another, even though his speed, effort and effectiveness of working are greater and his rating consequently higher. The following are some of the factors which can be the cause of this—

Effectiveness

Factors which will influence the effectiveness of a man's work must be clearly recognized according to whether or not they are within the worker's control—

(*a*) *Outside the worker's control*

1. Variations in quality or specification of the materials used although these materials are within prescribed tolerance limits.

2. Changes in the operating efficiency of tools or equipment within their useful life.

3. Minor changes in methods or conditions of operation.

4. Changes in lighting, temperature, climate and other temporary conditions of environment.

5. Variations in the mental attention necessary for the performance of certain elements of the work.

(*b*) *Dependent on the worker*

1. Variations in the quality of work within the specification.

2. The degree to which the worker is suited and accustomed to

his work, determined not only by his physical and mental faculties, but also by his past training, acquired skill and knowledge.

3. The attitude of mind of the worker which will affect his desire to get the work done quickly. This includes interest and pride in the job, the opinion held of supervisors, and many other psychological factors, some of which may have nothing to do with the job.

Speed

Factors which will affect speed are—

(a) *The type of effort demanded by the job*

Generally, a demand for increased physical effort will lead to a slower speed. For example, the speed of turning a particular handwheel will largely depend on the resistance to be overcome. The facility with which physical effort can be increased to overcome harsher resistance must influence rating, which is considering speed of working in terms of expenditure of energy. For example, there is a difference in carrying a heavy load comfortably balanced on the shoulders and carrying the same load by hand.

(b) *The care required on the part of the worker*

A need for increased care in carrying out an element of work will also reduce speed. For example, threading a piece of string through a curtain ring can easily be done using rapid movements, but if the string is to be threaded through the eye of a bagging needle it is necessary to control the movements carefully, and in consequence they are made less rapidly, even though no less effort may be involved.

Because various factors will influence a worker's motion patterns and speed and effectiveness in different ways, the observer must be familiar with the motion pattern followed by an average worker suited and accustomed to his work, and with how this pattern might change to meet the varied range of conditions.

In practice the work study officer will find no great difficulty in attaining consistency in the 75–110 range of ratings, between which the vast majority of assessments lie. To " rate " at higher and lower rates of working requires greater skill, and should be avoided if at all possible, or should be checked against a nearer average worker on the same work. By careful training of staff and by cross-checking of assessments, consistency of rating between observers can be assured to a high degree.

Time Study Procedure

Before work study is introduced in an organization, care should be taken to ensure that those who will be affected by it have been kept informed as to the intention and purpose of using it. In particular, no attempt should be made to apply the work measurement techniques without prior consultation between management and the work-people's representatives (*see* Chapter 3).

On first entry into each department the work study officer should be accompanied by a member of the management, who should introduce him to the foreman, who should in turn introduce him to the members of the works council or production committee, and to the shop stewards. The officer should then take the earliest opportunity to spend some time in the department gaining a knowledge of the work and forming his concept of standard for the purpose of rating.

Thereafter, whenever he is required to make a study of an operation he should always make a special point of seeing the foreman or his deputy before approaching any worker. With the assistance of the foreman or his deputy, and as a result of his own observations, the work study officer will then note which are the steady workers among those concerned. In consultation with the work-people's representative he will then select from among them one he considers temperamentally suited with whom to begin his study.

However much a worker wishes to help, he is likely to give an artificial performance when first observed. Helpful workers tend to show how good they can be and to omit normal breaks: workers passively accepting observation of their work are sometimes inwardly resentful, particularly in the early stages of the study. Thus, in any study it is as well to assume that the first studies made on the job serve only to familiarize the observer with the work and to accustom the worker to being observed.

The responsible work study officer should now plan the study taking into account the following factors—

1. Job breakdown.
2. Element break-points.
3. Establishing synthetic data both for cycle and element times.

This responsible work study officer should co-ordinate all future studies particularly of similar operations or operations with important elements in them.

The Tools of Time Study

The Stop-watch. In the design of watch recommended, whatever the time scale used, the winding knob returns both hands to zero when pressed and, immediately pressure is released, the watch restarts. This is known as a flyback type of watch. If it is desired to stop the watch completely, this can be done by means of a slide alongside the winder which halts the hands at the position they were in at the moment of bringing the slide into action.

Whatever type of watch is used, it is important that it should be checked for accuracy at regular intervals. After use the watch should be allowed to run down to preserve the spring. For safety in use, the stop-watch should be clipped to the study board, or held by a thong round the finger.

The Study Board. A study board is used to hold the study summary record sheet and the observation record (time study) continuation sheets which are shown in Figs. 34 and 35. It is made to give a good surface for writing without being large enough to interfere with observation of the worker being studied. The top may be shaped to facilitate holding in the left hand, and have a clip fitted into which the stop-watch can be securely fixed.

Taking the Study

The study summary sheet should now be filled in as far as is shown in Fig. 36. Note that although the observation record sheet illustrated has four columns (*W*, *X*, *Y* and *Z*), space may be saved if required by giving three columns only, in which case columns *X* and *Y* are combined and figures showing ineffective or check time are circled to distinguish them from observed times.

To facilitate rating the job should then be broken down into elements, which should be listed commencing on the first of the observation record (time study) continuation sheets, as in Fig. 37. At the end of each element description the break-point should be indicated whenever possible.

To start the study a clock must be found which is suitable for establishing a time check. Electric clocks of the impulse type which move visibly and audibly every 30 seconds are particularly suitable. When no clock is near another stop-watch can be used. The use of wrist-watches, because of the vagaries of some types, is not recommended.

The stop-watch is set in motion at an exact time observed on the clock, and must remain in motion until completion of the study. The exact time it is started is entered on the study summary record in the space headed " time check."

The work study officer then goes to the job and, after introducing himself to the worker, stands some distance away so as not to be in his way. The stop-watch and study board are held well up in line

STUDY SUMMARY RECORD

STUDY REF.	
SHEET REF.	

TIME STUDY		WORKS		DATE	
PRODUCTION STUDY		DEPARTMENT		TAKEN BY	
SYNTHESIS		PLANT/SECTION		LABOUR CLASSIFICATION	
		LOCATION			

TIME CHECK	OPERATION DESCRIPTION
TIME FINISHED____HR ____MIN	
TIME STARTED____HR ____MIN	
ELAPSED TIME=_____MIN	
TOTAL RECORDED TIME	
(Sum. of Cols. X + Cols. Y)____MIN	MATERIALS
TIMING ERROR=_____%	
AVERAGE RATING	EQUIPMENT
(Cols. Z/Cols. X) ×100=_____	MACHINE No. AND SPEED
No. OF CYCLES	WORKING CONDITIONS
QUANTITY	

QUALITY

ELEMENT REF.	ELEMENT DESCRIPTION	No. OF OCCASION	BASIC TIME (MIN)	R.A. COMPUTATION % FACTOR								TOTAL
				A	B	C	D	E	F	G	H	

FIG. 34. BLANK STUDY SUMMARY RECORD

	W	X	Y	Z	OBSERVATION RECORD (TIME STUDY)	SHEET REF.			

OBSERVATION RECORD (TIME STUDY)

SHEET REF.

STUDY REF.

DATE

ELEMENT DESCRIPTION	W RATING FACTOR	X OBSERVED TIME	Y INEFF. OR CHECK TIME	Z BASIC TIME	ELEMENT DESCRIPTION	W RATING FACTOR	X OBSERVED TIME	Y INEFF OR CHECK TIME	Z BASIC TIME
BROUGHT FORWARD					BROUGHT FORWARD				
TOTALS					TOTALS				

FIG. 35. BLANK OBSERVATION RECORD

STUDY SUMMARY RECORD				STUDY REF.	I.A.
				SHEET REF.	SR/1.
TIME STUDY	431	WORKS	CONTAINER	DATE	26 – 10 – 56
PRODUCTION STUDY		DEPARTMENT	12	TAKEN BY	E.J.C.
SYNTHESIS		PLANT/SECTION	DRUM	LABOUR CLASSIFICATION	
		LOCATION	GUILLOTINE		7/M

TIME CHECK	OPERATION DESCRIPTION
TIME FINISHED____HR ____MIN	Shear steel sheet for manufacture of drum type 201.
TIME STARTED____HR ____MIN	
ELAPSED TIME=____MIN	
TOTAL RECORDED TIME	
(Sum. of Cols. X + Cols. Y)____MIN	MATERIALS Stock size 70½" × 37" × 0·028"
TIMING ERROR=____%	Finished size 69⅞" × 36⅝" × 0·028" Weight 28 lb.
AVERAGE RATING	EQUIPMENT Guillotine shears. Armoured leather gloves.
(Cols. Z/Cols. X) × 100=____	MACHINE No. AND SPEED AB.146. Moon Bros. 6'6". Guillotine.
No. OF CYCLES	WORKING CONDITIONS
QUANTITY	Normal

QUALITY Speen. C.12.

ELEMENT REF.	ELEMENT DESCRIPTION	NO. OF OCCASION	BASIC TIME (MIN)	R.A. COMPUTATION % FACTOR								TOTAL
				A	B	C	D	E	F	G	H	

FIG. 36. STUDY SUMMARY RECORD: PARTIALLY COMPLETED

OBSERVATION RECORD (TIME STUDY)

ELEMENT DESCRIPTION	W RATING FACTOR	X OBSERVED TIME	Y INEFF. OR CHECK TIME	Z BASIC TIME	ELEMENT DESCRIPTION	W RATING FACTOR	X OBSERVED TIME	Y INEFF. OR CHECK TIME	Z BASIC TIME
BROUGHT FORWARD					BROUGHT FORWARD				
Check time					4. Operate foot pedal bar to cut. Grip edges of sheet with both hands–pull sheet clear of stops–slide sheet from guillotine table on to steel table for next operation and release. (Sheet moved approx. 3 ft).				
1. Release finished sheet–turn 180° and step to stock bench and with palm of left hand push forward top sheet–grip edges with both hands and slide sheet on to guillotine table–locate and position long side of sheet against stops of guillotine for long side cutting (sheet moved 5–6 ft through 90°).									
Breakpoint: As the left foot lifts to reach for the foot pedal bar.					Breakpoint: As the hands release the finished sheet on to the steel table.				
2. Operate foot pedal bar to cut. Grip edges of sheet with both hands–pull sheet clear of stops–turn sheet 90°–locate and position short side of sheet against stops of guillotine for end cutting.					5. Move round end of stock table–walk to raw material stockpile–with RH procure control pendant of electric hoist – LH. position "scissor grips" under edge of bundle of 80 sheets–operate hoist to clear bundle–operate hoist to lift and traverse to guillotine stock table (distance 15 ft). –position bundle on to table– release scissors grip–operate hoist to traverse back to stockpile, lowering–return to guillotine–pick up snips and cut fastenings–aside snips to table.				
Breakpoint: As the left foot lifts to reach for the foot pedal bar.									
3. Operate foot pedal bar to cut. Grip edges of sheet with both hands–pull sheet clear of stops– turn sheet 180°–locate and position second short side of sheet against stops of guillotine for end cutting.									
Breakpoint: As the left foot lifts to reach for the foot pedal bar.					Breakpoint: As the hand releases the snips to the table.				
TOTALS					TOTALS				

FIG. 37. OBSERVATION RECORD: PARTIALLY COMPLETED

with the operation being studied so that reading the stop-watch and recording the rating can be done while maintaining observation of all the worker's movements throughout the job.

Flyback Timing. As the worker commences the first element, the watch is clicked back to zero, the time which has elapsed between taking the time check and the start of the first element being entered in the column headed " Ineffective or check time " on the observation record sheet. This entry is marked " check time " in the column provided for description of the elements. (When using a decimal-scale watch, times should be expressed in one or two figures only, no decimal point being necessary at this stage.) The watch is zeroed similarly at the conclusion of each element.

Cumulative Timing. By this method the position of the stop-watch hand is recorded at the commencement of the study and at the end of each element without ever returning it to zero. The individual element times are afterwards arrived at by subtraction of successive readings.

Towards the end of the first element its number and rating are entered in the appropriate columns, and at the arrival of the break-point the time indicated is put down. Any unusual happening during or between elements, such as a fumble by the worker, must be mentioned in the element description column. It is most important that any time during which the worker is not performing one of the elements should be recorded in the ineffective time column of the study sheet, and a note made of the cause of the delay.

Ineffective time refers to periods during which the man is not working, or is doing work not forming a necessary part of the particular job being studied. Whatever the cause of the ineffective time, it should be most carefully noted. Some causes of ineffective time are as follows—

1. *Management responsible.* Waiting for work, instructions, material or equipment.

2. *Worker responsible.* Stopping work to talk unnecessarily with neighbour, etc.

3. *Contingencies.* Consultation with supervision, fellow workers, other departments. Obtaining special equipment, instructions, drawings, etc.

The remaining elements are then treated in the same way. Between cycles the work study officer should change his position so as to be sure that he is getting a full view of the work.

It should be an inflexible rule that no erasures are permitted on time study sheets. If an error in a time or rating figure is noticed at

OBSERVATION RECORD (TIME STUDY)				

ELEMENT DESCRIPTION	W RATING FACTOR	X OBSERVED TIME	Y INEFF. OR CHECK TIME	Z BASIC TIME	ELEMENT DESCRIPTION	W RATING FACTOR	X OBSERVED TIME	Y INEFF. OR CHECK TIME	Z BASIC TIME
BROUGHT FORWARD					BROUGHT FORWARD		45	58	
Check time			58		4. Operate foot pedal bar to cut. Grip edges of sheet with both hands - pull sheet clear of stops - slide sheet from guillotine table on to steel table for next operation and release. (Sheet moved approx. 3 ft).				
1. Release finished sheet - turn 180° and step to stockbench and with palm of left hand push forward top sheet - grip edges with both hands and slide sheet on to guillotine table - locate and position long side of sheet against stops of guillotine for long side cutting (sheet moved 5-6 ft through 90°).	100	17				95	13		
Breakpoint: As the left foot lifts to reach for the foot pedal bar.					Breakpoint: As the hands release the finished sheet on to the steel table				
2. Operate foot pedal bar to cut. Grip edges of sheet with both hands - pull sheet clear of stops - turn sheet 90° locate and position short side of sheet against stops of guillotine for end cutting.	95	13			5. Move round end of stock table - walk to raw material stockpile - with R.H. procure control pendant of electric hoist - L.H. position "scissor grips" under edge of bundle of 80 sheets - operate hoist to clear bundle - operate hoist to lift and traverse to guillotine stock table (distance 15 ft) - position bundle on to table - release scissors grip - operate hoist to traverse back to stock pile, lowering - return to guillotine - pick up snips and cut fastenings - aside snips to table.				
Breakpoint: As the left foot lifts to reach for the foot pedal bar.						—	—		
3. Operate foot pedal bar to cut. Grip edges of sheet with both hands - pull sheet clear of stops - turn sheet 180° - locate and position second short side of sheet against stops of guillotine for end cutting.	95	15			Breakpoint: As the hand releases the snips to the table.				
Breakpoint: As the left foot lifts to reach for the foot pedal bar.									
TOTALS		45	58		TOTALS		58	58	

FIG. 38. CONTINUATION OF COMPLETED OBSERVATION RECORD I

OBSERVATION RECORD (TIME STUDY)

SHEET REF. O.R/2.
STUDY REF. I.A.
DATE 26-10-56

ELEMENT DESCRIPTION	W RATING FACTOR	X OBSERVED TIME	Y INEFF. OR CHECK TIME	Z BASIC TIME	ELEMENT DESCRIPTION	W RATING FACTOR	X OBSERVED TIME	Y INEFF. OR CHECK TIME	Z BASIC TIME
BROUGHT FORWARD		58	58		BROUGHT FORWARD		526	83	
1 Worker fumble	95	20			1	105	16		
2	80	15			2	100	13		
3	95	16			3	95	16		
4	80	14			4	100	13		
1	95	19			Rest				80
2	95	13			1	105	15		
3	95	14			2	100	11		
4	100	12			3	100	13		
1	70	23			4	100	13		
2	95	13			1	105	15		
3	95	17			2	100	11		
4	100	14			3	100	14		
1	105	15			4	100	14		
2	100	11			1	105	16		
3	95	15			2	105	12		
4	100	14			3	105	14		
1	100	16			4	100	13		
2	100	11			1	100	17		
3	95	17			2	105	11		
Instruction (foreman)			25		3	105	13		
4	100	11			4	100	13		
1	100	15			1	95	20		
2	95	11			2	100	13		
3	95	14			3	80	17		
4	110	11			4	80	15		
1	100	17			Rest				300
2	95	13			1	80	20		
3	95	17			2	90	13		
4	100	13			3	100	13		
1	95	19			4 Rating doubtful	100	14		
2	95	13			1	100	15		
3	100	14			2	100	13		
4	105	11			3	90	16		
TOTALS		526	83		TOTALS		968	463	

FIG. 39. CONTINUATION OF COMPLETED OBSERVATION RECORD II

OBSERVATION RECORD (TIME STUDY)

ELEMENT DESCRIPTION	W RATING FACTOR	X OBSERVED TIME	Y INEFF. OR CHECK TIME	Z BASIC TIME	ELEMENT DESCRIPTION	W RATING FACTOR	X OBSERVED TIME	Y INEFF. OR CHECK TIME	Z BASIC TIME
BROUGHT FORWARD		968	463		BROUGHT FORWARD		1446	513	
4	100	14			3.	95	17		
1	100	17			4	80	15		
2	105	11			1	105	17		
3	105	12			2	105	11		
4	100	14			3	100	13		
1	100	17			4	90	15		
2	95	13			1	100	16		
3	90	16			2	100	13		
4	95	15			3	100	13		
1	105	15			4	100	13		
2	100	13			Check time			62	
3	100	15							
4	100	14			Totals	—	1589	575	
1	105	17							
2	100	13							
3	100	13							
4	105	13							
5	100	41							
1	100	17							
2	100	12							
3	90	14							
4	100	14							
1	100	14							
2	95	15							
3	100	15							
4	105	13							
1	105	14							
2	105	13							
3	100	13							
4	100	13							
Talk to neighbour			50						
1	105	15							
2	100	13							
TOTALS		1446	513		TOTALS				

FIG. 40. CONTINUATION OF COMPLETED OBSERVATION RECORD III

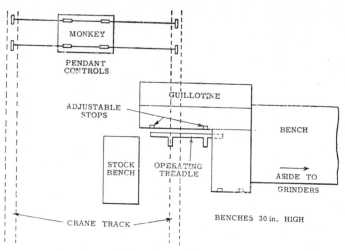

FIG. 41.   SKETCH OF LAYOUT OF OPERATION

the time it is made, it should be struck out immediately and the right value inserted alongside. If it is not noticed until some time later it can only be regarded as suspect and, as such, not valid for inclusion in the subsequent calculations. In particular, no attempt should ever be made to alter an observed time or rating figure after completion of the study.

Closing the Study

The cycle of elements should be repeatedly studied until the observer is satisfied he has sufficient data to proceed with the subsequent calculations which are involved.

When the last element of the last cycle is completed the watch is read and is left running until it can be compared with the clock by which it was started. At an exact time by the clock, the stop-watch is halted by use of the slide. The time by the clock is noted on the study summary record, and the reading indicated on the stop-watch entered at the end of the last sheet in the " Ineffective time " column and marked " check time." Columns *X* and *Y* are then totalled, after which the observation record sheets will be complete to the extent shown in Figs. 38, 39 and 40. At this stage a sketch of the layout of the operation with all the relevant dimensions will usually be made on the back of the sheet (as shown in Fig. 41). The information contained in this sketch is important since, together with the element breakdown, it defines the method observed.

The information in the " time check " section of the study summary record is now calculated to test the validity of the study. If the timing error is less than an agreed maximum (in the order of 1–2 per cent) then the information contained in the study can be used. If it is outside this limit the study must be discarded and a new one made.

From Fig. 42 it will be noticed that in the present example the timing error is just 1·5 per cent

STUDY SUMMARY RECORD				STUDY REF.	I . A .					
				SHEET REF.	SR/I .					
TIME STUDY	431	WORKS	CONTAINER .	DATE	26 - 10 - 56					
PRODUCTION STUDY		DEPARTMENT	12	TAKEN BY	E.J.C .					
SYNTHESIS		PLANT/SECTION	DRUM	LABOUR CLASSIFICATION						
		LOCATION	GUILLOTINE .	7/M						

TIME CHECK	OPERATION DESCRIPTION
TIME FINISHED 9 HR 52 MIN	Shear steel sheet for manufacture of drum type 201.
TIME STARTED 9 HR 30 MIN	
ELAPSED TIME = 22 MIN	
TOTAL RECORDED TIME (Sum. of Cols. X + Cols. Y) 21·7 MIN	MATERIALS Stock size 70½" x 37" x 0.028".
TIMING ERROR = 1·5 %	Finished size 69⅛" x 36⅝" X 0.028". Weight 28lb.
AVERAGE RATING	EQUIPMENT. Guillotine shears. Armoured leather gloves.
(Cols. Z/Cols. X) ×100 =	MACHINE No. AND SPEED AB . 146. Moon Bros . 6'6". Guillotine
No. OF CYCLES	WORKING CONDITIONS QUALITY Specn. C. 12.
QUANTITY	Normal

ELEMENT REF.	ELEMENT DESCRIPTION	NO. OF OCCURED	BASIC TIME (MIN)	R.A. COMPUTATION %								TOTAL
				FACTOR								
				A	B	C	D	E	F	G	H	

FIG. 42. STUDY SUMMARY RECORD WITH TIME-CHECK INFORMATION

" *Extension* " *of Observed Times*

After a number of observed times and corresponding ratings have been recorded for each of the elements of a job, and delays segregated and described, the next stage is to work out the basic time for each actual time noted. This process is termed *extension*, and as has been shown consists of finding out what time would have been taken to perform each element had the worker been working at exactly 100 rating. Each observed time for every element is multiplied by the corresponding rating, and the result divided by the standard rating (100 in the present instance)—

$$\text{Basic time} = \frac{\text{Observed time} \times \text{Observed rating}}{\text{Standard rating}}$$

In practice extension involves a great deal of repetitive work which is often done by juniors with tables or calculating machines so as to release the work study officer for more technical work. Each basic time should be entered in the appropriate column of the observation record sheet alongside the corresponding observed time and rating. If desired, coloured pencil can be used to distinguish between information obtained during study and calculations made afterwards.

The stage will now have been reached where the observation record sheets present the appearance shown in Figs. 43, 44 and 45.

Obtaining a Selected Basic Time per Element

The next step is to arrive at the *selected basic time* for each element. This is derived from an analysis of the list of basic times worked out for each element in the manner described, and choosing or calculating one for each which is considered to be representative.

Usually, and particularly in the case of highly repetitive work where variations in the basic times for each element are ordinarily very small, the straight arithmetic average is selected. This is obtained in the usual manner, by dividing the sum of the basic times for an element by the number of occasions it was observed.

In the present example this has been done in the time study analysis sheet in Fig. 46.

In certain operations, however, there may be frequent variations in the work involved in an element. For example, raw materials, steam pressure or machine speeds could vary within prescribed quality limits so as to make an appreciable difference in the times taken to perform the element.

In such cases the method of *graphic average* may be used. Observed times for the element are plotted against the reciprocals of

SHEET REF. OR./1
STUDY REF. I.A.
DATE 26-10-56

OBSERVATION RECORD (TIME STUDY)

ELEMENT DESCRIPTION	W RATING FACTOR	X OBSERVED TIME	Y INEFF. OR CHECK TIME	Z BASIC TIME	ELEMENT DESCRIPTION	W RATING FACTOR	X OBSERVED TIME	Y INEFF. OR CHECK TIME	Z BASIC TIME
BROUGHT FORWARD					BROUGHT FORWARD		45	58	.436
Check time			58		4. Operate foot pedal bar to cut. Grip edges of sheet with both hands—pull sheet clear of stops—slide sheet from guillotine table on to steel table for next operation and release. (Sheet moved approx. 3 ft). Breakpoint: As the hands release the finished sheet on to the steel table.	95	13		·124
1. Release finished sheet—turn 180° and step to stock bench and with palm of left hand push forward top sheet—grip edges with both hands and slide sheet on to guillotine table—locate and position long side of sheet against stops of guillotine for long side cutting (sheet moved 5-6 ft through 90°) Breakpoint: As the left foot lifts to reach for the foot pedal bar.	100	17		·170	5. Move round end of stock table—walk to raw material stockpile—with R.H. procure control pendant of electric hoist—L.H. position "scissor grips" under edge of bundle of 80 sheets—operate hoist to clear bundle—operate hoist to lift and traverse to guillotine stock table (distance 15 ft)—position bundle on to table—release scissors grip—operate hoist to traverse back to stock pile, lowering—return to guillotine—pick up snips and cut fastenings—aside snips to table. Breakpoint: As the hand releases the snips to the table.	—	—		—
2. Operate foot pedal bar to cut. Grip edges of sheet with both hands—pull sheet clear of stops—turn sheet 90°—locate and position short side of sheet against stops of guillotine for end cutting. Breakpoint: As the left foot lifts to reach for the foot pedal bar.	95	13		·123					
3. Operate foot pedal bar to cut. Grip edges of sheet with both hands—pull sheet clear of stops—turn sheet 180°—locate and position second short side of sheet against stops of guillotine for end cutting. Breakpoint: As the left foot lifts to reach for the foot pedal bar.	95	15		·143					
TOTALS	45	58	·436		TOTALS	58	58	·560	

FIG. 43. OBSERVATION RECORD SHOWING EXTENSION TO BASIC TIMES I

	W	X	Y	Z		W	X	Y	Z
OBSERVATION RECORD (TIME STUDY)					SHEET REF. O.R/2				
					STUDY REF. I.A.				
					DATE 26-10-56				
ELEMENT DESCRIPTION	RATING FACTOR	OBSERVED TIME	INEFF. OR CHECK TIME	BASIC TIME	ELEMENT DESCRIPTION	RATING FACTOR	OBSERVED TIME	INEFF. OR CHECK TIME	BASIC TIME
BROUGHT FORWARD	58	58		·560	BROUGHT FORWARD	526	83		5·021
1 Worker fumble	95	20		·190	1	105	16		·168
2	80	15		·120	2	100	13		·130
3	95	16		·152	3	95	16		·152
4	80	14		·112	4	100	13		·130
1	95	19		·180	Rest			80	
2	95	13		·123	1	105	15		·158
3	95	14		·133	2	100	11		·110
4	100	12		·120	3	100	13		·130
1	70	23		·161	4	100	13		·130
2	95	13		·123	1	105	15		·158
3	95	17		·161	2	100	11		·110
4	100	14		·140	3	100	14		·140
1	105	15		·158	4	100	14		·140
2	100	11		·110	1	105	16		·168
3	95	15		·143	2	105	12		·126
4	100	14		·140	3	105	14		·147
1	100	16		·160	4	100	13		·130
2	100	11		·110	1	100	17		·170
3	95	17		·162	2	105	11		·116
Instruction (foreman)			25		3	105	13		·137
4	100	11		·110	4	100	13		·130
1	100	15		·150	1	95	20		·190
2	95	11		·105	2	100	13		·130
3	95	14		·134	3	80	17		·136
4	110	11		·120	4	80	15		·120
1	100	17		·170	Rest			300	
2	95	13		·123	1	80	20		·160
3	95	17		·162	2	90	13		·117
4	100	13		·130	3	100	13		·130
1	95	19		·180	4 Rating doubtful	100	14		·140
2	95	13		·123	1	100	15		·150
3	100	14		·140	2	100	13		·130
4	105	11		·116	3	90	16		·144
TOTALS	526	83		5 021	TOTALS	968	463		9·398

FIG. 44. OBSERVATION RECORD SHOWING EXTENSION TO BASIC TIMES II

OBSERVATION RECORD (TIME STUDY)

ELEMENT DESCRIPTION	W RATING FACTOR	X OBSERVED TIME	Y INEFF. OR CHECK TIME	Z BASIC TIME	ELEMENT DESCRIPTION	W RATING FACTOR	X OBSERVED TIME	Y INEFF. OR CHECK TIME	Z BASIC TIME
BROUGHT FORWARD	/	968	463	9.348	BROUGHT FORWARD	/	1446	513	14.154
4	100	14		.140	3	95	17		.162
1	100	17		.170	4	80	15		.120
2	105	11		.116	1	105	17		.178
3	105	12		.126	2	105	11		.116
4	100	14		.140	3	100	13		.130
1	100	17		.170	4	90	15		.136
2	95	13		.123	1	100	16		.160
3	90	16		.144	2	100	13		.130
4	95	15		.143	3	100	13		.130
1	105	15		.158	4	100	13		.130
2	100	13		.130	Check time			62	
3	100	15		.150					
4	100	14		.140	Totals	→	1689	575	15.546
1	105	17		.178					
2	100	13		.130					
3	100	13		.130					
4	105	13		.147					
5	100	41		.413					
1	100	17		.170					
2	100	12		.120					
3	90	14		.126					
4	100	14		.140					
1	100	14		.140					
2	95	15		.143					
3	100	15		.150					
4	105	13		.137					
1	105	14		.147					
2	105	13		.137					
3	100	13		.130					
4	100	13		.130					
Talk to neighbour.			50						
1	105	15		.158					
2	100	13		.130					
TOTALS		1446	513	14.154	TOTALS				

FIG. 45. OBSERVATION RECORD SHOWING EXTENSION TO BASIC TIMES III

TIME STUDY ANALYSIS					STUDY No. 431/1A

DATE 26 - 10 - 56.

Element Ref:	1	2	3	4	5
p.1.	·170	·123	·143	·124	
	·190	·120	·152	·112	
	·180	·123	·133	·120	
	·161	·123	·161	·140	
	·158	·110	·143	·140	
	·160	·110	·162	·110	
	·150	(·105)	·134	·120	
	·170	·123	·162	·130	
	·180	·123	·140	·116	
p.2.	·168	·130	·152	·130	
	·158	·110	·130	·130	
	·158	·110	·140	·140	
	·168	·126	·147	·130	
	·170	·116	·137	·130	
	·190	·13	·136	·120	
	·160	·117	·130	·140	
	·150	·130	·144	·140	
	·170	·116	·126	·140	
	·170	·123	·144	·143	
	·158	·130	·150	·140	
	·178	·130	·130	·147	·413
	·170	·120	·126	·140	
	·140	(·143)	·150	·137	
	·147	·137	·130	·130	
	·158	·130			
p.3.			·162	·120	
	·178	·116	·130	·136	
	·160	·130	·130	·130	
	4·470	3·056	3·824	3·535	·413
	27	25	27	27	1
	·165	·122	·142	·131	·413

FIG. 46. TIME STUDY ANALYSIS

136

their corresponding ratings. A straight line is then projected from the origin of the graph and through the points plotted at such an angle as to equalize their scatter about it. The time corresponding to the position at which this line crosses the standard rating co-ordinate is taken to represent the selected basic time for the element concerned. Fig. 47 illustrates the procedure with an example taken from a different study.

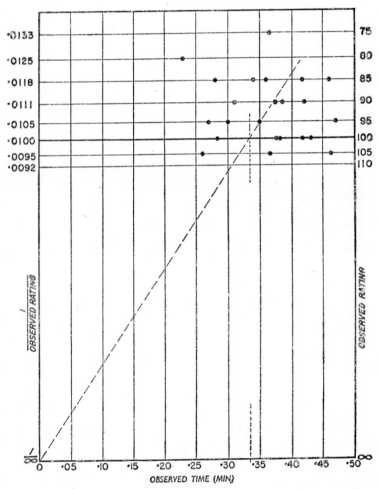

FIG. 47. GRAPHIC DETERMINATION OF SELECTED BASIC ELEMENT TIMES

STUDY SUMMARY RECORD				STUDY REF.	I.A.
				SHEET REF.	SR/1.
TIME STUDY	431	WORKS	CONTAINER	DATE	26-10-56
PRODUCTION STUDY		DEPARTMENT	12	TAKEN BY	E.J.C.
SYNTHESIS		PLANT/SECTION	DRUM	LABOUR CLASSIFICATION	
		LOCATION	GUILLOTINE		7/M

TIME CHECK		OPERATION DESCRIPTION
TIME FINISHED 9 HR 52 MIN		Shear steel sheet for manufacture of drum type 201.
TIME STARTED 9 HR 30 MIN		
ELAPSED TIME = 22 MIN		
TOTAL RECORDED TIME		
(Sum. of Cols. X + Cols. Y) 21·7 MIN		MATERIALS Stock size 70½" x 37" x 0.028"
TIMING ERROR = 1·5 %		Finished size 69⅛" x 36⅝" x 0.028" Weight 28 lb.
AVERAGE RATING		EQUIPMENT Guillotine shears. Armoured leather gloves.
(Cols. Z/Cols. X) ×100 = 98·1		MACHINE No. AND SPEED AB. 146. Moon Bros 6'6". Guillotine.
No. OF CYCLES 27		WORKING CONDITIONS QUALITY Specn. C.12.
QUANTITY 27		Normal

ELEMENT REF.	ELEMENT DESCRIPTION	No. OF OCCASION	BASIC TIME (MIN)	R.A. COMPUTATION % FACTOR								TOTAL
				A	B	C	D	E	F	G	H	
1.	Turn 180° - pick up sheet from stack and position under guillotine against stop to cut long side (Sheet moved 5-6 ft through 90°).	27	·165									
2.	Operate foot pedal to cut. Remove sheet turn 90° and position against stop to cut short side.	27	·122									
3.	Operate foot pedal to cut. Remove sheet turn 180° and position second short side against stop ready to cut.	27	·142									
4.	Operate foot pedal to cut. Remove sheet and aside to stack on bench on R.H. (Distance 3 ft).	27	·131									
5.	Procure stock of 80 sheets from storage and break fastenings (Distance moved 15 ft by overhead electric hoist pendant controls).	1	·413									

FIG. 48. STUDY SUMMARY RECORD: COMPLETED APART FROM RA

WORK MEASUREMENT SET-UP SHEET

CODE REF. **M/D/S**
SHEET REF. **SU/1.**

WORKS	CONTAINER.		
DEPARTMENT	12	OPERATION	
PLANT/SECTION	DRUM.	Shear steel sheet for manufacture of Drum type 201.	
LOCATION	GUILLOTINE.		

STUDY REF. **A1** TAKEN BY **E.I.C.**

SET-UP BY ...... DATE ......
WORK CONTENT .... SMs UT, ... MINS PER......
TIME AT STD PERF......... MINS PER......

ELEMENT REF.	ELEMENT DESCRIPTION	AVERAGE BASIC TIME PER OCCASION	FREQUENCY OCCUR-RENCE	AVERAGE BASIC TIME PER CYCLE	R.A.%	WORK CONTENT (SMs)
1.	Turn 180° – pick up sheet from stack and position under guillotine against stop to cut long side. (Sheet moved 5-6 ft. through 90°). ·165					
2.	Operate foot pedal to cut. Remove sheet, turn 90° and position against stop to cut short side. ·122					
3.	Operate foot pedal to cut. Remove sheet, turn 180° and position second short side against stop ready to cut. ·142					
4.	Operate foot pedal to cut. Remove sheet and aside to stack on bench on R.H. (Distance 3 feet). ·131					
5.	Procure stock of 80 sheets from storage and break fastenings (Distance moved 15 ft. by overhead electric hoist pendant controls). ·413					
						TOTAL

FIG. 49. WORK MEASUREMENT SET-UP SHEET: PARTIALLY COMPLETED

WORK MEASUREMENT SET-UP SHEET

WORKS CONTAINER. CODE REF. M/D/5

DEPARTMENT 12 SHEET REF. Su/1.

PLANT/SECTION DRUM.

LOCATION GUILLOTINE.

OPERATION: Shear steel sheet for manufacture of Drum type 201.

SET-UP BY

DATE

WORK CONTENT..............SMs. MINS PER..........

TIME AT STD PERF............. MINS PER..........

ELEMENT REF.	ELEMENT DESCRIPTION	A1 E.J.C.	B1 M.A.C.	B2 M.A.C.E.J.C.	A2 M.A.C.E.J.C.				AVERAGE BASIC TIME PER OCCASION	FREQUENCY OF OCCUR. RANGE	AVERAGE BASIC TIME PER CYCLE	R.A. %	WORK CONTENT (SMs)
1.	Turn 180° - pick up sheet from stack and position under guillotine against stop to cut long side (Sheet moved 5-6 ft through 90°).	.165	.162	.163	.170				.165	1/1	.165		
2.	Operate foot pedal to cut. Remove sheet, turn 90° and position against stop to cut short side.	.122	.130	.129	.126				.127	1/1	.127		
3.	Operate foot pedal to cut. Remove sheet, turn 180° and position second short side against stop ready to cut.	.142	.132	.141	.136				.138	1/1	.138		
4.	Operate foot pedal to cut. Remove sheet and aside to stack on bench on R.H. (Distance 3 feet).	.131	.131	.124	.127				.128	1/1	.128		
5.	Procure stack of 80 sheets from storage and break fastenings (Distance moved 15 ft. by overhead electric hoist pendant controls).	.413	-.458	—	—				.436	1/80	.005		

TOTAL

FIG. 50. WORK MEASUREMENT SET-UP SHEET: COMPLETED APART FROM RA

Summary of Time Studies

The elements, together with their respective selected basic times, are now listed on the study summary record together with a note of the number of occasions each was observed (Fig. 48). It is recommended at this stage that such times be expressed in minutes to three decimal places.

It now remains to carry forward the results to a " Work measurement set-up sheet " as shown in Fig. 49. At the head of this sheet information relating to the operation is filled in. The study number, together with the name of the observer, is entered in the first of the columns provided. The elements are then listed in turn in the " element description " column and the selected basic times for each entered in the manner shown.

When it is doubtful whether all normal variation and conditions of work have been taken account of and a good average work value can be obtained from the results of a single study, further studies, if possible by different observers and with different workers, should be made. The additional selected basic times so obtained should be added to the same set-up sheet.

When the responsible work study officer judges that sufficient studies have been made, the average basic time for each element is worked out by simple addition and division, after which the " frequency of occurrence " column, which refers to the number of times the element occurs per cycle of work, is filled in. In the next column the average basic time per cycle is then calculated by multiplying the average basic element time by the frequency. The set-up sheet in Fig. 50 has been completed to this stage, the results of three further time studies having been included.

Relaxation and Contingency Allowances

THE basic time per cycle required by the qualified worker to perform each element at standard speed and effectiveness of working has now been established. The next step is to find out what percentage of time should be added to each element to allow for fatigue and personal needs.

Relaxation allowance, abbreviated to RA, is an allowance of time made to a worker for personal needs and for recovery from the fatigue caused by doing his job. It will obviously vary from job to job according to the type of work; thus the heavier the work, and the higher the expenditure of energy, the greater will be this allowance.

As it is a principle of work study that the worker shall be able to achieve standard performance as an average over the day or shift without becoming more than reasonably tired, the period of rest allowed is calculated on this basis.

Basic time per cycle, relaxation and contingency allowances are then combined to give the units of work required.

Analytical Approach

Relaxation allowance is expressed as a percentage of the average basic time for each element. The elements are preferably considered separately on account of the frequently diverse nature of the work making up an operation.

The problem of fatigue is one to which a considerable amount of attention has been devoted in recent years, and research activity in this field is still in progress. For the purposes of work study it is unlikely, however, that much more of practical value will emerge for some time. To facilitate the assessment of relaxation allowances for inclusion in the work content, therefore, eight major known causes of fatigue have been listed, together with the main variations to which each is subject. Each of these variations has been given a percentage value by which to increase the average basic time for the element concerned. These percentages have been arrived at as a result of considerable experience in the application of work measurement techniques.

The causes themselves can be classified as follow—

A. Energy output	E. Personal needs
B. Posture	F. Thermal conditions
C. Motions	G. Atmospheric conditions
D. Visual fatigue	H. Other influences of environment

The table[1] on pages 144 and 145 shows the way in which these factors are used to determine suitable percentage values by which to increase the selected basic time for each element cycle time. The use of tables of this type has enabled different work study officers to attain a high degree of consistency when assessing relaxation allowance for the same job. It cannot be emphasized too strongly, however, that the satisfactory computation of RA is something for which considerable training and experience are necessary. The indiscriminate use of tables such as that given is something which management should actively discourage.

[1] (*a*) These tables are intended as a guide in assessing the relaxation allowances for individual elements.

(*b*) Although allowances are usually additive for individual elements, assessments for elements incurring high allowances *may* require reduction when followed by elements incurring less.

(*c*) The appropriate allowance for any factor present in an element should not be given until the influence of other factors upon it has been considered.

(*d*) Only in A, D and E has a separate allowance been indicated for women. Discretion should be used when assessing allowances for women under other factors.

(*e*) When special protective clothing such as gloves, footwear, suits or goggles have to be worn, additional fatigue may arise. Care should therefore be taken in making allowances under factors A, C, D, F and G.

FACTORS	TYPICAL EXAMPLES	Equivalent to handling	ALLOWANCES Men	ALLOWANCES Women	REMARKS
A. *Energy Output* (affecting muscular recovery)			per cent	per cent	When selecting the appropriate allowance for an element, the influence of the energy output in adjacent elements should be considered.
1. Negligible	Light bench work—seated	no load	0— 6	0— 6	
2. Very light	Light bench work—standing	0— 5 lb	6—7½	6—7½	
3. Light	Light shovelling	5— 20 lb	7½—12	7½—16	
4. Medium	Hacksawing or filing	20— 40 lb	12—19	16—30	
5. Heavy	Swinging heavy hammer 7—28 lb	40— 60 lb	19—30	—	
6. Very heavy	Loading weights	60—112 lb	30—50	—	
7. Exceptional	Loading heavy sacks	above 112 lb	requires special consideration		
B. *Posture*			per cent		When selecting the appropriate allowance for an element, the influence of the posture in adjacent elements should be considered.
1. Sit	Normal sedentary work		0— 1		
2. Stand (both feet)	Whenever body is erect and support on feet only		1—2½		
3. Stand (one foot)	Standing on one leg (using a foot control)		2½—4		
4. Lying down	On side, face or back		2½—4		
5. Crouch	When body is bent, but supported on feet or knees		4—10		
C. *Motions*					When selecting the appropriate allowance for an element, the influence of the restricted motions in adjacent elements should be considered.
1. Normal	Free swing of hammer		0		
2. Limited	Limited swing of hammer		0— 5		
3. Awkward	Carrying heavy load in one hand		0— 5		
4. Confined (limbs only)	Working with arms above head		5—10		
5. Confined (whole body)	Working at thin coal seam		10—15		

FACTORS	TYPICAL EXAMPLES	Lighting Good	Lighting Poor/Variable	REMARKS
D. *Visual Fatigue*		per cent	per cent	All colour contrasts wherever occurring must be considered in addition to light intensity.
1. Intermittent eye attention	Reading meters or guages	0	1	
2. Nearly continuous eye attention	Precision machine work	2	2	
3. Continuous eye attention—varying focus	Inspecting moving or stationary cloth for faults	2	5	
4. Continuous eye attention—fixed focus	Inspecting minute and/or moving objects	4	8	

E. *Personal Needs*

	Men per cent 2½	Women per cent 4

F. *Thermal Conditions*

	Temperature	Humidity Normal	Humidity Excessive	
		per cent	per cent	The selection of the allowance between the ranges given must be related to the type of work done which may offset the temperature effects, and to the type of ventilation.
1. Freezing	below 30°F.	over 10	over 12	
2. Low	32°—55°F.	10— 0	12— 5	
3. Normal	55°—75°F.	0	5	
4. High	75°—100°F.	0—40	5—100	
5. Excessive	above 100°F.	over 40	over 100	

G. *Atmospheric Conditions*

		per cent	
1. Good	Well ventilated rooms or fresh air	0	
2. Fair	Badly ventilated air, presence of non-toxic but foetid odours or non-injurious fumes	0— 5	Additional allowance will be necessary for special conditions of altitude and climate.
3. Poor	Presence of toxic dusts or heavy concentration of non-toxic dusts involving use of breathing filters	5—10	
4. Bad	Presence of toxic fumes or dusts involving use of respirator	10—20	

H. *Other Influences of Environment*

		per cent
1. Clean, healthy, dry and bright surroundings, low noise level. Influences without effect on work		0
2. Where work cycle is continuously repetitive and between 5 and 10 seconds		0— 1
3. Where work cycle is continuously repetitive and less than 5 seconds		1— 3
4. Where there is a complete absence of company Day—men		1
Day—women. Night—men		2— 5
5. Excessive noise, e.g. rivetting (allowance related to continuity of noise)		0— 5
6. Where effect of such disturbing influences might be detrimental to quality of output		5—10
7. Vibration of floors or machines, e.g. pneumatic drilling (allowance related to continuity of vibration)		5—10
8. Extreme conditions, e.g. dirt, noise, etc.		5—15

GUIDE TO RELAXATION ALLOWANCES

(See footnotes on page 143)

It is realized that in special cases the effects of other factors connected with fatigue, such as working at heights, cumulative fatigue and many others, are insufficiently understood. They are not, therefore, usually allowed for in such tables, since further research will be necessary before generally accepted values can be associated with them. For the present, when the exceptional circumstances in which they do occur are applicable, rough assessments are first made by extrapolation from the tables being used. From these assessments working values are eventually established by agreement between management and the representatives of the work-people concerned.

Special Considerations

In many companies it is customary, if the RA for any individual element falls below 10 per cent, to check that this would not have the effect of reducing the total RA for the complete task below the same value. If it is found that this would happen—which may be the case when the work is carried out under excellent physical and psychological conditions, or where substantial periods of waiting time are an integral feature of the job—the RA for the complete job is set at the minimum figure of 10 per cent of the total of the basic element times.

Short cycle repetitive work normally requires slightly more RA than long cycle work. This is because the repetitive use of a given set of muscles causes them to require a longer period of time for complete recovery from accrued fatigue. In very short cycle work monotony may also become an important factor, though it should be possible to reduce the relative effect of monotony by introducing small alternative duties such as arranging for a worker to obtain his own materials from stock.

Generally, when an RA of more than 30 per cent is necessary, it may be regarded as a criticism of management, and of designers in particular, since mechanical aids should have been provided or alternative methods found. Unfortunately there are still many cases in industry where RA of more than 30 per cent must be allotted.

Certain very exceptional types of work may demand RA of as high as 150–200 per cent. Such conditions could include high temperature, excessive humidity, the need for special protective clothing and the use of respirators. These cases must be examined very carefully before RA is allotted since, as they sometimes come outside the scope of the tables, the work study officer will be largely dependent on his own judgement.

Relaxation Allowance Computation

With these considerations in mind, the assessment of RA can now be made. This is done by filling in the appropriate values in the " RA Computation " section of the study summary record, every factor being considered in turn for each element.

When all the factors for each element have been considered and a percentage RA allotted as applicable, the total percentage for each element is summed and entered in the " Total " column, as shown in Fig. 51.

When more than one study is carried out, it may be considered sufficient to compute RA values once only, in which case it is done on the summary record for the last study made. The totals arrived at on this are then transferred to the work measurement set-up sheet. Alternatively, a separate assessment may be made each time a study is carried out. The final RA values entered on the work measurement set-up sheet are then determined from an assessment of all the separate computations.

Standard Time

The average basic time for each element on the set-up sheet is now increased by its appropriate RA percentage.

In the case of the first element of the operation under consideration this would give—

$$\underset{(0\cdot165 \text{ mins.})}{\text{Average basic time}} + \underset{(0\cdot035 \text{ mins.})}{21\tfrac{1}{2} \text{ per cent relaxation allowance}} = 0\cdot20$$

This is the work content (in standard minutes) for the element concerned and is entered in the appropriate column of the set-up sheet.

The work content for each remaining element is similarly calculated. The series is then totalled as shown in Fig. 52 to give the work content of the complete job. The final work content may include a contingency allowance of which a description is given below.

It is recommended that the work content for complete jobs should be expressed to two significant figures.

Contingency Allowances

In certain types of work a worker's job may include a number of minor activities which may be so spasmodic or infrequent that work measurement cannot be undertaken economically. To provide for this a contingency allowance expressed as a percentage of the basic times may be included in the work content for the job. The activities

STUDY SUMMARY RECORD				STUDY REF. I.A.
				SHEET REF. SR/1.
TIME STUDY	431	WORKS	CONTAINER.	DATE 26-10-56
PRODUCTION STUDY		DEPARTMENT	12	TAKEN BY E.J.C.
SYNTHESIS		PLANT/SECTION	DRUM.	LABOUR CLASSIFICATION
		LOCATION	GUILLOTINE	7/M

TIME CHECK		OPERATION DESCRIPTION
TIME FINISHED 9 HR 52 MIN		Shear steel sheet for manufacture of drum type 201.
TIME STARTED 9 HR 30 MIN		
ELAPSED TIME = 22 MIN		
TOTAL RECORDED TIME		
(Sum. of Cols. X + Cols. Y) 21·7 MIN		MATERIALS Stock size 70½" × 37" × 0·028"
TIMING ERROR = 1·5 %		Finished size 69⅞" × 36⅝" × 0·028". Weight 28 lb.
AVERAGE RATING		EQUIPMENT Guillotine shears. Armoured leather gloves.
(Cols. Z/Cols. X) × 100 = 98·1		MACHINE No. AND SPEED AB.146. Moon Bros. 6'6". Guillotine.
No. OF CYCLES 27		WORKING CONDITIONS QUALITY Specⁿ. C.12.
QUANTITY 27		Normal

ELEMENT REF.	ELEMENT DESCRIPTION	No. OF OCCASION	BASIC TIME (MIN)	R.A. COMPUTATION %								TOTAL
				FACTOR								
				A	B	C	D	E	F	G	H	
1.	Turn 180° – pick up sheet from stack and position under guillotine against stop to cut long side (Sheet moved 5–6 ft through 90°).	27	·165	9	2½	5	–	2½	–	–	2½	21½
2.	Operate foot pedal to cut. Remove sheet turn 90° and position against stop to cut short side.	27	·122	7½	2½	2½	–	2½	–	–	2½	17½
3.	Operate foot pedal to cut. Remove sheet turn 180° and position second short side against stop ready to cut.	27	·142	7½	2½	2½	–	2½	–	–	2½	17½
4.	Operate foot pedal to cut. Remove sheet and aside to stack on bench on R.H. (Distance 3 ft).	27	·131	7½	2½	2½	–	2½	–	–	2½	17½
5.	Procure stock of 80 sheets from storage and break fastenings (Distance moved 15 ft by overhead electric hoist pendant controls.)	1	·413	16	2½	–	–	2½	–	–	2½	23½

FIG. 51. STUDY SUMMARY RECORD: COMPLETED

WORK MEASUREMENT SET-UP SHEET

WORKS	CONTAINER		OPERATION		SET-UP BY	E.J.C.	CODE REF. M/D/5
DEPARTMENT	12		Shear sheet for manufacture of Drum type 201.		DATE 30.10.56		SHEET REF. 50/1
PLANT/SECTION	DRUM				WORK CONTENT ..67.. SMs		UT. — MINS PER SHEET
LOCATION	GUILLOTINE				TIME AT STD PERF. ..67..		MINS PER SHEET

ELEMENT REF.	ELEMENT DESCRIPTION	A1 E.J.C.	B1 M.A.C.	B2 M.A.C.	A2 E.J.C.	AVERAGE BASIC TIME PER OCCASION	FREQUENCY OF OCCURRENCE	AVERAGE BASIC TIME PER CYCLE	R.A.%	WORK CONTENT (SMs)
1.	Turn 180° pick up sheet from stack and position under guillotine against stop to cut long side. (Sheet moved 5-6ft. through 90°).	.165	.162	.163	.170	.165	1/1	.165	21½	.20
2.	Operate foot pedal to cut. Remove sheet, turn 90° and position against stop to cut short side.	.122	.130	.129	.126	.127	1/1	.127	17½	.15
3.	Operate foot pedal to cut. Remove sheet, turn 180° and position second short side against stop ready to cut.	.142	.132	.141	.136	.138	1/1	.138	17½	.16
4.	Operate foot pedal to cut. Remove sheet and aside to stack on bench on R.H. (Distance 3 ft.)	.131	.131	.124	.127	.128	1/1	.128	17½	.15
5.	Procure stock of 80 sheets from storage and break fastenings (Distance moved 15 ft. by overhead electric hoist pendant controls).	.413	—	.458	—	.436	1/80	.005	23½	.01
								TOTAL		.67

FIG. 52. WORK MEASUREMENT SET-UP SHEET: COMPLETED

covered by the contingency allowance must be clearly specified, and any such allowances must be carefully computed for the particular conditions relating to each job.

Examples of such activities are—

1. Consultation with supervision or other departments.
2. Sharpening of tools.
3. Obtaining special purpose equipment from a central pool.
4. Drawing special stores.

Allocating Rest

Although each unit of work or fraction thereof which goes to make up the work content of every job includes the appropriate percentage of relaxation allowance, it is, of course, seldom practicable for the worker to take this in small increments. What actually happens is that, while a small proportion may be taken between elements or cycles, the majority accumulates until it represents several minutes, when it may be used in a number of ways.

Sometimes managements arrange for tea and light refreshments to be available at certain times, though a proportion of the relaxation allowance must be left to the discretion of the workers. If workers are left to take the whole allowance at their own discretion they may work for too long a period before taking rest and so incur excessive cumulative fatigue.

12

Synthesis from Elemental Data

MANY jobs involve the manufacture or processing of products in which the work, while generally of the same type, is not continuously repetitive in the way referred to in Chapter 9. For instance, a worker in a boxmaking department may be given the job of making quantities of boxes which vary from batch to batch as regards size and shape, but for all of which the same general method of construction is used. Again, a machine worker may be required to produce articles which vary from day to day in some respects but remain identical in others.

In this and similar instances time study of every operation would be an extravagance, even if it were feasible. A characteristic of this type of work, however, is that, while a complete group of elements may not repeat itself for the days and weeks often necessary to justify separate study, certain individual elements may be common to the entire range of variations and recur repeatedly in different combinations. The situation has been likened to the alphabet, in which groups of letters common to many other words can, by suitable arrangement and repetition, be made to form the particular word required at a given moment. In fact, it may be found that many elements are common not only to variations in a certain type of work but also to many other jobs within a very wide range.

In order to take advantage of this characteristic it is necessary to have available a stock of data relating to the elements involved. It then becomes feasible to arrive at work contents by a process of synthesis for operations within the range covered. The means by which the required data are accumulated, stored and used calls for careful planning in what must be regarded in the nature of a long-term investment.

Establishing Synthetic Data

Most of the data required will be derived from time studies carried out generally along the lines already outlined. Since the rate of accumulation of data is slow if it relies on chance contributions from studies made entirely for immediate purposes, it is usual for a series of special studies to be made. These are carefully planned to cover as complete a range of conditions and specifications as will be met in practice, care being taken to ensure that like elements are identified with each other.

For instance, for an operation involving the filling of bottles, a series of time studies might be made covering varying sizes and types of bottle from the smallest to the largest and for the complete range of fluids encountered. The times for the human work will, for economy of application, be expressed in elements as large as possible, normally of seconds' duration and longer. Where, however, frequent repetition of very short elements is involved, the data should be expressed in terms of predetermined motion times. Such times are capable of universal application and in practice would, as far as possible, be used in conjunction with other synthetic data to assist in the computation of complete operation times.

Just as the first requirement of synthetic data is that work measurement studies shall be designed to produce them, so the second (and equally important) requirement is that the results are recorded in a way which will ensure complete understanding and facilitate application. While the other work measurement techniques require investigation of the job and a clear record of what has taken place, their results are not necessarily exposed to the tests to which synthetic data are subject. To ensure complete understanding, therefore, studies for this purpose really consist of analyses of the situations in which the data are produced relative to the way in which they are likely to be used. Everything of significance must be recorded explicitly so that the data may be used in complete independence of the authors of the original studies.

Classification of Synthetic Data

The simplicity with which synthetic data can be applied will depend very largely on the suitability of the classification system adopted. This will normally vary with the type of information recorded as well as the way in which it can be most conveniently used. Special consideration must be given to the clerical work involved in classification since, if this is excessive, it will nullify one of the particular advantages of this technique—economy of effort.

Although synthesis is sometimes performed with data incorporating relaxation allowance, there is a growing preference for basic element times to be used without any provision for RA. In addition to simplifying the method of classification, data in this form are much more satisfactory as the allowances appropriate to the circumstances can then be added and accounted for in the normal way at the usual stage of calculation.

The manner in which synthetic data are classified depends mainly upon the circumstances under which they will be used. For operations likely to be of a highly repetitive nature, careful element-by-element synthesis is necessary. An example of this, using element times taken from tables, is given in Fig. 53, where, it will be seen, provision is made both for constant elements and for those which are subject to variation in the job itself. In selecting the actual elements listed, account would be taken of the method, location and worker, as well as materials and equipment concerned, and full details of these would accompany the work content issued.

In the case of less repetitive work, where the same degree of detail is not necessary, it may be sufficient to use data represented in the form of a curve or even a family of curves. Again, however, very full information should be given respecting the conditions under which a value is applicable; a curve such as that given in Fig. 54, for instance, would be accompanied by a specification of paint type, surface characteristics, and the minimum area for which the data are valid. This system has the advantage that it enables intermediate readings which may not be on any of the curves to be estimated reasonably accurately; the number of variables which can be accommodated, is, however, limited.

In special circumstances synthetic data may be used as the basis of formulae or for the preparation of nomographs to enable element or operation times to be obtained by calculation.

For organizations who do not have the facilities to compile and classify data in the manner described, several proprietary systems have been developed which enable synthesis to be carried out using predetermined motion times as the basis of calculation. Whatever course is followed, too much emphasis cannot be laid on the necessity for work study officers who will be required to use synthetic data to be given a thorough training in their specialist application.

Operation: Drill through hole using ratchet gear.

Tools: Hand ratchet gear and stand.
             Morse taper drill and socket.
             Feed nut spanner.

Services: Soluble oil coolant.

	ELEMENT	Milliminutes	
		¼ in. thick plate	Per extra ⅛ in. thickness
A	Select drill and set up in ratchet . .	31	
B	Position ratchet under stand . .	172	
C	Check alignment of drill . . .	284	
D	Apply initial pressure and sink drill to full cutting diameter	420	
E	Make full power cuts and returns when cutting full diameter of drill . . .	673	802
F	Complete drilling after breakthrough .	1,740	
G	Remove drill and ratchet and lay aside .	71	
H	Remove drill from ratchet and box from drill	80	
J	Apply coolant as required . . .	73	36
		3,544	838

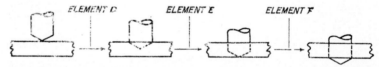

ELEMENT D   ELEMENT E   ELEMENT F

Fig. 53. Derivation of Operation Time Using Predetermined Motion Times[1]

(A complete set of data in respect of the operation described would include a separate table for each combination of drill size and material type encountered; elements A, B, C, G and H could be expected to remain constant over a wide range of these.)

[1] The above predetermined motion times are expressed in milliminutes at standard rating. In some systems the times given are expressed in time-measurement units (1 TMU = 0·00001 hour), and may or may not be at standard rating.

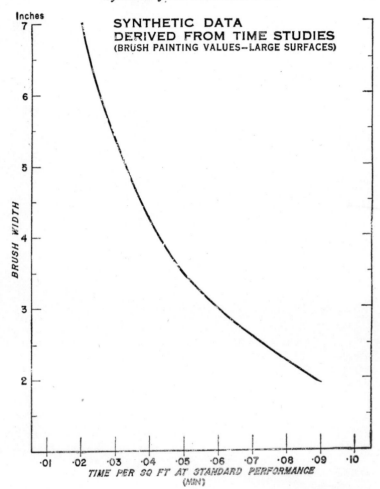

FIG. 54. SYNTHETIC DATA DERIVED FROM TIME STUDIES

Synthesizing the Work Content of Operations

It is most important that synthesis should only be applied to operations made up of elements coming within the range of studies (by dimension, shape, weight, etc.) to which the data are applicable.

The first stage of application is then to decide which elements are constant and are not influenced by changes in the physical characteristics of the object on which the operation is performed, and which elements are variable.

For constant elements, basic times should be available in the tables to be assigned without further consideration.

For those elements which are subject to variation in the work involved because of differences in the physical characteristics of different objects worked on (as, for example, in the case of painting different surfaces or using different kinds of paint), the basic times must be obtained from the available data by inspection. This requires a proper appreciation of the controlling factor before suitable times can be selected. Special cases may be found where a number of factors operate so that their combined effect is the significant variable. Such cases call for more detailed investigation involving the aid of statistical treatment.

When a basic time for each element of the operation has been obtained the sequence of elements should again be checked to ensure that it conforms to the prescribed method of working and fulfils the operation specification.

Relaxation allowance is then allotted and the work content of the operation determined in the usual way using the study summary record and set-up sheets already illustrated.

Advantages of Synthesis over Time Study

Although synthesis was originally developed to establish the work content for short-batch production and jobbing work, it can be used instead of time study to determine times for many other types of work, including repetitive work, provided the necessary data are available. The main advantage of synthesis is the reduced cost of application. It has been claimed that it has effected savings of up to 90 per cent of the cost of time study. The savings will depend very much on the type of operation but it is certain that, with practice, the synthetic method can be used to determine work content as satisfactorily and more economically than the time study method.

Apart from production applications, information on the human work content of different tasks is often required in connexion with the design of plant and the layout of shops and work-places, usually before production commences. By means of synthesis it is possible to establish times which are equally satisfactory for planning and production control purposes.

Analytical Estimating

ANALYTICAL estimating is used for measuring non-repetitive work when it has not been possible to compile sufficient data to enable basic times to be synthesized for all the elements involved. The same principle of breaking the job down into elements is observed as in other work measurement techniques, except that those elements for which times are to be estimated are of longer duration than elements for timing and rating. The technique serves all the basic purposes of other work measurement techniques, though it is slightly less precise owing to the greater reliance on judgement. It is being satisfactorily used in engineering maintenance as well as in engineering construction, and its use is likely to be extended to many aspects of process work and other fields.

Training for Analytical Estimating

The key to the whole technique lies in the character and ability of the estimator. If he has been a skilled craftsman in the type of work for which he is to estimate times, he is better qualified to form accurate estimates of the work involved. His judgements are also more likely to be accepted by workers.

It is important that, as soon as possible after his selection, an estimator should be given a status equal to that of a supervisor. He must also receive thorough training in work study to enable him to acquire a reliable concept of standard rate of working on which to base estimates of basic time.

As supervisors will have to co-operate closely with the estimator they too should be given some training in work study so that they understand the principles of the technique, and are able satisfactorily to describe jobs to the estimator well in advance. In particular, the

ANALYTICAL ESTIMATE SHEET			
WORKS/DEPT. A		ESTIMATE: S.236	
DESCRIPTION OF JOB *Clean and inspect head snub and tail bearings*			
PLANT OR EQUIPMENT: *No. 5 Conveyor*			

ELEMENT	MINS AT STANDARD RATING		
	TRADESMAN	MATE	LEAD TIME
1. *Proceed to job with tools, lock off switch*	3·00	4·20	4·20
2. *Remove head bearing cap – 2 × ⅝" bolts*	2·40	—	2·40
3. *Clean out grease and examine bearing*	1·80	1·20	1·80
4. *Replace bearing cap*	1·80	—	1·80
5. *Repeat elements 2–4 inclusive × 1*	6·00	1·20	} 9·00
6. *Clean snub pulley*	—	7·80	
7. *Remove guard – 2 × ⅝" nuts (awkward)*	3·00	3·00	3·00
8. *Place 2 bars through spokes and pack*	6·00	6·00	6·00
9. *Remove bearing cap – 2 × ½" nuts (very awkward)*	3·00	—	3·00
10. *Clean out grease and examine bearing*	3·00	1·80	3·00
11. *Replace bearing cap*	2·40	—	2·40
12. *Repeat elements 9–11 inclusive × 1*	8·40	1·80	8·40
13. *Remove bars and replace guard*	4·20	4·20	4·20
14. *Proceed to tail end*	1·80	1·80	1·80
15. *Remove guard – 4 × ⅝" bolts (very dirty)*	4·80	4·80	4·80
16. *Clean off round bearing*	—	4·20	4·20
17. *Remove bearing cap – 2 × ⅝" bolts*	2·40	—	2·40
18. *Clean out grease and inspect bearing*	2·40	1·20	2·40
19. *Replace cap*	1·80	—	1·80
20. *Replace guard*	4·20	4·20	4·20
21. *Repeat elements 15–20 inclusive × 1*	15·60	14·40	19·80
22. *Unlock switch and remove tools.*	3·00	3·00	3·00

LABOUR REQUIREMENTS:				
TRADESMEN 1	TOTAL @ STANDARD RATING	81·00	64·80	93·60
MATES 1	RELAXATION ALLOWANCE (17%)	12·16	9.72	14·04
	WORK CONTENT	93·15	74·52	107·64
	UNOCCUPIED TIME	16·36	35	
	OVERALL TIME FOR JOB AT STANDARD PERFORMANCE (Say)			110

FIG. 55. ANALYTICAL ESTIMATE SHEET: COMPLETED

method by which operations are to be carried out should always be discussed and agreed between supervisor and estimator. In the case of disagreement, the work study officer to whom the estimator is responsible may have to be consulted.

Element Breakdown

It will be shown that the elements listed cover the entire operation, including all tradesmen's and mates' work, as applicable. Once the best method has been agreed with the supervisor, the estimator can prepare an element breakdown on an estimate form of the type shown in Fig. 55. When a tradesman has a mate, as much unskilled work as possible should be allocated to him, and the standard times indicated for the mate are based on this policy, each standard time being derived separately for every member of the team.

Since it is convenient for the estimator to base his estimates on his knowledge of standard rate of working, i.e. in times at 100 rating, basic time is used throughout in analytical estimating.

When all the elements have been treated in this way the times are totalled as shown in the example, and a blanket RA added. This allowance is in fact a predetermined fixed allowance covering a group of similar jobs, usually varying from 10–20 per cent of the total basic time. Finally, if it is appropriate, a " policy allowance " (described in Chapter 16) may be added as a percentage of the total basic time, after which the allowed time of the job for each tradesman and mate and the time for the complete job can be calculated.

In construction and maintenance work where teams are frequently composed of several skilled and unskilled men working together, it is often worth while to prepare a multiple activity chart so that the most satisfactory method of working can be estimated for.

Abnormal Work and Team Work

When estimating, careful note must be taken of the conditions under which a job has to be carried out. This is particularly important in maintenance work. The degree of abnormality should be specified against each element for record purposes. For instance, times for removing a nut from a bolt might vary owing to the following conditions—

1. Easy—nut and bolt well greased.
2. Moderate—nut and bolt rusted.
3. Difficult—nut seized, requiring splitting off.

Each of these classifications can be further conditioned by factors such as accessibility, lighting, etc.

A feature of maintenance work in particular is the occurrence of factors which cannot always be foreseen and provided for in the original estimate, e.g., bad weather, excessive adjustment. Such factors have the effect of increasing the overall time required for the job, and should always be accounted for afterwards by requiring the tradesman to submit an " extra work authorization " detailing exactly what was involved. In this way it becomes possible to keep a check on the validity of issued times.

Use of Synthetic Data

When analytical estimating is first introduced into a department the work of the estimator is likely to be slow because of absence of synthetic data to assist in building up his estimates. These data will consist of overall basic times for groups of elements, some of which are derived from time studies and others from previous estimates. The availability of such data can substantially reduce the time required to prepare many estimates. It is important from the outset, therefore, to set up an efficient filing system to file records of jobs as they are done. Synthetic data should also be collected from all available sources, and sorted to ensure that proper use can be made of the times under conditions prevailing in the department concerned. The following are some of the lines along which an estimator can work—

1. Synthetic data can be used for walking to various areas of the site. These times can be evaluated from a site plan.
2. Times for climbing structures, ladders, etc., can be determined and filed.
3. Estimated times for the elements of a job can be filed for use again when they occur subsequently.

Many proprietary filing systems are available, and the majority of them can be adapted to enable the estimator to give the required information in a minimum of time. According to the type of work covered, data can be filed under main headings such as—

1. Plant or sections of plant
2. Categories of jobs

Each main heading can have subsections for similar work. Further subdivision should be made if subsections become unwieldy. Data in day-to-day use should be collected in book form and kept close to hand for ease of reference.

Estimator Loading

It is not possible to give firm figures regarding the number of workers an estimator can cover satisfactorily as the number is largely determined by the type of work covered—

1. *Routine work.* Once initial estimates are made for work of this nature, little further work is required from the estimator apart from checking at specified intervals that no changes have occurred.

2. *Planned work of a repetitive nature.* For such work the estimator is only involved in the preparation of the original estimates.

3. *Breakdown work.* For a section in which work is well planned, breakdown work will be small. However, when estimates are required for general planning or for incentive application, because such work is of a non-repetitive nature an estimator must be in a position to prepare an estimate without delaying execution of the job.

4. *Work consisting of many jobs of short duration.* Such jobs can often be grouped within one estimate but generally take up a high percentage of an estimator's time.

For work covered by the first two headings the estimator's work is proportionately less, and in such cases a group of twenty or more workers may be dealt with. If there is much breakdown work or work of short duration, however, ten workers may be a maximum.

The quantity of synthetic data available will also exercise a considerable effect on the number of estimators required for a given number of workers.

14

Activity Sampling

IN certain types of work it may not be practicable to use the work measurement techniques so far described, either to establish work contents directly or for the purpose of building up a fund of synthetic data. This might be the case in plants and departments where a number of heterogeneous operations are taking place, for example, in stores and warehouses, or for certain types of office work, especially if team working is involved.

Often, however, it is desirable for management to know reasonably accurately what is taking place in such situations in terms of the proportion of time being devoted to each type of activity. When this is the case, the work study officer can have recourse to a technique similar to that used in the field of statistical quality control where, by examining the results obtained from a comparatively small sample of the product, it has been found feasible to estimate within specified limits of accuracy the proportion of defective articles in the very much larger quantity from which the sample was taken. Subject to the adoption of a satisfactory procedure, the proportion of defects in the sample can be taken as representing, within the definable limits, the proportion existing in the total quantity.

In the same way, time spent doing work can be considered as being made up of a number of individual *moments*, during each of which a particular state of activity or inactivity (delay) prevails. On this basis a similar sampling technique calling for only a fraction of the time and effort which would be required by a full-time study can be used, the sample in this case consisting of a number of individual moments selected at random intervals from a representative period of the job. From direct observation a record is made of the particular activity in progress at each of these moments; subject again to the adoption of a satisfactory procedure, the results for the sample can be used to estimate within definable limits the proportion of job time being occupied by each type of activity and delay recorded.

Studies Using Activity Sampling

The particular technique most often used in this type of study is known as Activity Sampling. A characteristic of this type of study is that it is aimed at providing a record of what is actually taking place at the instant the job is observed; it is not a record of what the observer thinks should be happening, nor what has just happened nor is about to take place, no matter how close to the moment of observation such other activities actually occur. For instance, even if the worker is on the point of starting his machine when the observer arrives, unless the machine has actually started the entry made on the observation sheet records the appropriate type of machine inactivity.

The principle can be illustrated by means of a simple example—

In the case of a single machine the only information which may be required is how its total time is divided between two types of activity, working and not working, during an 8-hour day. Continuous observation over this period might show the following state of affairs, where the shaded portions indicate working time—

4 HOURS   4 HOURS

Total period of continuous observation = 8·0 hours
Total non-working time = 3·7 hours
Non-working time as a percentage of total time $= \dfrac{3\cdot7}{8\cdot0} \times 100 = 46\cdot3$ per cent

Now, suppose activity sampling had been carried out independently, taking thirty random observations over the same 8-hour period as follows—

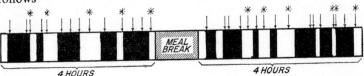

4 HOURS   4 HOURS

Number of random observations $\quad = 30$
Number of non-work observations
(marked *) $\qquad\qquad\qquad\qquad = 11$
Number of non-working observa-
tions as a percentage of total number $= \dfrac{11}{30} \times 100 = 36\cdot7$ per cent
of random observations

$\therefore$ Proportion of non-working time estimated as a percentage of total time $= 36\cdot7$ per cent.

Accuracy of Results

It is evident that the result obtained by activity sampling in the foregoing example differs from that obtained by continuous study. Had the observer made more frequent visits and obtained a larger number of random observations, then his estimate of the non-working time would have been closer to the result obtained by continuous study. In fact it can be shown that the number of random observations to be made depends on the degree of accuracy required. In practice it has been found that a ninety-five per cent guarantee of the specified limits of accuracy (commonly known as the "ninety-five per cent confidence limits ") is acceptable for most purposes. This means, in effect, that the accuracy of the figure obtained can be guaranteed to be within $\pm L$ nineteen times out of twenty, L representing the limits of permitted variation stated as a percentage of total time. The number of observations (N) necessary to achieve such a result is then obtained from the following formula[1]—

$$N = \frac{4\,p\,(100 - p)}{L^2}$$

which can be re-written as $L = 2\sqrt{\dfrac{p\,(100 - p)}{N}}$

p being the occurrence of the specified activity expressed (approximately) as a percentage of N.

Thus, in the example it can be stated with ninety-five per cent confidence (nineteen times out of twenty) that the non-working time lies within the limits $(36\cdot7 \pm 17\cdot6)$ per cent

since $L = 2\sqrt{\dfrac{37 \times 63}{30}} = \pm\ 17\cdot6$ per cent approximately.

---

[1] The formula, which is derived from elementary statistics, varies according to the confidence limits required. The ninety-five per cent value has been used throughout the examples in this chapter.

These limits are wide owing to the small number of observations. To obtain a similar result within $\pm 8 \cdot 8$ per cent it will be necessary to take 120 observations, i.e. in order to double the accuracy it is necessary to quadruple the number of observations.

Scope of the Technique

Since the technique requires only spot observations, it is possible to use it to study groups by visiting the individuals in sequence, recording in each case what activity or delay is occurring at the instant of observation. In fact this procedure is usually a feature of activity sampling, since the fairly large numbers of observations required for reasonable accuracy are accumulated more rapidly with groups than with individuals. Activity sampling is a much cheaper method of obtaining information about groups than continuous observation, since a small number of observers can cover a relatively large group.

This fact-finding technique can be used to determine the properties of time devoted to different activities and delays by groups of either men, machines or pieces of equipment.

Breakdown of Activities for Sampling

Having decided that activity sampling should be resorted to, the first step is to plan a " tree " of activities and delays. This tree sets out the headings under which the random observations will be recorded. For example, it has already been seen that one may wish to know simply the average proportion of time during which a group of men or machines are working and not working. The tree in the simplest of all cases would then be—

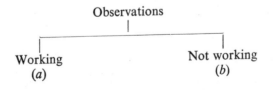

Normally it is desired to obtain rather more detail than this, and an example of a tree used in investigating the occurrence of a number of different types of activity might be as follows—

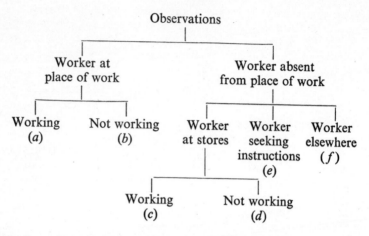

A planned tree of this kind becomes the basis for the random observations. Every observation would be recorded under one or other of the headings (*a*) to (*f*) on an observation sheet of a type similar to that illustrated in Fig. 56.

Representative Period of Study

One of the advantages of using activity sampling is that the required observations can be spread over a longer period than would be economical when continuous studies are carried out. In this way it is possible to obtain a more representative sample of the activities and delays under investigation. This advantage normally leads to an activity sampling investigation being extended over several days or weeks; obviously the length of period should be a multiple of any work cycle time.

It is most important, too, that observations should cover the whole of the working period. Thus, in the case of twenty-four-hour shift work over a period of one fortnight, observations should be taken throughout the $24 \times 7 \times 2$ hours of this period.

Required Number of Observations

If the general pattern of activity and inactivity is to be investigated, the required accuracy can be expressed in terms of the percentage time devoted to all activities. Thus, supposing it is anticipated that about seventy-five per cent of the total time of a group of men or machines is devoted to various activities ($p = 75$), then if

C

ACTIVITY SAMPLING STUDY

STUDY No. 542/1 SHEET 4 OF

OBSERVER CGW DATE 10-1-56

ROUND No.	TIME		WORKER / ~~MACHINE~~								OBSERVATIONS						
	ON	OFF	1	2	3	4	5	6	7	8	a	b	c	d	e	f	No.
25	7.40	7.48	✓										✓				1
				✓								✓					2
					✓								✓				3
						✓								✓			4
							✓									✓	5
								✓								✓	6
									✓		✓						7
										✓	✓						8
26	7.55	8.02	✓												✓		1
				✓									✓				2
					✓						✓						3
						✓					✓						4
							✓						✓				5
								✓								✓	6
									✓			✓					7
										✓	✓						8
27	8.05	8.12	✓								✓						1
				✓							✓						2
					✓								✓				3
						✓										✓	4
							✓				✓						5
								✓			✓						6
									✓		✓						7

FIG. 56. ACTIVITY SAMPLING: OBSERVATION SHEET

a satisfactory degree of accuracy would be ± 3 per cent of the total time ($L = 3$) with ninety-five per cent confidence, the required number of observations, using the equation given, would be—

$$\frac{4 \times 75 \times (100 - 75)}{3^2} = 833$$

One would thus aim initially at making about 850 observations.

It may be, however, that the main interest centres on one particular kind of activity in the tree described. If, for example, this was suspected to occupy about five per cent of the total time ($p = 5$), and a result accurate to ± 1 per cent of the total time ($L = 1$) with ninety-five per cent confidence would be acceptable, then the required number of observations would be—

$$\frac{4 \times 5 \times (100 - 5)}{1^2} = 1,900$$

The initial aim, therefore, would be to obtain about 2,000 observations. This rough estimate can be checked after the first 100 or so observations have been made to see whether the five per cent estimate is reasonable. If it is not, a new calculation can then be made with the more accurate figure available.

Study Programme

The activity sampling technique is particularly suited to the investigation of multiple activities, either of men or machines. If the subjects being studied are close together so much the better since this will facilitate the accumulation of observations. Whatever the arrangement, careful planning of the study programme is essential to ensure it is carried out in a systematic manner.

Each round of the department or plant will result in as many observations as there are men or machines. If, for example, 7,500 observations are required to investigate the combined activities of ten workers over a period of fourteen days, it will be necessary to make 750 rounds during that period. In order to ensure reasonable distribution it is usually advisable roughly to equalize the number

of rounds made per day, in this case $\frac{750}{14}$ or 54.

Thereafter, the times during each day at which observers are to start on their rounds are determined by random selection. There are various ways in which this can be arranged, such as by marking slips of paper with actual times (say at 5- or 15-minute intervals) throughout the day and selecting them at random, or by making use of a suitable table of random numbers.

If the time for a complete round takes longer than the minimum possible interval (five minutes in the foregoing example), two or more observers will have to be appointed. In such a case a day's programme of rounds might be set out as shown in Fig. 57.

Having more than one observer is also a means of reducing the likelihood of error, since it enables the results obtained by different observers to be compared with each other and any significant differences noted.

ACTIVITY SAMPLING PROGRAMME

STUDY No. 24/C   DATE APPLICABLE 14-2-56

OBSERVERS (1)   RJE

            (2)   SW

OBSERVER 1		OBSERVER 2	
ROUND	TIME	ROUND	TIME
1	7·35	1	7·45
2	7·50	2	8·00
3	8·05	3	8·10
4	8·15	4	8·30
5	8·40	5	8·45
6	8·50	6	9·05
7	9·20	7	9·30
8	9·35	8	9·40
9	9·45	9	10·00
10	10·05	10	10·15
11	10·25	11	10·30
12	10·35	12	10·40

FIG. 57. ACTIVITY SAMPLING: DAY'S PROGRAMME OF ROUNDS

Analysis of the Results of Activity Sampling

This process can best be demonstrated by continuing with the hypothetical example already referred to in which two observers have been detailed to make approximately 7,500 observations of a team of ten workers over a period of fourteen days. In the first place, the results would be summarized as shown in Fig. 58.

The percentages in column 3 of Fig. 58 are derived simply from the formula—

$$\frac{\text{Number of observations recording the particular activity}}{\text{Total number of observations}} \times 100$$

e.g. $\dfrac{2,500}{7,560} \times 100 = 33{\cdot}1$ per cent for activity (*a*)

ACTIVITY SAMPLING SUMMARY

STUDY No. *24/C*   DATE *20-2-56*

SUBJECT *Issue of expendable materials*   LOCATION *Main Stores (D)*

OBSERVERS *2*   WORKERS *10*

REQUIRED No. OF OBSERVATIONS *7500 (approx.)*

REPRESENTATIVE PERIOD *14 days*

No. OF ROUNDS *27 per observer per day*

ACTIVITY REF.	No. OF OBSERVATIONS	ESTIMATED % OF TOTAL TIME	95% CONFIDENCE LIMITS AS % OF TOTAL TIME
a	*2500*	*33·1*	*± 1·1*
b	*971*	*12·8*	*±0·8*
c	*1472*	*19·5*	*±0·9*
d	*1678*	*22·2*	*±1·0*
e	*226*	*3·0*	*±0·4*
f	*713*	*9·4*	*±0·7*
TOTAL	*7560*	*100·0*	*—*

FIG. 58.   ACTIVITY SAMPLING: SUMMARY OF RESULTS

ACTIVITY REF.	ESTIMATED % OF TOTAL TIME FOR WORKERS										TOTAL PER ACTIVITY
	1	*2*	*3*	*4*	*5*	*6*	*7*	*8*	*9*	*10*	
a	0·9	2·3	3·1	5·0	5·2	1·9	3·7	2·6	4·2	4·2	33·1
b		2·6			2·3	2·3		1·5	0·4	3·7	12·8
c		1·7	1·4	0·8		4·6	4·8	2·8	1·5	1·9	19·5
d	5·9	3·1	2·7	3·1	1·6	1·1	0·9	0·2	3·6		22·2
e	3·0										3·0
f	0·2	2·9	0·2	0·7	0·9	0·1	0·6	2·9	0·3	0·2	9·4

FIG. 59. ACTIVITY SAMPLING: COMPARISON OF WORKERS' ACTIVITIES

The ninety-five per cent confidence limits are calculated in each case using the formula—

$$L = 2\sqrt{\frac{p(100-p)}{N}}$$

Again for activity (*a*) therefore—

$$L = 2\sqrt{\frac{33·1 \times 66·9}{7,560}} = \pm 1·1 \text{ per cent of total time.}$$

Thus, it could be stated with ninety-five per cent confidence, that activity (*a*) occupies (33·1 ± 1·1) per cent or between 32·0 per cent and 34·2 per cent of the total time spent on the job by the ten workers concerned.

It is possible also to use the information obtained from the study in a number of different ways. For example, the activities of each of the ten workers can be set out for comparison in the manner shown in Fig. 59.

In the same way, the results could be analysed by days or by the time of day.

A useful advantage of analysis on these lines is that it sometimes indicates whether significant " bias " errors—i.e., errors due to the presence of the observer or because of the choice of an unrepresentative period—are present.

Using the Results of Activity Sampling

The activity sampling technique was devised for the purpose of getting information about the time spent by groups of men or machines on various activities and delays. For this purpose it can be very useful, and in many cases it has been found most valuable as a method of reconnaissance prior to the use of more detailed work study techniques. Among the many applications of activity sampling are numbered the investigating work necessary in—

1. Improving the arrangement of duties and general organization of work.
2. Indicating the directions in which improvements in methods and equipment should be sought, and assessing the value of proposed changes.
3. Assessing the value of introducing group incentive schemes.
4. Examining the causes of unsatisfactory performance figures.

A further category of application which requires special mention, since it was the field to which activity sampling was first applied, is the measurement of *machine interference*. There are sometimes occasions when it is economically desirable to put a worker in charge of a number of automatic machines, each subject to unpredictable stoppages which will call for his attention before starting up again. This can be done provided no damage results from the stoppage, either to the equipment or to the material being worked on. Machine interference refers to the way in which these stoppages, because of their random occurrence, sometimes result in several machines being affected simultaneously. Since the worker can only attend to one machine at a time, any others not working while he is occupied have to stand completely idle until he is able to give them attention in turn.

As will be shown in a later chapter, before work contents can be established for work of this kind, it is essential to have an accurate idea of the likely occurrence of machine interference, since its incidence will affect not only the amount of work the worker is called upon to do, but also the total output of the group of machines for which he is responsible.

Rated Activity Sampling

As an extension of the normal uses of activity sampling, attempts have been made to modify the technique so that it may be used to determine the work content, and standard times for jobs. After recording the appropriate activities, observers have made rating assessments by watching workers for short periods of time (say ten to twenty seconds); the assumption has then been made that such ratings are applicable to the corresponding activities recorded; the difficulties of such a procedure will be apparent. The main problem, however, is that because activity sampling records in general terms only what actually happens, even if workers are rated the broad context of existing methods of working must be accepted. If these methods are not sound then the work contents obtained will be correspondingly affected.

In general, therefore, at the present stage of its development this technique, to which the name Rated Activity Sampling is given, while it has in an increasing number of cases provided data suitable for the establishment of standard times, should be used for this purpose with the utmost caution until further research has established its reliability.

Economics of Activity Sampling

Where only one machine or worker is being studied, then in order to make the required number of observations within a reasonable period, activity sampling might require the whole time of one observer. In this case little or no gain results from using activity sampling in preference to making continuous studies. It may be possible for several different activity sampling studies, none of which would be economic on its own, to be carried out simultaneously by a single observer who is able to arrange his programme in a way which will enable him to make observations for more than one study on the same round.

The activity sampling technique is most effective when several observations for the same study can be obtained during one visit or round. Even where an observer spends the whole of his time in the working area, the fact that he is studying several workers or machines simultaneously is an advantage which cannot be claimed for any other work measurement technique. It will, of course, be apparent that the full benefit of this can only be obtained when the layout of the plant is such that the observer spends the minimum amount of time travelling between different locations.

15

Target Times for Jobs

WHEN planning the supply of services and raw materials, delivery dates, etc., management is interested in the overall time to be issued for a job using the specified method and adhering to defined standards of quality. Situations will often arise where this time is outside the control of the individual worker; it may be controlled by plant or machine running time; in team-work it may not be possible for certain workers to work until others have completed some part of the job; again, total time for a job may be complicated by a mixture of team and plant times.

The two decisive factors in working out an overall target time for a job are therefore—

1. An accurate knowledge of plant running time.
2. A knowledge of the likely performance of workers.

In the present calculations standard performance of workers has been assumed. For those who have reasons for not basing their plans on standard performance, the time applicable to any other level of performance can be obtained in the manner shown in the first two examples which follow.

Planning Times for Simple Jobs

The following examples will illustrate the means by which overall times are derived for straightforward types of job—

174

1. *A worker engaged only on manual work.* In cases where the only limitation on output is the worker's individual capacity, and there is ample work available, the time for the operation at standard performance will simply be the standard time.

2. *A worker engaged on work which is machine or process controlled.* Finding the time for a job at standard performance, where a worker attends an item of plant and has work both inside and outside plant running time, can be illustrated by the example of a worker attending a mixer for which the multiple activity chart is reproduced in Fig. 60. Suppose he loads a batch of materials into a mixer, starts the mixer, and, after mixing is completed, unloads it. The overall time will be the actual machine running time (in minutes) plus the time-equivalent of the worker's *outside work* at the level of performance aimed at. Outside work refers to those of the worker's duties which are carried out when the machine is not producing and being human work they will be expressed in units of work.

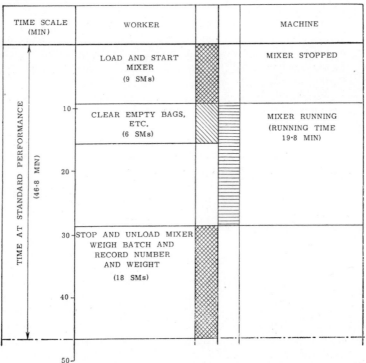

FIG. 60. MULTIPLE ACTIVITY CHART: ONE WORKER

Because in this case the time-equivalent of the *inside work* of clearing away empty bags, positioning containers and attending to the process at the anticipated level of performance is less than the plant running time this will not affect the overall time. If the time-equivalent of the inside work at the performance level concerned equals the machine running time the overall time for the job would, of course, be based entirely on the work content.

3. *A team engaged only on manual work*. If a team is working together on some job such as unloading a lorry, which does not involve plant running times, the time for the job will be the sum of the times for the limiting elements when they are carried out at standard performance.

An example will make this clear. Three men work as a team to unload a lorry carrying forty sacks each weighing 1 cwt. The specified method of operation is as follows: Worker *A* stands on the lorry and dumps the 1-cwt sacks on to the pallet of a fork lift truck. Each pallet holds ten sacks. Workers *B* and *C* each drive a fork lift truck. In turn each drives his truck alongside the lorry, positions the sacks as worker *A* dumps them, drives to the stores, and, after releasing the pallet, returns with an empty one. When the forty sacks are unloaded, *A* climbs down and reports to the checker's office, and *B* and *C* report to the chargehand for further instructions.

With the knowledge of the work contents of the various jobs the multiple activity chart shown in Fig. 61 can be drawn up.

From the multiple activity chart it will be seen that at certain stages in the task each worker is obliged to wait while one of the other two completes some limiting element. The time at standard performance for the complete task is the sum of the times for the limiting elements, which can be picked up from the heavily shaded portions of the multiple activity chart.

The values of these in SM are—

$1 \cdot 50 + 0 \cdot 56 + 0 \cdot 38 + 2 \cdot 06 + 0 \cdot 38 + 2 \cdot 06 + 0 \cdot 38 + 2 \cdot 06 + 0 \cdot 38 + 2 \cdot 06 + 1 \cdot 50 = 13 \cdot 3$ SM which is equivalent to $13 \cdot 3$ minutes at standard performance.

4. *A team engaged on work which is machine or process controlled.* When a team of workers is attending a unit of plant, work which has to be done outside plant running time will be done by the team. The time at standard performance for the operation will be the plant running time plus the time-equivalent of the limiting elements on the outside work. The procedure is therefore one of combining the factors described in Examples 2 and 3.

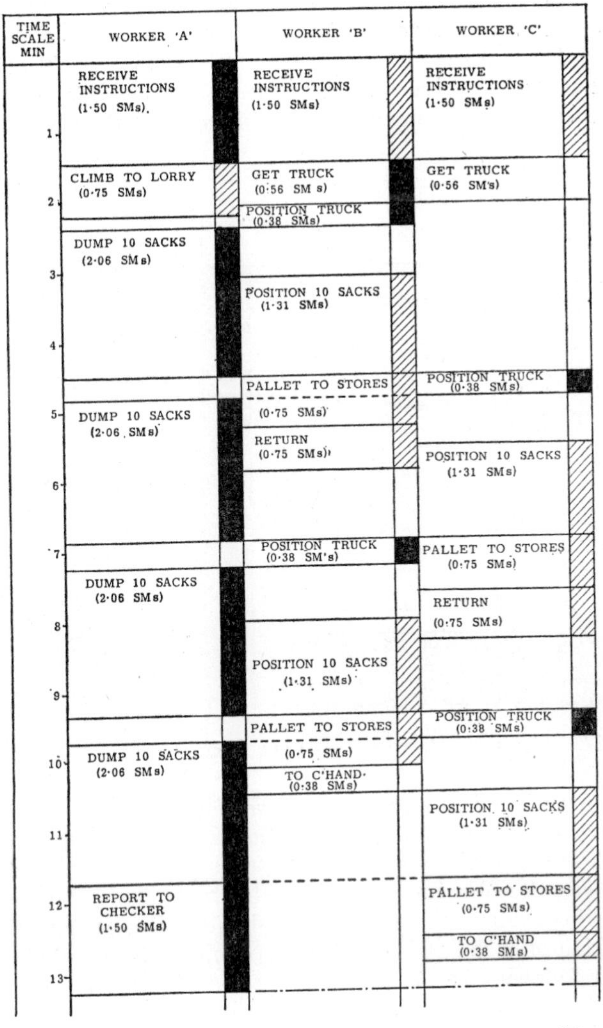

TIME SCALE MIN	WORKER 'A'	WORKER 'B'	WORKER 'C'
	RECEIVE INSTRUCTIONS (1·50 SMs).	RECEIVE INSTRUCTIONS (1·50 SMs)	RECEIVE INSTRUCTIONS (1·50 SMs)
1			
2	CLIMB TO LORRY (0·75 SMs)	GET TRUCK (0·56 SMs)	GET TRUCK (0·56 SMs)
		POSITION TRUCK (0·38 SMs)	
3	DUMP 10 SACKS (2·06 SMs)		
		POSITION 10 SACKS (1·31 SMs)	
4			
		PALLET TO STORES (0·75 SMs)	POSITION TRUCK (0·38 SMs)
5	DUMP 10 SACKS (2·06 SMs)	RETURN (0·75 SMs)	POSITION 10 SACKS (1·31 SMs)
6			
7	DUMP 10 SACKS (2·06 SMs)	POSITION TRUCK (0·38 SMs)	PALLET TO STORES (0·75 SMs)
8			RETURN (0·75 SMs)
		POSITION 10 SACKS (1·31 SMs)	
9			POSITION TRUCK (0·38 SMs)
		PALLET TO STORES (0·75 SMs)	
10	DUMP 10 SACKS (2·06 SMs)	TO C'HAND (0·38 SMs)	POSITION 10 SACKS (1·31 SMs)
11			
12	REPORT TO CHECKER (1·50 SMs)		PALLET TO STORES (0·75 SMs)
			TO C'HAND (0·38 SMs)
13			

FIG. 61. MULTIPLE ACTIVITY CHART: TEAM OF THREE WORKERS

Setting Times for More Complex Jobs

The jobs so far examined have been separate from one another, but in practice they are often combined, so that after one is started another is begun before the first is completed. The following more complicated instances are typical—

W.S.

G

1. *Worker does other work during the machine controlled part of the cycle.* As an example, during the plant running time of the power driven mixer shown in Fig. 60, the worker might be doing some general cleaning up. The overall time would not be affected, however, if the cleaning up could be done inside the plant running time.

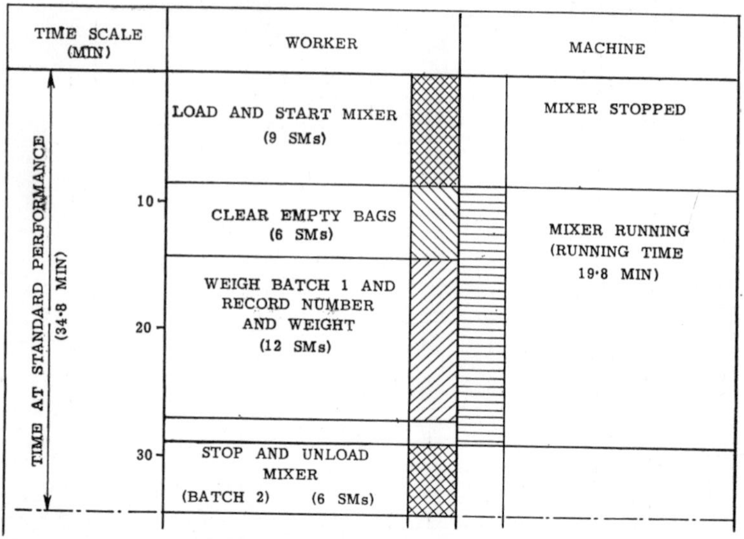

TIME SCALE (MIN)	WORKER		MACHINE
	LOAD AND START MIXER (9 SMs)		MIXER STOPPED
10	CLEAR EMPTY BAGS (6 SMs)		MIXER RUNNING (RUNNING TIME 19·8 MIN)
20	WEIGH BATCH 1 AND RECORD NUMBER AND WEIGHT (12 SMs)		
30	STOP AND UNLOAD MIXER (BATCH 2) (6 SMs)		

TIME AT STANDARD PERFORMANCE (34·8 MIN)

FIG. 62. MULTIPLE ACTIVITY CHART: ONE WORKER, COMPLEX JOB

2. *Repetitive jobs where work on previous unit of product can be finished during a subsequent machine controlled cycle.* In jobs which are repetitive some work on the previous unit of product can very often be done during a subsequent plant running time. Referring again to the mixing operation, if this were repetitive the weighing of each batch could be left until the plant running time of the following batch. Some of the outside work of each batch would then become inside work of the next.

This is illustrated in the new multiple activity chart, Fig. 62. It will be noted that, while the time at standard performance for the first batch will be 46·8 minutes, the time would be reduced to 34·8 minutes for each subsequent batch.

3. *Worker attends several units of plant each performing the same operation.* Sometimes a worker attends several similar units of plant each performing the same operation. For instance, in

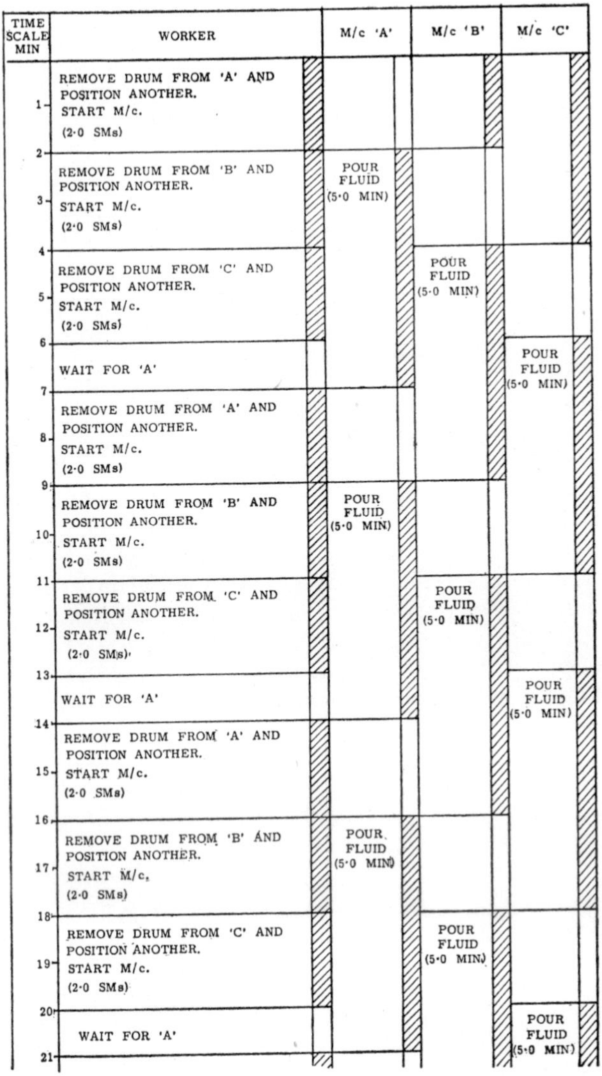

TIME SCALE MIN	WORKER	M/c 'A'	M/c 'B'	M/c 'C'
1	REMOVE DRUM FROM 'A' AND POSITION ANOTHER. START M/c. (2·0 SMs)			
2				
3	REMOVE DRUM FROM 'B' AND POSITION ANOTHER. START M/c. (2·0 SMs)	POUR FLUID (5·0 MIN)		
4				
5	REMOVE DRUM FROM 'C' AND POSITION ANOTHER. START M/c. (2·0 SMs)		POUR FLUID (5·0 MIN)	
6				
7	WAIT FOR 'A'			POUR FLUID (5·0 MIN)
8	REMOVE DRUM FROM 'A' AND POSITION ANOTHER. START M/c. (2·0 SMs)			
9				
10	REMOVE DRUM FROM 'B' AND POSITION ANOTHER. START M/c. (2·0 SMs)	POUR FLUID (5·0 MIN)		
11				
12	REMOVE DRUM FROM 'C' AND POSITION ANOTHER. START M/c. (2·0 SMs)		POUR FLUID (5·0 MIN)	
13				
14	WAIT FOR 'A'			POUR FLUID (5·0 MIN)
15	REMOVE DRUM FROM 'A' AND POSITION ANOTHER. START M/c. (2·0 SMs)			
16				
17	REMOVE DRUM FROM 'B' AND POSITION ANOTHER. START M/c. (2·0 SMs)	POUR FLUID (5·0 MIN)		
18				
19	REMOVE DRUM FROM 'C' AND POSITION ANOTHER. START M/c. (2·0 SMs)		POUR FLUID (5·0 MIN)	
20				
21	WAIT FOR 'A'			POUR FLUID (5·0 MIN)

FIG. 63. MULTIPLE ACTIVITY CHART: ONE WORKER, THREE MACHINES

179

G 2

the case of filling drums, using three automatic weighing machines which stop the flow when the correct quantity has been run in, the work sequence might be as shown in Fig. 63.

Here it will be seen that the time at standard performance on any one machine includes " position drum," " pour fluid," and " remove drum," and that these require 7·0 minutes. But as the fluid is running into the drum a further two drums can be positioned. The unit of product when working to this method is thus three drums, not one, and the time at standard performance for this multiple operation is 7·0 minutes for three drums, if the work is continuously repetitive.

4. *The worker attends several dissimilar units of plant.* Sometimes a worker attends a number of dissimilar units of plant which are automatically controlled, and for which plant running times can be accurately established. In such cases the time for the job at standard performance can be worked out on similar lines to the example already given of the three automatic weighing machines referred to in Fig. 63.

If, however, the dissimilar units of plant are not automatically controlled, it may be impossible to draw up a multiple activity chart foretelling the work sequence, or indeed to break up the work into separate tasks on any unit of plant. Under such circumstances a worker gives attention to each item of plant as and when he is able, and for planning purposes the time per unit of output at standard performance is calculated over the day or shift on the basis of average conditions over the period concerned.

Unoccupied Time (UT) and Various Allowances

WHEN men work in a team or on machine operations which do not require constant attention, they are frequently unoccupied for short periods while the machine or other members of the team complete certain jobs. If nothing were done to take account of this time the effect would be a lowering of the worker's unit hour for the day or shift during which such waiting time occurred.

When this is the case unoccupied time for a job can be expressed as—

$$\text{Overall time for job} - \frac{\text{Standard time for}}{\text{carrying out the work}} = \text{UT}$$

Thus, in the example of a multiple activity chart for a simple mixing operation (Fig. 60), the period of 13·8 minutes, i.e. for running time less time for inside work, which is the time the worker is forced to wait for the machine if he has been working at standard performance, represents the UT applicable to the job if done in the manner recorded.

The Undesirability of UT

In certain types of work it may be inevitable that some unoccupied time will occur. From the point of view of management, however, such time is wholly undesirable, representing as it does an imbalance in the use of labour or labour/machine resources. Since production plans should normally be based on the best possible use of labour, every opportunity should therefore be taken to reduce UT to a minimum.

Even where unoccupied time has previously occurred, a thorough method study of the job may suggest various means of reducing or eliminating the need for it. There is the possibility of allotting other useful work during plant running times, while team-work which is seriously unbalanced may be rearranged to achieve better balance. Sometimes it is found possible, after due consultation with the technicians responsible, to speed up certain items of plant or, in more serious cases, for one worker to control an extra machine. The multiple activity charts already used for obtaining the time for a job at standard performance, by clearly indicating where unoccupied time occurs, may be specially useful in helping to suggest where improvements can be made.

When considering these matters, however, it should be remembered that it is sometimes more important to keep an expensive item of equipment functioning continuously than to make maximum use of the service of workers. When formulating plans management must view the whole economic picture in order to achieve the best balance. Cases where there is a high figure of unoccupied time should nevertheless be kept continuously under review.

For convenience of application, unoccupied time is regarded either as fixed, that is to say, as an integral feature of the operation, or as variable. Calculating fixed unoccupied time for individual workers and for jobs as a whole is a simple matter so long as the times at standard performance are known. Where the time for a job at standard performance is not known until after the operation has been completed on each occasion, unoccupied time is variable and special rules apply.

Fixed UT for Simple Jobs

The following further examples may help to make the calculation of process allowance more clearly understood—

1. *One worker engaged only on manual work.* In such cases, where there is no plant running time or team-work to worry about, there cannot be any unoccupied time.

2. *A team engaged only on manual work.* Referring to the multiple activity chart for unloading a lorry (Fig. 61) unoccupied

time for each worker and the complete job are calculated as
follows—

Worker A: Work content $= 1 \cdot 50 + 0 \cdot 75 + 2 \cdot 06 + 2 \cdot 06 +$
$2 \cdot 06 + 2 \cdot 06 + 1 \cdot 50 = 12 \cdot 0$ SM
Time for this work at standard performance $= 12 \cdot 0$ min
Time for complete job at standard performance $= 13 \cdot 3$ min
$\therefore$ Unoccupied time $= 13 \cdot 3 - 12 \cdot 0 = 1 \cdot 3$ min

Worker B: Work content $= 1 \cdot 50 + 0 \cdot 56 + 0 \cdot 38 + 1 \cdot 31 +$
$0 \cdot 75 + 0 \cdot 75 + 0 \cdot 38 + 1 \cdot 31 + 0 \cdot 75 + 0 \cdot 38 = 8 \cdot 1$ SM
Time for this work at standard performance $= 8 \cdot 1$ min
Time for complete job at standard performance $= 13 \cdot 3$ min
$\therefore$ Unoccupied time $= 13 \cdot 3 - 8 \cdot 1 = 5 \cdot 2$ min

Worker C: Work content $= 1 \cdot 50 + 0 \cdot 56 + 0 \cdot 38 + 1 \cdot 31 +$
$0 \cdot 75 + 0 \cdot 75 + 0 \cdot 38 + 1 \cdot 31 + 0 \cdot 75 + 0 \cdot 38 = 8 \cdot 1$ SM
Time for this work at standard performance $= 8 \cdot 1$ min
Time for complete job at standard performance $= 13 \cdot 3$ min
$\therefore$ Unoccupied time $= 13 \cdot 3 - 8 \cdot 1 = 5 \cdot 2$ min

3. *A team engaged on work which is machine or process controlled.*   When a team of workers is attending an item of plant,
unoccupied time will be arrived at for each member of the team
in the same way as in Example 2.   The total unoccupied time for
the job will take account of time resulting from the machine and
that due to imbalance of work within the team.

Fixed UT for more Complex Jobs

1. *Workers do other work during the machine controlled part of
the cycle.*   Where it is found that a job contains a large proportion
of unoccupied time, it may be possible to give the workers other
necessary work to do during plant running times, such as cleaning.
The UT will then be the plant running time less the work connected with the plant.

2. *Repetitive jobs where previous unit of product is finished during
a subsequent machine controlled cycle.*   Similarly, in the example
of loading a mixer shown in Fig. 62, when this job is continuously
repetitive the process allowance is the cycle time of $34 \cdot 8$ min less
the $33 \cdot 0$ min representing the man's work at standard performance,
that is $1 \cdot 8$ min per batch.

3. *Worker attends several units of plant making the same
product.*   When a worker is attending several units of plant each
performing the same process, the factors which must be considered
were shown in Fig. 63.   It should be noticed that, when the

operation is being performed as part of a continuously repetitive process, in which starting and finishing delays are of such short duration as to be negligible, the normal unoccupied time is 1·0 min for every three drums filled. (If the starting and finishing delays are of any significance they are averaged out over the day or shift concerned as unoccupied time per unit of product processed.)

4. *Worker attends several dissimilar units of plant.* When a worker attends several dissimilar units of plant, provided they are all automatically controlled, unoccupied time can be worked out in exactly the same way as the previous example.

Variable UT

In some instances, where a number of fixed cycles may be intermingled in a variety of ways, it may not be economic to calculate the unoccupied time for each possible combination. In such cases, it is usual to establish the unoccupied time using the hour or the day or shift time as the fixed cycle. This method is used in dealing with that type of work which requires workers to carry out a number of jobs in a variety of sequences. The UT arrived at is known as " variable unoccupied time," which may be derived in the following ways—

1. *Using the hour as the fixed cycle.* The assumption is made that a process takes exactly one hour during which the worker is present. Unoccupied time is then simply the period left in the hour after deduction of the time-equivalent of the work content of the human work. Thus, for a job requiring 42 SM in one hour, unoccupied time would be $60 - 42 = 18$ min.

For jobs occupying more or less than one hour process time, the same procedure can be used if the total number of units of work called for in the complete job is converted into the average number required per hour. The corresponding unoccupied time per hour is converted into total UT for the job by multiplying it by the number of hours required for the process.

2. *Using the day or shift as the fixed cycle.* A factory clock can be used to record the total time a group of operations takes. The number of cycles of each operation performed in that time will be known. If the work content of each operation is also known the total unoccupied time can be obtained by subtracting the time equivalent of the total units of work from the overall time taken to complete the operations—

$$\text{Unoccupied time} = \frac{\text{Overall time}}{\text{(by clock)}} - \frac{\text{Total units of work at}}{\text{standard performance.}}$$

Operations where unoccupied time must be treated in this way include continuous processes where the worker gives intermittent attention to an instrument panel; cases where the worker takes and records readings and does some routine work as well; tradesmen's mates in a workshop assisting a number of tradesmen, and men responsible for keeping other workers supplied with materials and for taking away work.

Interference Allowance

In the type of work where machine interference is a factor, the total amount of machine running time will usually be somewhat less than would otherwise be the case. If the worker's job is assessed on the assumption that he will always be available immediately a machine stoppage occurs, a misleading picture of his attainable performance will be shown by reason of the period when some machines have to wait for attention and production is lost.

The effect of such machine interference, therefore, is to increase the average time needed for the operation. The amount of this increase, known as *interference allowance*, is usually expressed like unoccupied time as a period of time additional to the work content of the operation. Its actual value can be determined by activity sampling or other suitable method of observation or calculation.

Excess Work Allowance

Allowances of this type are generally concerned with some non-standard feature of the conditions under which a job is performed. Typical instances might be because of extra time required for processing a batch of poor quality material, or because of the malfunctioning of a particular item of plant.

Excess work allowances are temporary, and, of course, apply only for the duration of the conditions concerned.

Policy Allowance

Policy allowance is defined by the British Standards Institution as " a factor applied to standard time, to provide a satisfactory level of earnings for a specified level of performance."

Such allowances, particularly when they have a relationship to workers' earnings, are usually decided upon by management and are not the responsibility of the work study officer except inasmuch as it is his task to see they are included wherever appropriate.

The Application of Allowances

The following diagram may help to clarify the way in which the different allowances are applied—

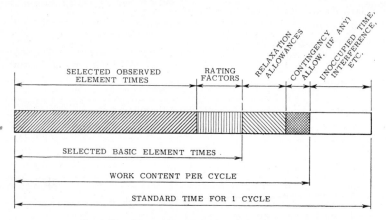

FIG. 64. THE APPLICATION OF ALLOWANCES

The manner in which unoccupied time and the various allowances, while affecting the overall time for the job, are excluded from the work content should be particularly noted. The necessity to make such allowances is usually an indication that labour and/or machine capacity is not being used to full advantage. By isolating these allowances in this way, and at the same time indicating clearly the conditions under which they apply, any change in those conditions can be investigated and the requisite adjustments made without necessarily affecting the work content of the job.

Contingency allowance, as has already been pointed out, is made in respect of an integral feature of the task for which measurement in detail may not be justified. As such it is included in the work content where it can only be considered for change if the method is altered.

17

Confirming Work Content and Standard Times

BECAUSE time study is the basic technique of work measurement it is of the greatest importance that means should be available for checking standard times arrived at by means of it so that, if the need arises, this can be done in the most effective way and with the minimum disturbance.

Since a check on observed times is always included when making the time study, by comparing the elapsed time with the total of the recorded times, the factor to which attention must be directed is the assessment of performance rating. Because the accuracy of the standard times set for a job is largely dependent upon the degree of accuracy as well as the consistency with which rating is done, a method has been devised whereby a worker's performance in practice can be checked against the total units of work of the output he achieves.

The procedure is to make a *production study* of the job under actual operating conditions. This is a protracted but simplified form of time study extending over at least a completely representative part of the job and for a period of suitable duration, during which the worker's mean rating is assessed at regular intervals (say, every half minute) without recording details of the individual elements. A careful record is maintained of all ineffective time. The average estimated rating obtained in this way is compared with the rating figure as calculated from the record of the worker's production during the same period. If there is a wide discrepancy between the two figures the cause of the disagreement must be traced.

Making the Study

It will be recalled that by definition, a worker who carries out the work involved in a job at standard rating, and takes the appropriate relaxation allowance, achieves standard performance, i.e. 60 units of work (SM) per hour.

Hence, where *gross working time* includes both net working time (actual time spent at the operation) and also relaxation allowance taken (recorded waiting time and time spent on unmeasured work being specifically excluded)—

$$\frac{\text{Average rating during net working time}}{100 \text{ (i.e. standard)}} \times \begin{array}{c}\text{Gross working time}\\\text{in minutes}\end{array}$$
$$= \begin{array}{c}\text{Total units of work}\\\text{produced by the worker}\end{array}$$

If, therefore, a comparison is made between the total units of work recorded during a production study (based on the issued standard time for the job) and the number which would correspond to the worker's rating during the same study, it is possible to detect if there is a discrepancy.

Example

Production study of can-making operation—

1. Data from original time study—
   Work content of job: 3·6 SM per can
   Average percentage of RA included in work content (SM): 20 per cent
2. Data from production study—
   Working day (duration of production study): 8 hours
   Waiting time recorded: $\frac{1}{4}$ hour total
   ∴ Gross working time: $7\frac{3}{4}$ hours
   RA taken: $1\frac{1}{4}$ hours
   ∴ Net working time $= 6\frac{1}{2}$ hours
   Average rating estimated during net working time: 105
   Actual output for day: 112 cans

3. Comparison between units of work actually recorded and units of work calculated from production study—

$$\text{Actually recorded} = \frac{112}{(\text{cans})} \times \frac{3 \cdot 6}{(\text{SM})} = 403 \text{ SM}$$

$$\text{Calculated} = \frac{105}{\frac{(\text{rating})}{100}} \times \frac{7\frac{3}{4} \text{ hours} \times 60}{(\text{gross working time})} = 488 \text{ SM}$$

4. Extent of Discrepancy—

Standard time calculated from production study

$$= \frac{488 \ (\text{SM})}{112 \ (\text{cans})} = 4 \cdot 4 \text{ SM per can}$$

Issued standard time $= 3 \cdot 6$ SM per can

This study suggests that the issued value of $3 \cdot 6$ SM per can may be too low, the cause for which will most likely be found to be one of the following—

1. An arithmetical error.
2. An incorrect or altered method of performing the job (e.g. " inside cycle " work being done as " outside cycle " work).
3. Incorrect machine speed (e.g. due to belt slip).
4. Slight changes in materials or product specification.
5. A change in the frequency of occurrence of occasional or variable elements of work.

Duration of Production Study

The necessary duration of a production study is dependent upon the class of work being performed. For short cycle repetitive work an hour may be adequate, for other repetitive work perhaps one day, and for non-repetitive work a period sufficient to ensure a representative run, which may possibly extend to several days.

Some short cycle repetitive work for which the standard times have been set by work study may not require production studies to be taken as well, providing the original studies were adequately recorded and of sufficient duration, and that they include the relaxation and contingencies applicable to that work.

For most classes of work, the cost of making production studies is small, and the advantages to be obtained from them are many.

Checking Consistency of Standard Times

The following are the main uses of production studies made for checking consistency—

1. *"Loose" or "tight" standard times.* A time study observer may not have acquired a satisfactory concept of standard. Too great a divergence from a true concept of a 100 rating would introduce looseness or tightness into standard times, although this might also be caused by excessive or insufficient margins for relaxation or other allowances. Production studies will sometimes help to reveal the cause of loose or tight standard times.

2. *Variations in quality.* It is essential that quality standards specified with the issue of standard times should be in accordance with those obtained in practice. Production studies are often useful in revealing whether or not the quality standards laid down are being maintained in practice, and if, where times have become loose, it is because the work involved in maintaining those standards is not being carried out.

3. *Variations in standard times.* It is essential that standard times remain fair to management and workers. If the quality of the raw material, or the tools of production vary, time study may have revealed to a great extent such variation, but a longer observation is sometimes necessary to prove that standard times will remain fair under all normal working conditions. Production studies may be used to reveal whether the standard times set in fact cover all such variations on a long-term basis.

Demonstrating the Fairness of Standard Times

If required, production studies may also be used to demonstrate the fairness of standard times for the following purposes—

1. *To inspire confidence.* It is most important that everyone concerned should have confidence in the fairness of standard times set. Such values may form the basis of an agreement between management and workers, and both parties must place their trust in them. It is also vital that the work study staff should gain confidence in the accuracy of the times which they are setting.

2. *As a production record for subsequent reference.* Production studies provide evidence of past production rates. They should be dated, certified correct by a responsible executive, and filed away. The time may come when the output of the department shows appreciable variations for some reason or other, when complaints may be made that the standard times of certain jobs are

unrealistic. Reference to production study records may help to clear up any misunderstandings of this kind.

Special Purposes

If, after application, the *performance index*[1] on a certain operation shows a marked upward or downward trend, a production study may be desirable as a check that the *work specification* (described in the next chapter) is being adhered to.

If work is being carried out in excess of specification, the performance index will be low. For example, the operation of spot-facing holes in a mild steel flange may be performed by the worker who drills the holes, purely because it is customary to do so, and despite the fact that no allowance for doing so is included in the work unit value of the drilling operation.

If operations which have been allowed for are being omitted or neglectfully performed, due perhaps to relaxed or inadequate inspection, the performance index will be high. For example, a worker may fail to remove burrs on articles that have been turned in a lathe. Here it might be necessary to enforce the quality standard required and specified or, alternatively, to amend the work specification and reduce the standard time if the high quality originally specified proves to be unnecessary.

[1] Performance indices are referred to in Chapter 19.

18

The Work Specification

THE final stage of carrying out work measurement is for the work study officer to present the results in a form suitable for use by management. This is the *work specification*. In addition to stating the work content and standard time of the operation concerned, this should describe in detail the method by and conditions under which the work is to be performed, including layout of the work-place, and particulars of the machines, tools, appliances, materials and services used. Reference should also be made to the duties and responsibilities of the worker while doing the work involved. This information is filed for record purposes so that the effect of any changes in the way of doing the job can be determined and the method and work content and standard time amended accordingly.

Although the work specification is primarily considered here in relation to time study, in the use of all work measurement techniques an adequate work specification must be prepared for each job. The detail will vary according to economic considerations. A work specification for a non-repetitive work job, for example, will take a much briefer form than that for a repetitive operation.

Although it is not possible to develop a standardized form of work specification, since each must be prepared for the particular job it describes and the context in which it will be used, a general pattern can be set and matters which should be included outlined.

Purpose of the Work Specification

The work specification is prepared in order to relate standard times to the conditions on which they are based. It is not intended to be a report of work study activities, nor should it include estimates of savings. These can be recorded separately, and, if necessary, have attention drawn to them in an official report to management.

The conditions under which standard times are set may bear a close resemblance to those under which a similar operation is being performed in a different location or at a different time. A further purpose of the work specification, therefore, is to provide a means of checking to what extent the values it records may be used elsewhere. Thus, it may be possible to avoid repetition of some time study work.

When a financial incentive scheme is to be based on work measurement, the work specification may also be used as a contract between management and worker.

Particulars of the Job

Under particulars of the job it is necessary to consider a number of factors. Relevant details with regard to each point should then be included in the work specification under the appropriate headings—

1. Purpose of the job.
2. Design and condition of plant, layout of work-place.
3. Nature and quantities of incoming materials and services.
4. Type and condition of equipment, tools, and appliances used.
5. Method employed.
6. Quality specifications for the product, outgoing condition.
7. Ambient conditions.

1. *Purpose of the Job*

As complete details are given under " method employed," a brief description of the job, sufficient only to identify it from other jobs, is all that is needed under this heading. Where possible, the words used should conform to those in general use in the organization concerned to enable the job to which they refer to be easily recognized.

2. *Design and Condition of Plant, Layout of Work-place*

Changes in any of these factors may affect the specified method for a particular job. Information concerning design and condition of plant and layout of work-place should be included in the work specification in the form of drawings and photographs. In respect of condition of plant, it may assist if reference is made to frequency of overhaul.

3. *Nature and Quantities of Incoming Materials and Services*

Specific information regarding the nature and quantities of incoming materials and services should appear relating them to the appropriate parts of the job.

4. *Type and Condition of Equipment, Tools and Appliances Used*

Specification of tools, equipment and appliances is important. The life of tools, for example, will have a bearing on standard times, and reference to frequency of their inspection, replacement and overhaul should be included. Types of equipment and appliances should be entered and listed by reference to plant inventories.

5. *Method Employed*

Full information regarding the particular method is essential, especially for jobs for which differing methods are available.

6. *Quality Specifications for the Product, Outgoing Condition*

Quality specifications should be obtained from management prior to work study as a matter of routine. It is important that these should be clearly identified and dated, as the standard times are based on current specifications. The outgoing condition of the product, particularly when it has an effect on a succeeding operation, should always be carefully described.

7. *Ambient Conditions*

The ambient conditions under which the job may be performed should be closely defined, and the standard time adjusted to provide for probable variations from the conditions prevailing when the study is made.

Specification of the Method

Misuse of standard times, arising from inadequate specification of methods of working, can cause both management and work study personnel considerable embarrassment. The difficulty can be avoided by careful definition of the job and the conditions under which it is to be performed. At the same time specification of the method should not be allowed to contain unnecessary detail. For highly repetitive work, however, analysis of method in terms of basic motions may be necessary to obtain precise definition.

Generally the document should be detailed enough for changes affecting standard times to be identified as a method alteration, and so justify a reassessment.

The various types of process charts used in method study provide simple ways of describing methods, and they can be prepared to whatever degree of detail is required. Whenever it is considered necessary, copies of the appropriate charts should be included in any work specifications.

It is essential in describing a method to refer to any safety precautions and regulations which may be applicable. Reference should also be made to good housekeeping standards.

Specifying Standard Times and Allowances

Information required for production planning, cost control, methods improvement, financial incentive schemes, etc., and which should be available from the work specification are, in general, as follows—

1. *The time for the job at standard performance.* This may be given directly in SM per part or per 100 parts, or it may also be shown as an output rate in units of product per hour.

In the case of an incentive scheme based on work measurement, it is particularly important that job times should be issued in a form capable of complete understanding by workers.

Thus, a job comprising

5·0 SM + 1·3 min UT per part

would require a standard time of

5·0 + 1·3 = 6·3 min per part (6 min 18 sec per part)

which is equivalent to

$\dfrac{60}{6·3}$ or 9·5 parts per hour

or   10·5 hours (i.e. 630 min) per 100 parts

The use of a table is often resorted to to reduce the work of calculating the number of parts per hour for different standard times.

2. *The work content of the job.* This is taken from the summary sheet. Special reference should be made to the reason for and extent of any contingency allowance included in the work content. Any criterion of work efficiency or acceptable percentage of rejected product on which the work content is based should also be shown.

In some cases of team-work it may be necessary to show the work content for the work of the various members of the team separately. In other cases the total work content for the job may be all that is required.

3. *Unoccupied time.* Any unoccupied time, like the work content, should be shown either in respect of each worker or for the job as a whole, depending on which is appropriate. In general the extent of unoccupied time is coupled with the work content as shown in the example used above to illustrate how job times should be expressed.

4. *Interference allowance.* The amount of interference allowance should be detailed. Delays due to plant or machine synchronization are inherent in the method specified for some jobs; interruptions to the process due to breakdowns, for example, are not covered.

5. *Policy allowance.* Details of policy allowance (*see* Chapter 16) should be filed with the work specification.

Whenever it is intended to audit the work contents at regular intervals, the date after which the published figures become invalid should be clearly quoted.

Provision of Tabular Summary

The work specification for each job carried out in a section should be made available to the worker's representatives for reference. For general administrative purposes, however, it is unnecessary to refer to it each time the standard times are required. It is convenient to prepare a summary, in tabular form, for each operation which should contain—

1. The work specification reference number.
2. A brief description of the purpose of the operation.
3. The standard time.
4. The work content.
5. The extent of unoccupied time.
6. The extent of interference allowance.

Maintenance of the Work Specification

It is in the interests of all concerned that work specifications should be complete and unambiguous. Conditions under which a product is made cannot be expected to remain unchanged. To facilitate the maintenance of values, conditions during the period of observation must be properly defined.

It will be obvious that a work specification must contain a very detailed description of the process that is being carried out. In many cases this information may be highly confidential. The number of copies of the work specification prepared should, therefore, be strictly limited, and a decision obtained from higher management as to where they are to be retained. Any part of a specification should be available for inspection by representatives of management or workers, whenever there is good reason, but care should be taken, when such inspection takes place, that no copies are made of information which is of a confidential nature.

Work specifications are documents of value containing the results of considerable expenditure of time and money. Filing should be such as to ensure that there is no danger of loss by fire or theft. The standing of a work study department is dependent to no little extent on the care with which work specifications are maintained as well as on that put into their preparation.

Work Study as a Service to Management

As was pointed out in Chapter 2, the British contribution to the development of the productivity techniques grouped under the heading of Work Study has been twofold. In Chapter 3 reference is made to the great importance attached in the British system of work study to the human factors. But while this in itself constitutes a major advance over previous attitudes, equally important is the way in which the work study attitude of mind has been applied to spheres of activity far wider than the original objective of the effective use of manpower.

Fig. 65 gives a general picture of the way in which work study can be of service to management in all spheres. Necessarily, the developments have not been as intense on some fronts as they have on others; but in respect of many functions shown in Fig. 65—and in many other fields not mentioned, there—the value of objective analysis and measurement, and of the constructively critical attitude embodied in work study, has been proved time and time again. In this chapter we consider briefly those fields of application of the work study service that are most highly developed at the present time and which are most likely to be met by the student joining a progressive organization. They are—

(*a*) Incentive schemes   (*b*) Labour control   (*c*) Materials handling
(*d*) Planning   (*e*) Plant and product design

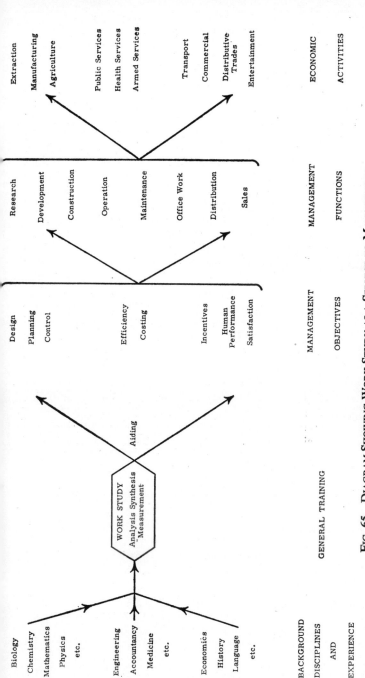

Extraction
Manufacturing
Agriculture

Public Services
Health Services
Armed Services

Transport
Commercial
Distributive Trades
Entertainment

ECONOMIC
ACTIVITIES

Research
Development
Construction
Operation
Maintenance
Office Work
Distribution
Sales

MANAGEMENT
FUNCTIONS

Design
Planning
Control
Efficiency
Costing
Incentives
Human Performance
Satisfaction

MANAGEMENT
OBJECTIVES

Aiding

WORK STUDY
Analysis Synthesis
Measurement

GENERAL TRAINING

Biology
Chemistry
Mathematics
Physics
etc.

Engineering
Accountancy
Medicine
etc.

Economics
History
Language
etc.

BACKGROUND
DISCIPLINES
AND
EXPERIENCE

FIG. 65. DIAGRAM SHOWING WORK STUDY AS A SERVICE TO MANAGEMENT

(*Note*: This diagram is intended to suggest possible areas of application and is not of course exhaustive. It gives a picture of the way in which general training in work study can help bring academic knowledge to bear more effectively in the various tasks of management.)

Financial Incentives Based on Work Study

Because standard times enable jobs of differing type and duration to be expressed in terms of the same denomination, they provide an exceptionally useful basis for the operation of a system of payment by results. The availability of the work specification for use as the contract between management and worker in this connexion is particularly convenient, since it establishes precisely the conditions under which a job is to be performed as well as the method to be employed. In the event of a change in either or both of these it can be a routine matter to determine the extent and effect on the work content or standard times and make the necessary adjustments.

From the worker's point of view the ability easily to calculate bonus earnings is important. Standard times are perfectly straightforward in this respect and their use in incentive schemes is discussed below.

Although they are no substitute for good planning and supervision, incentive schemes of this type have the added advantage that there is every encouragement for workers to pay attention to delays and record waiting time, thus making it apparent to management when and where action may be necessary to prevent their recurrence.

Principles of Incentive Schemes

Work study incentive schemes are designed so that an employee is paid a reward, additional to the job hourly rate, systematically related to his own effective contribution to the achievement of objectives specified by management. The employee's contribution to the achievement of management's objectives (i.e. the amount of work he, personally, does) is measured in terms of units of work performed. The schemes are therefore based on work measurement data which must, of course, be obtained by proper application of the appropriate techniques.

The various techniques of work measurement are explained in Chapters 9–14. It is made clear therein (pages 105–107) that the average worker, trained and accustomed to his job, should be able to perform 60 units of work per hour, i.e. the standard rate of working (exclusive of waiting time) while doing measured work.

In representative industries, it has been agreed with the trades unions concerned that the appropriate additional reward, or bonus, to be paid under work study incentive schemes for the performance of 60 units of work per hour is $33\frac{1}{3}$ per cent of the employee's job hourly rate.

In most work study incentive schemes an employee's bonus is

related to a direct index of his performance which is known as Operator Performance (O.P.). This and other indices are described below under the heading of " Labour Control."

Natural Teams

The results of incentive schemes generally show clearly that those schemes under which the individual is rewarded for his own efforts are more effective than those under which groups of people share equally in some communal bonus.

In some cases, however, a number of men work as a team; the team being of such a nature that the work of the individual members is interdependent and it is impracticable to define their duties separately. Under such circumstances bonus must be calculated on a team basis. Teams covered collectively by an incentive scheme should be as small as possible and should always consist of members of an interdependent group and not be based purely on geographical location. It has been found in practice that provided such a team does not exceed six to eight men there is no significant deterioration in the feeling of individual incentive.

Additional Objectives

The earlier types of incentive schemes in the main covered straightforward repetitive work and had as their objective simply an improvement in the rate of output of product per man-hour. In many cases, however, objectives such as improvement in use of materials, services and plant may be much more significant financially than an increase in rate of output per man-hour. Where possible, factors relating to these objectives should be included in specific schemes provided that the employee's bonus is still based on his own, or his team's, effective measured contribution.

Effect of Incentive Schemes

They provide to management an increase in the output of effective work of the employees; a sound basis of labour control in that changes in the levels of performance of employees are measured and made available; and a consistent and acceptable means of rewarding an employee in relation to his own effective contribution of work.

They provide to the employee the opportunity to earn for himself and his dependants a higher standard of living in the form of increased purchasing power.

Properly designed and administered work study incentive schemes have indirect results difficult to evaluate but nevertheless of the greatest importance. They can effect dramatic improvement in

W.S.   **H**

labour turnover, absenteeism and management-labour relations generally.

Calculation of Bonus Earnings and Performance

In most cases, bonus is calculated separately from the base rate wages and other earnings such as overtime premiums, etc. This ensures that the guaranteed minimum wages, where they apply, are in fact paid and the worker can see clearly that his pay covers both his guaranteed minimum and the bonus he has earned. Usually arrangements are also made to provide certain indices of labour performance which are calculated at the same time as the bonus.

The basis of the calculation is the work performed by the worker and the time taken to carry it out. The first stage is to record the quantity of work actually done and from this to calculate the number of units of work produced. The actual time taken to do this measured work may be recorded or may be ascertained from the total attendance time (clock hours) by deducting waiting time and time spent on un-measured work, etc.

As an example, consider a *straight proportional* payment-by-results incentive scheme—one, that is to say, in which the worker's total earnings are in direct proportion to the number of units of work he has produced.

Guaranteed base rate (say) 3s. 9d. (45d.) per hr

A bonus of (say) $33\frac{1}{3}$ per cent of base rate is to be paid for standard performance (i.e. 60 SM per hr)

Then earnings rate per SM

$$= \frac{\text{3s. 9d.} + 33\frac{1}{3} \text{ per cent}}{60 \text{ SM}} = \frac{60\text{d.}}{60 \text{ SM}} = 1\text{d. per SM}$$

If the worker is given a batch of 72 parts to process at (say) 2·0 SM per part and completes them in a recorded time of 2 hr 20 min, his bonus would amount to—

(Actual earnings)

$$= \left\{ \begin{array}{ccc} \text{number of} & \text{SM value} & \text{Earnings} \\ \text{parts} \times & \text{per} \times & \text{rate per} \\ \text{processed} & \text{part} & \text{SM} \end{array} \right\}$$

less (time rate earnings)

$$- \left\{ \begin{array}{cc} \text{Time taken} & \text{Base Rate} \\ \text{to complete} \times & \text{per} \\ \text{batch} & \text{hour} \end{array} \right\}$$

$$= (72 \times 2 \cdot 0 \times 1 \cdot 0)\text{d.} - (2\frac{20}{60} \times 45)\text{d.}$$

$$= 144\text{d.} - 105\text{d.}$$

$$= 39\text{d. or 3s. 3d.}$$

Similarly, if a worker receiving the same base rate performs various operations totalling (say) 448 SM in an 8½-hr day, out of which 1 hr 15 min has been booked on waiting time, his bonus for the day would be—

$$(448\text{d.} \times 1 \cdot 0)\text{d.} - (7\frac{15}{60} \times 45)\text{d.}$$

$$= 448\text{d.} - 326\text{d.}$$

$$= 122\text{d. or 10s. 2d.}$$

And his average performance level in measured work

$$= \frac{448}{435} \times 100 = 103$$

TABLE SHOWING
BONUS RATES AT VARIOUS PERFORMANCES

Base rate: 3s. 9d.

Operator Performance	Bonus in Pence per Hour	Operator Performance	Bonus in Pence per Hour
75	0·0		
76	0·6	91	9·6
77	1·2	92	10·2
78	1·8	93	10·8
79	2·4	94	11·4
80	3·0	95	12·0
81	3·6	96	12·6
82	4·2	97	13·2
83	4·8	98	13·8
84	5·4	99	14·4
85	6·0	100	15·0
86	6·6	101	15·6
87	7·2	102	16·2
88	7·8	103	16·8
89	8·4	104	17·4
90	9·0	105	18·0

(N.B. This table applies to a particular base rate or group of base rates. A set of such tables will normally be required.)

In addition the worker would, of course, receive his time rate of 3s. 9d. per hour in respect of the whole period of $8\frac{1}{2}$ hours he is recorded as being present.

An alternative method of arriving at the bonus is to calculate first the average performance level (103 above) and then compute the bonus by reference to a table setting out bonus rates per hour which are equivalent to various performance levels. Part of such a table is shown on page 203 and reference to it indicates a bonus rate of 16·8d. per hour for 103 performance. Since the time on measured work is 7 hrs 15 min—

$$\text{Bonus earned} = 16·8 \text{ (d. per hour)} \times 7·25 \text{ (hours)}$$
$$= 122\text{d. or 10s. 2d. as before.}$$

There are of course, other ways in which bonus earnings may be calculated, but it is felt the two illustrated will be adequate to demonstrate the relative ease with which these calculations can be made.

Labour Control and Work Study

Labour Control is a system based on clerical procedures which provides vital information regarding production and labour performance, so that a constant control of labour deployment can be exercised.

Use of Work Measurement

As the relative cost of labour in all fields is continuously rising the measurement of work is essential in order to deploy, and record the effectiveness of, labour.

A satisfactory means of measuring work has been found in the techniques of work measurement and the unit of work is a yardstick applicable to most kinds of work. If past records and experience or broad guesswork are used to arrive at the amount of work involved in operations, the delays, frustrations and injustices commonly found in industry are likely.

The day-to-day effectiveness with which labour is used is an important responsibility of junior management (or supervision, as it is often termed). Admittedly, in a small business or in small departments, direct visual supervision can achieve some degree of effectiveness. But information submitted for Labour Control tells supervision (and, in turn, management) how the duties delegated are being carried out in comparison with established standards. Equally important, the worker can be shown how his efforts compare with an optimum standard.

By proper analysis of deviations from standards, the true causes and extents of losses are disclosed and supervision can see what action, if any, should be taken to improve labour utilization and performance. Furthermore, the greater confidence thereby engendered, by the removal of frustrations for the men and surmise and doubt regarding performance, assists in improving labour relations.

Factors Affecting Performance

Various factors may interfere with the achievement of a performance to the optimum standard, giving rise to " excess " times, and " excess " costs. The factors causing such excesses may be divided roughly into three categories—

1. *Ability and willingness of the worker to achieve optimum performance.* Proper selection and training should ensure the development of worker's ability. An equitable incentive scheme based on work measurement will provide an inducement to the worker to give of his best.

2. *Availability of plant and equipment.* Workers can produce optimum performance only if they have the plant and equipment available to them to do so. This can be ensured as far as possible by proper plant overhaul and maintenance or, where economic considerations allow it, by provision of stand-by resources.

3. *Availability of supplies of work to be done.* The provision of the right amount of work at the right time and in the right place, to enable the worker to maintain optimum performance over his day, is achieved by proper organization and planning.

Information for Labour Control

The *unit of work* has been found to be the most satisfactory measure of work for overall labour control, as it enables fair comparisons to be made of performances on any type of work, regardless of character or location. Other systems based on measurements such as tons, yards or cubic feet have a limited local use for control on one product or process. They do not however, enable performances on different kinds of work to be compared.

In recording a worker's activities, the achieved production is converted to units of work, and time spent otherwise than on production is also carefully recorded. When this information has been analysed and condensed, the salient features are presented to management at periodic intervals for comparison with standards. The basic information presented to management is as follows—

1. Performance indices, showing the levels of performance reached and maintained by the labour force, expressed either as

units of work per hour or as a percentage of standard performance (*see* below).

2. Analysis of time spent otherwise than on productive work, showing the causes and duration of such delays.

3. Labour costs of production showing wages cost of producing 1,000 units of work at actual performance for comparison with wages cost at optimum performance.

Presentation of Control Data

In presenting information to management and supervision, care must be taken to include only data covering activities for which they are directly responsible and which they, by their efforts, can influence. Different information must therefore be supplied at different levels and the intervals at which the information is presented will depend on the type of work. The following are suggested for the more usual types of work—

1. Supervision—generally weekly but daily if desirable and if the type of work lends itself.

2. Section Management—weekly and sometimes daily.

3. Factory Management—monthly.

Supervision (i.e. foremen and chargehands) is responsible for the performance of the individual worker. Information about each worker's output of work and how his time was spent is given on a return often called the *posting sheet*. Various other names can be given to this document, but it takes the form of a return showing (for each man) hours, output, and average performance. Where financial incentives (*see* page 200) are in operation, the bonus earned is usually appended. This information is passed to the section concerned immediately after the completion of the period to which it applies. After inspection by supervision the information is given to the workers, either individually or by posting the sheet up in the section.

Section Management, having delegated individual control of the men to supervision, will not require such detailed information. Section Management's primary interest is to see that each group is carrying out its allotted task. The average figures for each group may appropriately be presented weekly. An analysis of waiting time may also be given under headings showing the amount of time lost on account of each cause and also unit labour costs of production for comparison with set standards. Figures may be submitted daily in some instances.

Factory Management requires an even broader view than that

given to Section Management. This is supplied on a monthly summary which consolidates the average figures for each group presented on the weekly basis. In addition to man-hours worked, output and performance indices, labour costs of production are given for comparison with set standards. Being expressed in money values, some of this information is suitable for incorporation in an overall cost control statement embracing all cost factors, such as materials, machinery and overheads.

Labour Control: Use of Performance Indices

As has been shown, once a job has been measured and the human work in it expressed in units of work, it is possible to devise a system of labour control based on unit of work. The principles of this procedure are as follow—

A comparison is made between the number of units of work which should be produced by workers and departments, worked out on the basis of whatever target performance has been set, with the number of units of work which have actually been achieved. The principle is that a careful analysis is made of any failure to achieve the target set, and in practice use is made of performance indices.

Reliable performance indices greatly assist management in making the most effective use of labour. Standard times which a worker can maintain are established by work measurement. These are essential to management for the planning of production; and they also help the worker in his understanding of the task set him. For both they provide a fair means of measuring achievement.

The purpose of performance indices is to measure levels of performance for the information of management. These indices can be designed to take account of various factors affecting output and input.

The factors most likely to affect the attainment of standard performance over the working day or shift are—

1. The effort and attention given by the worker to the job.
2. The incidence of waiting time, during which the worker is prevented from working due to interruptions beyond his control.
3. The incidence of times during the process at which the worker can do no more work pending completion of the operation. This time is termed unoccupied time (*see* pages 181–185).

There are three main performance indices used for control purposes, and below we give definitions based on British Standards and examples of two different methods by which they can be arrived at— either as percentages of standard performance or in units of work per hour. (Note that " measured " and " estimated " in the B.S.I. definitions mean " arrived at by the appropriate work measurement techniques.".)

Operator Performance

Operator performance, or *true performance*, is an indication of the effectiveness of a worker (or group of workers if required) while on measured or estimated work. It is the ratio between *total standard times for all measured and estimated work done* and *time actually spent on this measured and estimated work* (*i.e. excluding diverted and waiting time and any time on unmeasured work*).

A very simple example may make the procedure clearer: after it had been measured by one of the techniques of work measurement, a simple job, unaffected by team or process times, was found to have a work content of 15 SM per part processed. That is to say, the worker is expected to take a quarter of an hour to complete each part at the standard performance.

Supposing the worker is at his work bench eight hours a day, at standard performance he will therefore do the job—

8 (hr) $\times$ 4 (parts processed per hour)
= 32 times per day, which is equivalent to 480 SM per day.

By expressing the work content of any job in this way it is possible to make valid comparisons between different levels of output. Thus, if in this example the job is only done twenty-four times in eight hours the SM accumulated will total—

24 (number of times job was done) $\times$ 15 (value in SM) = 360, representing a performance only 75 per cent of standard,

(i.e. $\dfrac{360}{480} \times 100$).

Calculated on this percentage basis, operator performance is arrived at as follows—

$$\text{Operator performance} = \frac{\text{Units of work actually produced by worker}}{\text{Units of work producable at standard performance}} \times 100$$

To find the number of units of work actually produced is simply a matter of multiplying the number of times the specified job has been done by its work content. The calculation of the denominator is based on that part of the attendance time when the worker is engaged on measured work, i.e. attendance time less waiting time and less time on unmeasured work.

Note: On the basis of the work units used in this book, where

60 SM per hour are expected to be produced as standard performance, the denomination is in fact equal to the number of minutes in which the work has been done, i.e.

$$\text{Operator performance} = \frac{\text{Units of work produced}}{\text{Number of minutes to produce them}} \times 100$$

The resultant operator performance can be entered on the worker's daily work card, and notified to him on a daily basis, while analysis of the time spent on unmeasured work, waiting time and unoccupied time, is a daily guide to management of how effectively they are planning.

Another method of expressing operator performance is—

$$\text{Operator performance} = \frac{\text{Units of work produced}}{\text{Number of hours to produce them}}$$

or, using the figures from the example above

$$= \frac{360}{8} = 45 \text{ units of work per hour.}$$

Departmental Performance

This is used to indicate the effectiveness of a department or a section, and is a ratio between *total standard times for measured and est.mated work done* and *time actually spent on measured and estimated work plus any waiting or diverted time for which the department is responsible.* Departmental performance is concerned with the average performance of the department on measured work and includes the effects of any waiting time. On a percentage basis the index is arrived at thus—

$$\frac{\text{Departmental}}{\text{performance}} = \frac{\text{Units of work actually produced by department}}{\text{Units of work producable at standard performance}} \times 100$$

Note that in this case the calculation of the denominator is based on the attendance time less only the time on unmeasured work, i.e. not less the waiting time as in operator performance above. The same applies to the denominator when calculating the index on the units of work per hour basis—

$$\frac{\text{Departmental}}{\text{performance}} = \frac{\text{Units of work produced}}{\text{Attendance hours less hours on unmeasured work}}$$

This performance index is useful as it presents a picture of the efficiency of a department, and can be used to compare the performance of different departments.

It also shows the general effect on performance of waiting time and in some cases time during the process when the worker can do no work.

Comparing the appropriate operator performance with the departmental performance shows up the effect of enforced idleness, due to waiting time or unoccupied time, where applicable, on the rate at which the worker is willing to work. As neither waiting time nor unoccupied time is in the control of the worker but is, in fact, the responsibility of supervision, this comparison forms a ready check on the effectiveness of supervision and may lead to improved planning of work.

Overall Performance

This gives, on a basis of units of work against time, an indication of the net utilization of labour in producing useful output. It is the ratio between *total standard times for measured work plus unmeasured work at assessed performance* and *total attendance time* expressed in percentage form; therefore—

$$\text{Overall performance} = \frac{\text{Units of work produced (measured and estimated)} + \text{unmeasured at assessed performance}}{\text{Units of work producable at standard performance}} \times 100$$

In this case the denomination is based on the whole of the attendance time. The same again applies when calculating the index on the units of work per hour basis—

$$\text{Overall performance} = \frac{\text{Units of work produced}}{\text{Attendance hours}}$$

The overall performance is intended to reveal the net result in terms of useful output which it has been possible to obtain. Whereas the operator performance shows the rate of output obtainable while work is available, the overall performance shows what this has been over the whole of the attendance time. The difference thus indicates the loss due to all causes, such as waiting time, unoccupied time, etc. Similarly, the difference between departmental performance and overall performance reveals losses in potential output which have come about from causes other than those attributable to the department.

All three indices described above may be calculated for individual workers or groups of workers, and for departments or whole factories, by totalling the enumerators and denominators as defined.

Materials Handling and Work Study

In recent years increasing attention has been directed to the effective handling of materials as a means of increasing productivity and reducing overall costs. Materials handling concerns the movement of both material and people throughout a complex concern—raw materials; components between the various activities; finished products; materials for maintenance and construction work; and scrap. Handling embraces movement from the supplier to the incoming stores, through the various stages of manufacture into finished products, to the warehouse, and then on to the customer. Handling, and the study of handling, is by no means confined, therefore, to the processing operations or the confines of the factory itself.

Importance of the Process Operation

Activities in any kind of concern can be broadly classified under two headings—process operations, and handling operations. Work study is, in effect, the tool which has been developed to analyse and measure these operations and thereby devise ways and means of increasing productivity. Method study offers a quick and effective way of making this analysis.

In this form of analysis, process operations, referred to in work study as " do " operations, are the first to be considered because if these are changed in nature and sequence, combined or eliminated at any point, the associated handling and movement operations are at once affected. A very simple example will illustrate the importance of this approach.

Example: Assume there are two consecutive operations performed some distance apart at points *A* and *B*, and it has been suggested that the method of handling material from one to the other should be investigated. The first questions requiring to be answered are—

1. Can *A* or *B* be eliminated?
2. Can *A* or *B* be combined in one operation?
3. Can *A* be brought next to *B*?

If the answer to any of these questions is " yes," then handling is not necessary.

Handling studies are carried out by means of the method study charting technique and the questioning sequence (Chapters 5 and 6).

Two points are of particular note about the application to materials handling problems of the method study questioning sequence. Firstly, some of the questions may not apply to a particular activity. In such instances there is no need to dwell laboriously on them; but they should be asked to ensure that no aspect is neglected or overlooked. Secondly, some of the questions may need further elaboration beyond the simple initial question to arrive at a complete understanding of the situation. For example, to appreciate fully the implication of these answers it may be necessary to consider such factors as—

1. The form in which materials are supplied.
2. The estimated utilization of new handling equipment.
3. The effect of changed methods on overall cost.
4. Handling methods in other departments.

Applying the questioning sequence in this manner establishes the need, place, order, person—finally the means of carrying out what the best method requires. All possibilities of falling into the error of considering handling equipment first and endeavouring to fit it into a particular situation are thereby eliminated.

Use of Charts

The fundamental analysis of the job is carried out by applying the questioning sequence to the process chart in the appropriate way. It may be desirable, however, to supplement the process chart with other aids, such as the flow diagram, string diagram or multiple activity chart (*see* Chapter 5). In a materials handling problem the paths of movement will in general be of major interest and a flow diagram may be of considerable help when dealing with the question "Where?" This device enables the problem to be viewed in plan or elevation and is valuable in that it helps appreciation of such features as unnecessarily long routes, backtracking, poor or excessive use of traffic aisles, points of unreasonable congestion, hold-ups, and danger hazards. In addition, the suitability of collection and delivery points for materials and products in course of manufacture, and the relative siting of a department, can be readily studied.

In certain instances when it is required to examine complex inter-departmental or inter-section materials movement, the flow diagram may become a maze of lines and difficult to follow. In particular the flow diagram is not suitable when such quantitative factors as distances, weight and frequency of movement have to be studied. An alternative device on such occasions is the Travel Chart, an example of which is shown in Fig. 66.

The particular areas being studied are marked out along the horizontal and vertical axes as shown, both commencing from the same point. Movement is always plotted by reading from the horizontal to the vertical axis. If in the example it is assumed that the initial movement was from department 5 to department 3, the X at the junction of the columns joining department 5 to department 3 records this move. The same procedure is then followed for all other moves that take place during the chosen period of time for the study.

The number of *X*s in each vertical column is then added up and the bar chart constructed to show the movement *from* each department. Horizontal columns are similarly added up and the second bar chart constructed to show the movement *to* each department. These charts not only provide an at-a-glance picture of the volume and nature of the movement to and from each department, but also form the basis for further analysis and investigation.

Substituting the *X*s for distances, weights, number of journeys, or other quantitative figures presents an even more realistic picture of the movement. The effect of rearrangement of machines and departments to eliminate or reduce movement can readily be studied from this type of chart.

From method study it is, therefore, possible to decide the optimum qualitative requirements and compare alternative methods in this

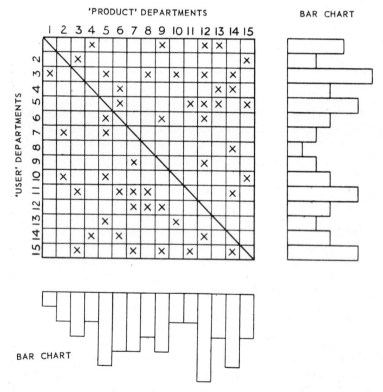

FIG. 66.   MATERIALS HANDLING TRAVEL CHART

respect. This applies equally whether the materials are handled manually or with power-driven equipment.

Work Measurement Contribution

When an alternative method is being evaluated quantitative as well as qualitative data will be required. Work measurement provides the means of obtaining this information and a means for comparing the work content of alternative methods regardless of the nature of the work performed. In this way it is possible to obtain the best balance between operations and thereby ensure the best possible work flow. By comparing alternative methods on this basis the most economic method can also be selected and an accurate estimate made of the anticipated savings. In addition work measurement provides a sound factual basis for decisions on future action, a particularly valuable feature where decisions involve capital expenditure.

Planning and Work Study

As a result of the division of labour into grades and specialist functions, together with more complex equipment and buildings, etc., there has been a growing realization that a measure of formal planning of all the functions of a productive enterprise was necessary to ensure the maximum use of all the available resources.

The techniques which have developed into modern work study were evolved to meet the need for a more accurate knowledge of two fundamental planning requirements—the methods to be adopted to achieve specified objectives, and the time required to carry out such methods.

Basic Planning Steps

1. Establish and specify the *objective*. Determine the desired result and the time by which it has to be achieved.

2. Consider the *method* by which the objective may best be achieved and the *times* required to carry out each stage of the chosen method.

3. Devise the *programme*.

4. Arrange *resources* and initiate *action*.

5. *Control* progress to ensure the desired result is achieved.

The five steps of planning should be undertaken in the stated sequence although it will be necessary frequently to refer back to one of the preceding steps for further consideration. All the steps can be undertaken by a single person or department, or by a number of separate units in the organization, depending on the magnitude of the project. Specialized planning staff may or may not be justified. Whoever undertakes the work, it is most important that all of the five steps should be considered and continuously co-ordinated if planning is to be successful.

Contributions of Work Study to Planning

Because of the versatility possessed by modern work study resulting from a continuous and successful search for refinements, developments and additions to the techniques, it is worth while to examine in detail the contribution which work study can now make to planning, considering briefly each of the five basic planning steps in turn.

1. *Establish and specify the objective of the plan.* Objectives may result from policy decisions by management arising from new inventions, technical developments, market requirements, sales trends, analyses of orders or salesmen's reports. It is necessary to specify this objective in terms capable of being translated into executive action by means of designs, models, drawings, schedules, bills of quantities and the like.

The value of work study in the design field is described below. By the application of work study techniques at this stage of planning more accurate times can be obtained, hence improved and more accurate target dates can be forecast.

In certain types of production work the availability of suitable work study data can help greatly in assessing feasible delivery dates at closer specifications and keener prices.

2. *Consider the method by which the objective may be achieved and the times required to carry out each stage of the chosen method.* The method may in turn depend on the time available or the materials most readily obtainable. Hence, not only must a study be made of individual operations and their sequence but also of the three physical resources—labour, materials and capital equipment—needed to implement the methods. For example, it will be necessary to specify the type and category of labour; the effective working rate expected, which in turn can be significantly influenced by the adoption of work measurement and incentive schemes; the form, shape, size and state of material; the methods of handling materials; the equipment and plant items to be used and the best layout.

This is the field of method study. The method must be studied to make sure it is the most economical in all the circumstances.

For all manual operations a knowledge of standard times and the performance to be expected from the labour is required. (Synthetic data are of great value in establishing the standard times for novel jobs (*see* Chapter 12).) This is essential to establish how long it should take to carry out the specified methods with a certain labour force. This is the field of work measurement.

It is also necessary to have basic performance data available to show process-controlled and machine-controlled cycle times. In establishing this data work study will provide a more realistic approach for obtaining the true range, capacity, capabilities and characteristics of all equipment in the inventory.

3. *Devise the programme.* When it is established exactly what has to be done, how it will be done and how long each stage or operation is likely to take, the overall production cycle can be laid out in proper sequence as a programme, taking account of the machine and labour loading involved. The quantities and times at which raw materials are required must be considered in relation to this programme.

Where more than one job is to be done simultaneously, they can most conveniently be fitted together by displaying the work load on a Gantt chart or other programming device.

The accuracy and efficiency of the programme devised will largely depend on the proper use of work study at the previous planning step.

4. *Arrange resources and initiate action.* Various recording systems can show with accuracy what materials are currently available or when they will become so. But economy in the stocking of material resources is not possible unless there is knowledge of when and at what rate they are to be required. Reference to the programme produced at the previous step supplies this information. Labour and equipment resources should be considered in similar fashion.

If certain materials cannot be obtained when required, alternatives will have to be examined and only if supply dates are unacceptable, will the programme have to be amended. If the necessary labour or equipment is not readily forthcoming overtime, shift-working or subcontracting may become necessary.

The programme can only be implemented by issuing instructions to proceed with the prescribed methods at the right time and rate. To do this, forms or documents are required which conform to a logical and coherent system or procedure. The procedure must be one most suited to all circumstances.

Work study techniques can be used to great advantage in devising the most effective clerical procedures and also checking (by activity sampling) that they are being operated and maintained satisfactorily.

5. *Control progress to ensure the desired result is achieved.* In addition to initiating action the procedure—and if necessary the documentation—must be so devised as to feed back vital information dealing with the progress of the work. In order that all concerned

may clearly see the progress being made, the information is best utilized by posting it to the Gantt chart or other programming device, mentioned in (3) above. When this has been done the achieved results can be compared with the planned expectation. It is then possible to see how effectively the programme is being met and what remedial action is required to correct or accommodate any deviations.

Effective accomplishment of the programme should not generally be obtained at the expense of efficient usage of labour, materials and capital equipment. It is necessary therefore to compare regularly the results achieved with the stated objective in order to measure the overall effectiveness of planning. The determination of performance indices (*see* above) is essential to reveal where improvement is possible and in this work study can play a large part.

Plant Design and Work Study

The basic principles of work study are the same whether applied to design, construction, operation or maintenance. In other words, critical analysis of the recorded data is fundamentally the same in the four fields listed. The subject for study is selected, all the relevant facts are recorded, the facts are examined critically in an ordered sequence, the most practical solution is then developed and the final result of the analysis is installed. With this in mind it will be seen that work study can be applied to the design of plant in any field of activity, but the particular techniques used, the method of their use, and the basic data to which they are applied must necessarily vary.

More specifically, the following targets are aimed at in the application of work study to design of a new plant or project or modification or extension of an existing one—

(*a*) Shorten project time.
(*b*) Reduce capital and operating costs.
(*c*) Ensure efficient maintenance.
(*d*) Ensure efficient construction.
(*e*) Predict correct initial manning.
(*f*) Reduce alterations.
(*g*) Improve quality of design.
(*h*) Economize in technical manpower.

The work study techniques used to help achieve these aims are all based on method study and work measurement, but adapted to the particular needs of the designer. For instance, the charting techniques are often elaborated and may include scale models and other advanced two- or three-dimensional methods of display, while the critical examination phase may well be extended to cover special conditions.

In the selection of the aspects of the design which should be studied and in the assessment of the most efficient design from the many alternatives costs must not be overlooked. Inevitably, on design the problem arises, for example, of choosing between increased capital cost and lower maintenance costs. The best conclusions can only be reached by measuring each of these costs in like terms, e.g. return on capital plus depreciation per annum against the annual maintenance cost, and equating them.

The following broad steps may be considered as illustrating the use of work study in design.

Examine Basic Design Data

The recording of the basic process as an outline process chart (*see* page 41) followed by a critical examination of each operation in order to develop an improved basic plant, is the first step. Capital costs and operating costs are reduced by simplification and by the combination of operations in the same item of plant, when perhaps separate and costly items were originally specified. The final agreed plan records the full facts to enable the design to go ahead smoothly with the minimum alteration at later stages. The first step has been called a " coarse scale " method study of the process and it becomes more and more obvious that this critical appreciation should be carried out as early as possible, certainly well before sanction to spend capital is requested.

As design proceeds " fine scale " method studies of minor process operations using detailed flow process charts and critical examination (*see* Chapters 5 and 6) should be carried out. These studies give worth-while economies in minor plant items, storage facilities, services usages, materials handling, etc.

Examine Operators' Work

A detailed study of the methods to be used in operating the plant and the measurement of the work involved leads to better methods being developed so that the plant design can be improved from this point of view. Reductions in process costs and in labour problems, and improvements in working conditions and safety result from this type of study.

Examine Maintenance Work

By listing the possible failures of all the plant items, the efficiency of the design in giving cheap maintenance can be assessed. Each plant item design can be analysed to reduce the maintenance work necessary. The methods of carrying out the essential maintenance can then be studied and measured to develop the most economic. This work can be expanded in the later detailed design stages to form the framework for maintenance manning, planning (*see* page 214) and incentive schemes (*see* page 200). Such points as the accessibility and space provided to carry out maintenance work quickly and effectively and the amount of spare plant it is economic to purchase prove to be fertile grounds for the reduction of capital and operating costs.

Examine Construction Work

A close examination of construction methods early in the design of a project, using an experienced construction engineer, leads to improvements in the speed and efficiency of the erection work. This study serves as a very good basis on which to build better construction planning programmes.

Two further points at which work study can make itself felt are concerned with the organization and administration of design.

Design Planning

The planning of design work, as a part of the whole planning of a project through design, procurement and construction can be improved by the use of planning as applied to any type of human work.

The timing, sequence and integration of the efforts of all concerned in the design of a project is a complex problem and can only be resolved efficiently by detailed planning, probably down to one man, one week (or even one day) and one drawing. The plan when programmed must then be controlled day by day to ensure that the target is met. This detailed integration of effort depends to a great extent on good work study practice applied to the work of the team, and hence contributes to the more efficient use of technical manpower.

Examine Design Office Activities

The use of activity sampling (*see* Chapter 14) to find out the proportion of time spent on all the jobs in the design office provides signposts to more detailed method studies. Critical examination shows that the time spent on paper-work procedures, drawings, material listing, etc. can be reduced and that costing systems can be improved.

Work Study Applied to Product and Tool Design[1]

The foregoing section has dealt mainly with the design problems associated with the location and erection of a whole project on a large-scale site. This leads to consideration of the work of an engineering drawing office engaged in the design of the components which make up this large equipment, as well as numberless other products and the tools that produce them.

Product and tool designers are well aware of the necessity to simplify and standardize as far as possible; yet method study investigations into manufacturing problems frequently throw up useful recommendations for improvements in design to products and tools. This suggests that the method study approach has a contribution to make, if its techniques can be adapted to the special problems of the designer.

It is evident at once that the task of the product designer is a difficult one. He is given a specification of requirements which may be very general or quite specific, and he has to convert abstract ideas into lines on paper. He may have to create something different from anything previously made. Referring to the method study procedure, he has very little to *observe* and *record*, except perhaps the manufacturing process for a similar product, if one exists.

Work study is no substitute for knowledge, hard thinking and inspiration, and inevitably the designer first has to give free play to his thoughts to conceive the general idea which will fulfil the requirements of the job. It is when the rough design has begun to evolve and is being developed in its constructional form that the method study procedure can be introduced.

Critical Examination the Key

Critical examination is the key step, but it is first necessary to expose the problem in such a way that it can be analysed systematically. The best way to do this is by means of a straightforward process chart showing the operations that would be needed to convert the design into the product. This is a salutary exercise in itself for any designer, for it demands up-to-date practical knowledge of manufacturing processes, and it obliges him to visualize and record the work necessary to produce his brain-child.

In analysing and questioning every item and operation, the designer must concentrate on achieving simplicity through elimination, where-

[1] Specially contributed by G. P. Wade, Esq., B.SC., M.I.Prod.E., A.M.I.E.E., Director of Work Study and Staff Training, Engineering and Allied Employers' West of England Association.

ever this is practicable and economic. In method study terminology, he is primarily concerned with *what* his drawing says must be done, and *why*. He must continually be challenging the purpose of each part and each operation to see whether it can be eliminated. He is initiating a process and his task is to simplify his demands as far as possible, paying due regard to the economics of the problem—how many have to be produced and how much can be spent on machines and tools.

After the product designer has decided *what* is essential and un-avoidable, the secondary questions, *how, when, where,* and *who* have to be answered by those whose job it is to plan the processes, tools, layouts and detailed methods of manufacture. However difficult these problems, they are at least unavoidable ones, if the product is well designed. So often complicated methods have to be evolved for work which should never have been called for in the first place.

Designing the Tools

This leads to the work of the tool designer, who is given the draw-ing of a product to make and has to devise the tools and equipment to do it efficiently. However well they work from a mechanical point of view, those which are operated and controlled by human beings will not be efficient unless they are designed for easy and comfortable use. The tool designer must therefore take account of the movements of the worker, and he must adapt his design accordingly. He should prepare a process chart showing in detail what movements will be needed and he should analyse and criticize his design until it fulfils the principles of motion economy (*see* pages 88–92). In developing tools and equipment which require rapid, complex or highly repeti-tive movements on the part of the worker, the techniques of micro-motion analysis are available for observing and recording work which cannot be adequately studied visually.

The product designer who is working on articles for human use is also vitally interested in ease of operation and control. He needs the same approach as the tool designer and should apply the method study procedure to analysing the way his product will be used, as well as to the way it will be made. In all cases the designer has to balance the demands of the function against those of economy, and their relative importance will vary with every job.

Method Study Fundamental

The analytical procedures which have been outlined, and which are inherent in method study, are entirely general. They are funda-mental to the rules which good designers endeavour to follow, such as reducing the number of components, using standard parts, and forming material instead of cutting it. These are all particular applications of the general principle of elimination. It is not unreasonable to hope that the form and appearance of the finished product, designed with these aims of simplicity and convenience constantly in mind, will approach those other and older canons of good design—fitness for purpose and pleasantness in use.

Other Fields for Work Study

There are many other fields in which work study has proved of value. For example, in the personnel technique of Job Evaluation, much use is made of the factual information given by work study as to what a job really consists of. This assists with the planning of a hierarchy of work, according to the complexity of jobs and the qualities necessary to perform them, upon which an equitable wages structure may be based. Similarly, the information used in labour control can also be used in cost control, since it enables the " value " of different kinds of work to be expressed to a common base.

Another use of work study is in Budgetary Control. The basis of every operating budget is the quantity of the product to be manufactured or services to be supplied. Where every product, or quantity of service is identical, the output may be measured directly in terms of quantities of product or service, otherwise some other measure is required. This is provided by work study in the form of the work content of each product or unit of service. By this means it is possible to measure in terms of a common unit the budgeted or actual total output of a factory, department, process, etc. Also standard times enable targets to be set, both for productive processes and operations and for service departments such as maintenance.

Work Study and Management

It cannot be too strongly emphasized that work study is no more a substitute for good management than it is for technical knowledge and experience in the different specialist functions. Provided this is continuously borne in mind, the various techniques it includes together comprise one of the most powerful tools at management's disposal in the day-to-day business of developing and directing an organization whether industrial, commercial or otherwise.

Sometimes method study investigations can be carried out by local management (provided it has received adequate training) since the techniques have been particularly designed to highlight the type of information in which management often has direct interest. More often, however, management is too much occupied with a variety of other responsibilities to be able to spare the time necessary for making detailed studies. As a result, it is usual for method study investigations to be regarded as a specialist function, and for responsibility for them to be delegated to someone who is not only adequately trained and experienced but is able to devote the whole of his time to the subject and to see that findings of particular significance are brought to management's attention, together, when necessary, with appropriate suggestions for improvement. The ability to understand the extent and nature of the work that has gone into each investigation will be of immense assistance to management at all levels when evaluating the information supplied and deciding on the course of action.

Work measurement techniques cannot be successfully applied except on a continuing basis by specialist personnel. These specialist personnel do not constitute a profession on their own. On the contrary, the best results are often obtained by using personnel who have long experience of the work concerned and who have undergone thorough work study training; intensive specialization in the techniques alone is certainly not a qualification. In the same way as with method study, management will find it of considerable benefit to be familiar with the general techniques so that it can better appreciate the significance of work values and of the different factors involved in their derivation.

The whole success of work study, in fact, depends upon management possessing not only sufficient knowledge for executive control, but sufficient understanding to stimulate the application of the techniques, to decide " what " is to be studied (the work study staff will decide " how "), and to appreciate work study's possibilities as well as its limitations.

The Work Study Department

Where a work study department exists within an organization it should be regarded as an advisory group which can be called in to make investigations as required by management. Although such a department may suggest subjects for investigation, it should not start on them independently but must first obtain management authorization to do so. It will be seen, therefore, that work study is essentially a functional activity which will be dependent for its success very much on the degree of collaboration it is able to achieve with the planning, operational, inspection, safety and other specialist functions. In addition, as has been shown above, the work study department is available to preview and give advice on the work study aspects of specifications and designs for new plant and equipment, methods and products (or services).

The number of personnel employed on work study in an organization will, of course, have a very close bearing on the way in which the responsibility for the function is allocated. In some small concerns one individual only is able to carry out on his own all the investigations and make whatever studies are required. In such cases it frequently happens that he passes his findings straight through to top management and is closely concerned with the implementation of any recommendations he makes.

When the number of work study personnel increases it is often the practice to divide responsibility for the different fields, and many large organizations have both method study and work measurement sections in their work study departments. Further subdivision may sometimes be justified within these sections to provide better service to different parts of the organization. It is most important, however, that this division of responsibility within a work study department should be understood for what it is—to make for convenience of working—and not used as a means of applying either the method study or the work measurement techniques as completely separate activities. The danger of this happening will be reduced and the work study officers made more effective if they are moved from time to time between sections. This will help them to maintain an appreciation of all the various factors applicable to each task they study, apart from those with which they may be immediately concerned.

Selection and Training of Personnel

The most desirable personal qualities required of the work study officer are tact, honesty and enthusiasm, since in most cases his work will consist of obtaining information from others and, after analysing it, getting other people to accept and act on his suggestions. It is an advantage that he should have practical experience in the type of work he will be investigating, but in small concerns, where he may be required to study a variety of different trades, this may not be possible. What is more important, therefore, is that he should possess the ability quickly to appreciate what is involved in any task in terms of the skill and effort called for to achieve a given result.

The length of specialist training required will vary according to the capacity of the individual and the extent of his responsibilities, but experience has proved that even under favourable circumstances it may take about two years to make a highly-trained work study officer. While much less time than this is required to provide training in the techniques themselves, considerable practice and experience are usually necessary before the best results are achieved. Practice can only satisfactorily be obtained in actual working conditions and under the guidance of an experienced senior officer.

Costs of Application of Work Study

Costs of application naturally vary according to the techniques used, which is a good reason why management should be familiar with the alternative techniques available and their main advantages and disadvantages in any particular instance. In the case of method study, once the cost of introducing new methods and equipment has been met, the expenses of maintaining a scheme are usually small. Work measurement may incur a continuing cost in connexion with the maintenance of values for control and other purposes, but this should seldom exceed a small percentage of the total wage bill.

In general, it can safely be predicted that the results of work study will pay many times over for the costs of its application. It should be remembered also that in the majority of cases the savings are cumulative.

Conclusion

The point is often made that there is nothing new in work study, and that it is, after all, only common sense. It is true that the ideas behind some of the techniques have their origin as long ago as the beginning of the nineteenth century, while there are a number of companies operating today who have been applying one or other technique for more than forty years. It is true also that work study is largely common sense.

What the modern work study approach does is to establish a relationship between the various techniques in a way which not only makes for their more effective application but is a useful guide and aid to the work of actually directing and controlling that application. It is an attempt to make order of common sense by devising a system of analysis which will ensure that the employment of that attribute is more a matter of routine and less the product of inspiration. Work study is not designed for the contemplative, but for the busy executive who often has insufficient opportunity to examine his command critically.

In itself work study can achieve nothing. For success it depends entirely upon what use is made of it by responsible management. Hence, it must be integrated into the normal process of management. At the same time it must be realized that work study is no " once and for all " technique which can be used and then discarded. On the contrary, if it is to be part of the normal process of management it must be used continuously. In each case, too, the principles must be moulded to suit the nature of the particular problem; success in one instance does not imply automatic success in another, for no two cases are exactly the same.

In this book only the basic introduction to the subject has been given, but it is hoped that sufficient explanation of its potentialities has been made to encourage its widespread adoption wherever the opportunity exists. Sufficient experience has already been gained in many fields to show that work study can play a significant part in the continuous process of raising the general level of productivity, without which economic progress is impossible.

Index